Microsoft® Office Live

Take Your Business Online

KATHERINE MURRAY

PUBLISHED BY
Microsoft Press
A Division of Microsoft Corporation
One Microsoft Way
Redmond, Washington 98052-6399

Library of Congress Control Number: 2007924654

Printed and bound in the United States of America.

1 2 3 4 5 6 7 8 9 QWT 3 2 1 0 9 8

Distributed in Canada by H.B. Fenn and Company Ltd.

A CIP catalogue record for this book is available from the British Library.

Microsoft Press books are available through booksellers and distributors worldwide. For further information about international editions, contact your local Microsoft Corporation office or contact Microsoft Press International directly at fax (425) 936-7329. Visit our Web site at www.microsoft.com/mspress. Send comments to mspinput@microsoft.com.

Acquisitions Editor: Juliana Aldous Atkinson
Developmental Editor: Lynn Finnel
Project Editor: Lynn Finnel
Editorial Production: Online Training Solutions, Inc.
Technical Reviewer: Kelly Quirino; Technical Review services provided by Content Master, a member of CM Group, Ltd.
Cover Design: Laurie Vette

Body Part No. X13-24202

Contents

Introduction

WELCOME TO *Microsoft Office Live: Take Your Business Online*! If you've been putting off the idea of getting your business on the Web or are just getting started in the business world and want a fast, inexpensive starting point, I have good news for you. Now creating, hosting, updating, and working with a Web site is so easy that you can do it before lunch (no kidding). And now, designing a professional Web site doesn't require a truckload of talent or confidence—you can simply click a few links, make a few choices, and you're on your way.

This book introduces Microsoft Office Live Small Business, a completely Web-based way to get your business on the Web and begin growing your business by reaching customers, vendors, and coworkers in a fast, efficient, and professional way. Along the way, you'll learn how to create an e-commerce site; create and manage online marketing programs; and manage all your business documents, schedules, and contacts in a way that fits into your fast-paced world of small business ownership.

What Is Office Live Small Business?

Not too long ago, designing a Web site was something only people with specialized skills (or very deep pockets) were able to do successfully. *Standards* and *coding* and *server space* were foreign concepts that most small business owners didn't have time to explore. We needed something simple, fast, and cost-effective that would help us create, update, and fine-tune Web pages for our businesses. We needed something flexible but powerful, intuitive enough that we could remember how to use it in a snap.

Reader, meet Office Live Small Business. Office Live Small Business, meet the reader.

Office Live Small Business is portable, flexible, convenient, powerful—and simple. By the time you finish this book, you can have a professional, effective, interrelated business management system that smartly connects your Web site and your vendors, clients, coworkers, marketing, sales, and communications. All online, right now! And it will cost you nothing to get started. (Monthly charges do apply for some Office Live Small Business features, as you'll learn in Chapter 3.)

Does that sound like something you've been looking for? Well, let's get started. Your business could be online by this afternoon!

Who Is This Book For?

Microsoft Office Live: Take Your Business Online is for you if you are looking for a simple but powerful (and customizable) way to get your company on the Web. Here are a few assumptions I'm making about the type of book you want and need:

- As the owner of a small business, you don't have a lot of time to spend wading through complex descriptions or complicated steps. For that reason, the ideas, procedures, and explanations you'll find here are short, to-the-point, and practical.
- You wear many hats as the owner of a business, and you need ideas that reflect that—so this book covers topics ranging from Web design to data management to communication with vendors and coworkers. You'll find business articles and how-to's on virtually every area of the program. Why? Because in business, more is usually better, and more is especially better when it's fast.
- You like to know how other business owners handle their businesses. We all love to hear stories and behind-the-scenes info about choices others make on their road to success, and so this book provides you with a few interviews with business owners who give some insight into how they use Office Live Small Business. Their stories may inspire you to try new things or use the program in a way you hadn't envisioned before.

What's In This Book?

Microsoft Office Live: Take Your Business Online helps you explore all the features and capabilities of this easy-to-use but powerful offering from Microsoft. Here is a chapter-by-chapter overview of what you will find in the various chapters.

Chapter 1, "Your Small Business on the Web," tells the story of the Web today—how people are using it, ways in which they are connecting, what the benefits look like, and what you may be missing. Specifically, you'll get some of the latest statistics and cost comparisons (as well as inspiring bits such as the numbers related to sales and marketing online) so you can explore how the world of the Web connects with the real world of your budget.

Chapter 2, "Introducing Microsoft Office Live Small Business," shows you how Office Live Small Business takes the best capabilities the Web has to offer and brings them together into a low-cost way to create, manage, update, and promote your site with one easy-to-use program.

Chapter 3, "Getting Started with Microsoft Office Live Small Business," shows you how to sign up for the program, get a domain name, choose the features you want to use with your site, set up permissions and security features, work with e-mail and user accounts, and more. You'll also learn how to find and work with the help system available with Office Live Small Business.

Chapter 4, "Designing Your Site," gets into the heart of the program by walking you through the process of using the Web tools included with Office Live Small Business. Even if you've never designed a site before, you'll find the design tools easy to understand and use. By the time you finish this chapter, your basic pages will be finished, and you'll have a presence online! That's a pretty exciting idea when you've been waiting months—or years!—to take the leap.

Chapter 5, "Taking Your Site to the Next Level," builds on the basic site you created in the previous chapter by showing you how to add features to the overall functionality and to specific pages on your site. You learn how to change the layout of your pages, add Web modules of all sorts, and add tables to your site.

Chapter 6, "Tracking Your Web Statistics," shows you how to keep an eye on the flow of traffic that finds its way to your site. Who is coming and why? What's attracting them? What messages are they seeing? And will they come back? These are all important questions to consider as you nurture your Web site into a successful destination online. Office Live Small Business includes a Web reporting feature that enables you to view your Web traffic from a variety of perspectives.

Chapter 7, "Staying in Sync with Microsoft Office Live Small Business Mail," provides steps and examples that show you how to make the most of Web-based e-mail by pulling everything together in one easy-to-use interface (that you can view any place you have Web access). Use Office Live Small Business Mail to reach customers, vendors, coworkers, and more—directly from within your Office Live space. Nice—and convenient!

Chapter 8, "Selling Products Online," is all about the dream of online shopping. How can your business be part of the craze? Online purchasing has risen exponentially in the last five years; online traffic is surpassing even holiday mall traffic. This chapter shows you how to prepare items to sell online, create your own store, manage sales and customers, and more. You learn to create and manage product listings for your site as well as for eBay.

Chapter 9, "Promoting Your Business," gives you a whirlwind tour of the world of online advertising and e-mail marketing. What have you been missing? In this chapter, you'll learn how to use Office Live AdManager to create and track your ads and fine-tune your keywords. You also find out how to use the E-mail Marketing feature to create, send, and track e-mail marketing campaigns.

Chapter 10, "Working with Business Applications," shows you how to use the smart, simple, and interrelated Business Applications you have at your disposal. Learn to manage time, projects, files, and people (!) using the intuitive online applications covered in this chapter.

Chapter 11, "Working with Microsoft Office Live Workspace," introduces you to creating and sharing workspaces with coworkers, clients, vendors, and peers. A workspace gives you a central online space for important documents, meetings, brainstorming sessions, and more.

Chapter 12, "Using the Resource Center," provides you with a number of helpful resources for growing your business online. Participate in the Office Live Small Business community, find additional articles on specific business topics, watch small business seminars, and read the latest blog posts from Office Live Small Business experts.

Special Features

Throughout this book, you'll find a number of special features that are designed to help you learn the program quickly, make the most of program features, and find answers to some of your business questions along the way:

- **Tips** provide ideas you can try immediately to improve the look or function of your site.
- **Notes** offer ideas and resources you may want to check out for your own site or business use.
- **See Alsos** steer you toward additional information elsewhere in the book.
- **Your Business Online: Q&A Interviews** let you know how other Office Live Small Business users like you are working with the various features in the program.

Your Small Business on the Web

IN THIS CHAPTER, YOU WILL

- Learn why your business needs a Web site.
- Discover the benefits of having a great Web presence.
- See what you're missing with online sales and marketing.

HELLO! AND welcome to Microsoft Office Live Small Business, the first complete, connecting, online resource that helps you pull together everything you need to get your business on the Web; increase your visibility; work with vendors, staff, and customers; and much more. The software is easy to learn and use and brings you a wealth of resources designed to make your daily tasks easier to manage and give you the time you need to focus on growing your business.

Life is busy, and as the owner of a small business, you always have more to do. You might be working in your "off hours" to get your business off the ground. Or perhaps you've taken the leap and gone into business full time for yourself (and now you *really* need to make sure you're investing your time and money in something that's sure to bring a good return). Chances are your days are long and you forgot what "weekends" were long ago. Office Live Small Business can help with that.

Maybe you are learning, like many of us, that good intentions do help you steer your business in the right direction, but they don't necessarily keep a roof over your head. Making a splash in your neighborhood, your niche, or your nation requires visibility, and visibility usually costs money. Office Live Small Business can help with that, too.

And perhaps you, like many of us, jumped into Web design with both feet, thinking, as those of us with the entrepreneurial gene tend to say, "How hard can this be, anyway? I'm sure I can figure it out." If that worked for you, great! But most small-business owners quickly run into the reality that adding anything beyond basic Web functionality is no walk in the park, and expensive Web hosting contracts—and even more expensive Web design contracts—aren't priced affordably for most startups. To top it all off, you run the risk of investing lots of time and money with a third-party designer and winding up with a site that doesn't thrill you (and that you can't change easily).

Office Live Small Business can *really* help with that!

Throughout this book, you will find out how Office Live Small Business, in a smart, elegant, and low-cost way, can help take the sting out of many of the hassles you face as you take your business online and increase your visibility. And along the way, as your business starts bursting at the seams, you'll need a handy, smart way to manage all the data and relationships you will be gathering. Guess what? Office Live Small Business can help you there, as well.

The State of the Web Today

The Web is more than 20 years old now (isn't that hard to believe?!). Although people in the 1980s wondered how (and whether) the Internet would ever make money, that particular question is answered every second as millions of clicks are heard around the world—people buying, selling, researching, reading, connecting, reviewing, and ordering what they need and want.

The Global Web

It didn't take long for the Web to begin to earn its keep for businesses, large and small alike. Recent statistics show that the worldwide Internet audience has reached more than 1 billion users (!), an increase of more than 100 percent in the last five years. According to the *Computer Industry Almanac*, 2 billion users are projected by 2011.[1] Table 1-1 lists the top 10 countries/regions in Internet usage. If you have a product that's marketable worldwide, there's a huge potential audience for you!

---

1 "Worldwide Internet Users Top 1 Billion in 2005." *Computer Industry Almanac*. Available online at *www.c-i-a.com/pr0106.htm*.

TABLE 1-1 Top 10 Countries/Regions in Internet Use[2]

RANK	COUNTRY/REGION	USERS (IN MILLIONS)	PERCENTAGE
1	United States	197.8	18.3
2	China	119.5	11.1
3	Japan	86.3	8.0
4	India	50.6	4.7
5	Germany	46.3	4.3
6	United Kingdom	35.8	3.3
7	South Korea	33.9	3.1
8	Italy	28.8	2.7
9	France	28.8	2.7
10	Brazil	25.9	2.4

Today, even small businesses that have something to offer on the world stage can compete with large companies if they have the business supports and processes in place to make a worldwide reach possible. The Web helps to level the playing field in that regard—who will capture the potential customer's attention? How will you market your products and services? When you have a Web site, e-mail marketing, social networking, and more, you can demonstrate your business services and products on any computer that has Internet access, anywhere in the world.

Improvements on the Local Scene

The Internet isn't just crossing oceans and continents; it's also burrowing ever deeper into your own neighborhood. Today, local interactive mapping sites such as Windows Live Maps help you to find specific businesses in your area, along with a map right to their door. The results display not only the map and directions, but address, phone number, and other Web results that include the business name or location.

For example, you can use Windows Live Local Search to look for cooking classes in Atlanta. Instantly, a list appears, offering sites that meet the criteria you entered. When you click a link, you find the address and phone number of the business, as well as a link for directions. The Web Results area provides you with links to blog posts, Web articles, and more in which the business you selected has been referenced. Voila—instant recommendations! Why shouldn't that be *your* business?

2 *Computer Industry Almanac.*

Today, whether you are targeting a global or local market, your potential customers are likely to look you up online as soon as they hear about you. They will want to see your site in order to get a sense of the quality of your products and services, to find out how personable or professional your company is, and to seriously consider whether they want to do business with you. Being able to present a professional site that inspires buyer confidence is essential. Office Live Small Business can help you do just that—and more—without a huge expense of time or money.

DID YOU KNOW...

Internet users accessing the Web from home average

- 35 different browsing sessions per month, per person.
- 69 different domains visited each month.
- 1,511 unique pages viewed each month.
- 43 page views per browsing session.
- 32 hours browsing per month.
- 55 minutes per browsing session.
- 46 seconds spent on each page visited.[3]

Small Businesses on the Web

A Web site gives your business visibility, presence, and—if you do it well—credibility. Your site lets your customers know who you are, what you offer, and what you stand for. All this communication is very valuable—customers need to know where to find you and how to reach you if they are interested in your services and products.

The development of the Web has been a real boon to cottage industries. Twenty years ago, it was possible to run a business from your kitchen table. But chances are that you spent a boatload of money on overnight mail services and long-distance phone calls, not to mention the ultra-expensive, four-color, professionally printed marketing materials you had designed and printed to give your business a professional look.

3 Nielsen NetRatings, October 2007. Available online at *www.nielsen-netratings.com/press.jsp?section=pr_netv&nav=3*.

Today, thank goodness, a home-based business can have as much credibility as a large corporation if it offers quality products and services, works to put customer satisfaction up near the top of the list, and faithfully provides the type of experience it promises. We no longer have to use expensive design firms for our marketing materials. We can produce appealing, effective documents, worksheets, presentations, and more by using programs on our desktop and laptop computers.

But the more you invest your time and energy in your business, the more you create—which means the more you have to manage. Combine documents, worksheets, products, clients, suppliers, staff, and a Web site, and what do you get? A mass of churning, hard-to-keep-up-with tasks, unless you have an effective way of dealing with it all.

Office Live Small Business answers this need for small-business owners by giving you not only a way to create, manage, update, and work with a professional Web site but also a place online that can serve as the hub for all your business activities. Your Office Live Small Business Home page (shown in Figure 1-1) can be the center of all your business tasks, whether you want to e-mail clients, share marketing materials with prospective customers, update employee information, create Web ads, add new product photos to your site, design an e-mail marketing campaign, or sell products or services online.

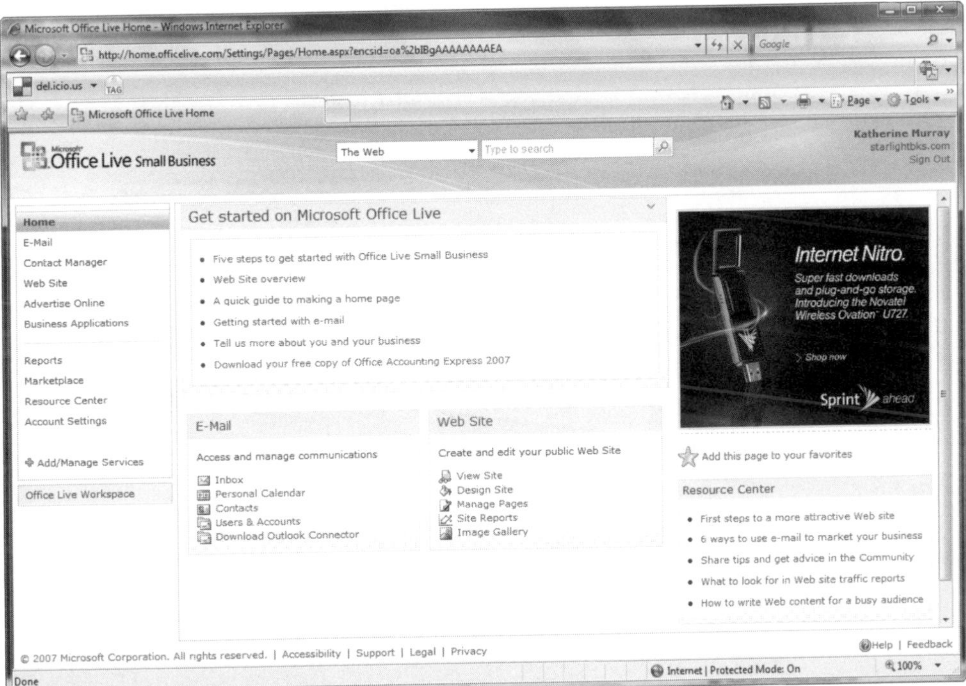

FIGURE 1-1 Your Home page provides a central dashboard for all activities in Office Live Small Business.

SEE ALSO For a detailed look at the way all the Office Live Small Business features work together to support your business, see Chapter 2, "Introducing Microsoft Office Live Small Business."

Web Challenges for the Small Business

If you've been thinking about getting your business online for a long while but haven't taken the plunge, chances are that you are very aware of all these practical challenges going online presents:

- You need to find a dependable Web hosting service, which requires time (in research) and money.
- You need Web design software (again, more investment) and the time and patience to learn it.
- If you don't have writing or graphics skills, you need to create or delegate the creation of your pages.
- You need to be able to troubleshoot Web problems, get your questions answered, and be able to respond to customer queries.
- You need to update your Web content regularly to show your business as a living presence on the Web.

Getting Your Business on the Web

If your business doesn't yet have a Web presence, consider these very real benefits of getting your business online:

- Potential customers can find you whenever it's most convenient for them.
- Placement in search engines gives you constant, 24/7 marketing.
- You can demonstrate your work online —with photos and write-ups of products or through customer testimonials and portfolios—without making a trip to visit a new client.

- You can provide ongoing customer support from your Web site, offering news, downloads, sale information, and more on your site.
- You can create a sense of community in your industry or among your customers and vendors by providing forums, videos, and more that foster good communication and give people a chance to meet.

If your business already has a Web site, answer these questions to determine whether you're really getting the maximum benefit you might receive from your online presence:

- How many new contacts do you get in a week from your Web site?
- How often do you update site content?
- How many hours per month do you spend updating and revising your site?
- How many comments have you received on the overall look and functionality of your site? Have they been largely positive or negative?
- How easy is it to keep track of and follow up on client contacts by sending marketing materials, proposals, and more?
- Are you using your site as effectively as you could be in communicating your mission to existing customers and those you hope to attract?
- Have you been hanging back from using the latest technologies or incorporating new features because you don't have the time to spend learning the techniques?

Your business is a unique entity, springing from your inspiration, your initiative, and your sense of what's needed in the world. Not every site needs all the bells and whistles the latest Web technologies can offer. But every business, small or large, benefits by being on the Web in three very real and important ways:

- Your Web site tells the world who you are and what you offer.
- Your Web site works around the clock and can reach any location with Web access.
- Search engines bring customers to your site who would never find you on the street.

Identity, accessibility, and exposure—three things no business can do without. And these things are available for your business, right now, *free*, with Office Live Small Business. Figure 1-2 shows a business Web site created by using Office Live Small Business. It's easier than you might think, and the long-term gain might just surpass your expectations.

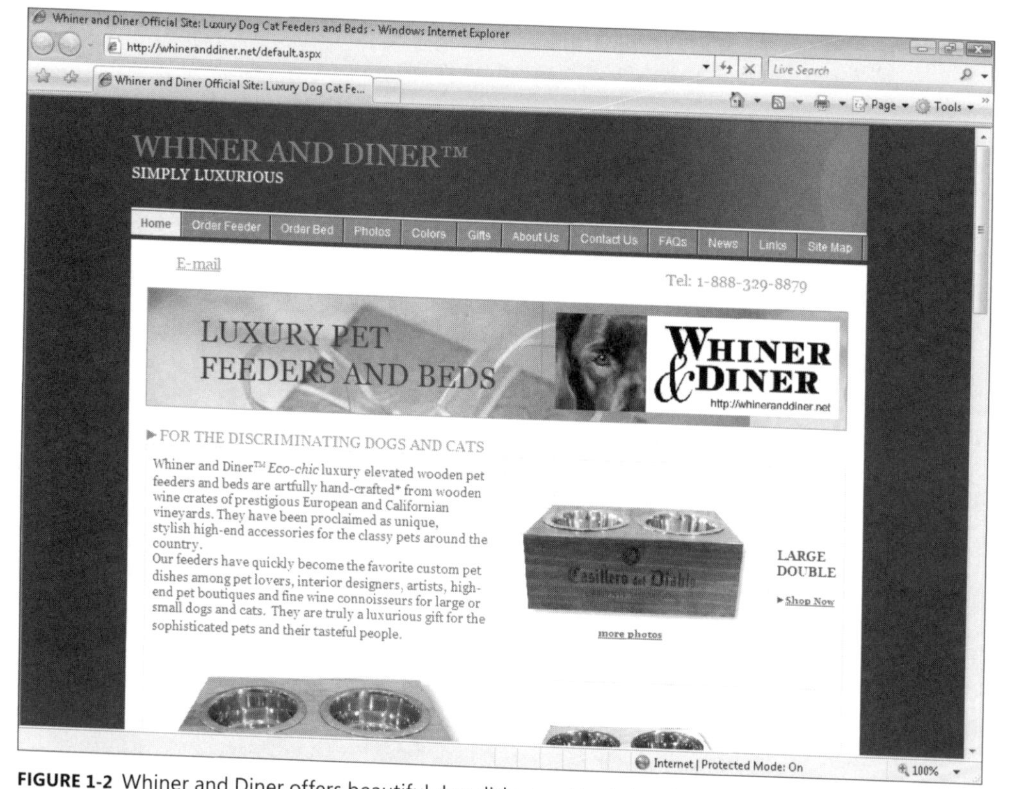

FIGURE 1-2 Whiner and Diner offers beautiful dog dishes and beds hand-crafted from fine wine crates.

Your Online Identity

Of the many potential benefits of getting your business online, none of them beats this: people get to know you through your Web site. If you present an inviting, professional, helpful space online where people can find out about your products and services, get a sense of the reliability of your business, and generally reduce the sense of risk they feel in giving a company they're unfamiliar with a chance, you will be well on your way to establishing a Web presence that really works for you.

Everything on your Web site communicates something to your site visitor:

- The colors you choose can convey a sense of fun and adventure, stability and responsibility, or any number of things in between, depending on the text, background, and image colors you select (see Figure 1-3).
- The font you use—and the spacing you select—goes toward helping you present your ideas clearly, consistently, and with focus.

- The photos you include might be just for fun, or they might showcase your products or services; either way, they help your site visitors know what you think is important to show them.
- The ease with which a visitor can navigate your site could have some connection with how easy you are to deal with. If potential customers get lost on your site or can't find what they need, what will that say to them about getting their questions answered when they have a customer service issue?

FIGURE 1-3 This site shows how color, images, and layout all work together to create a professional look.

Working Around the Clock

As the owner of a small business, you probably feel like *you* work around the clock (I know I do!), but by having a Web site, you literally can communicate information about your business 24 hours a day. And if you have a site equipped with e-commerce features, you might be selling products across all time zones as well.

Here are a few examples of the way your Web site continues working for you long after you've stopped burning the midnight oil:

- Your site provides customers (and potential customers) with information about the types of products and services you offer. Figure 1-4 provides an example of a site that does just that.
- Your site functions as an always-on receptionist for your business, answering questions, providing directions, and helping visitors find the department and/or person they need to reach.
- Your site can offer downloads of catalogs, presentations, bug fixes, and more that can help support your customers when it's convenient for them.
- Your site can bring together groups you work with—for example, your staff, your vendors, or your clients—and enable them to share thoughts, interests, and questions in a forum format.
- You can offer ongoing training if your business warrants it, in the form of articles, classes, videos, and more.

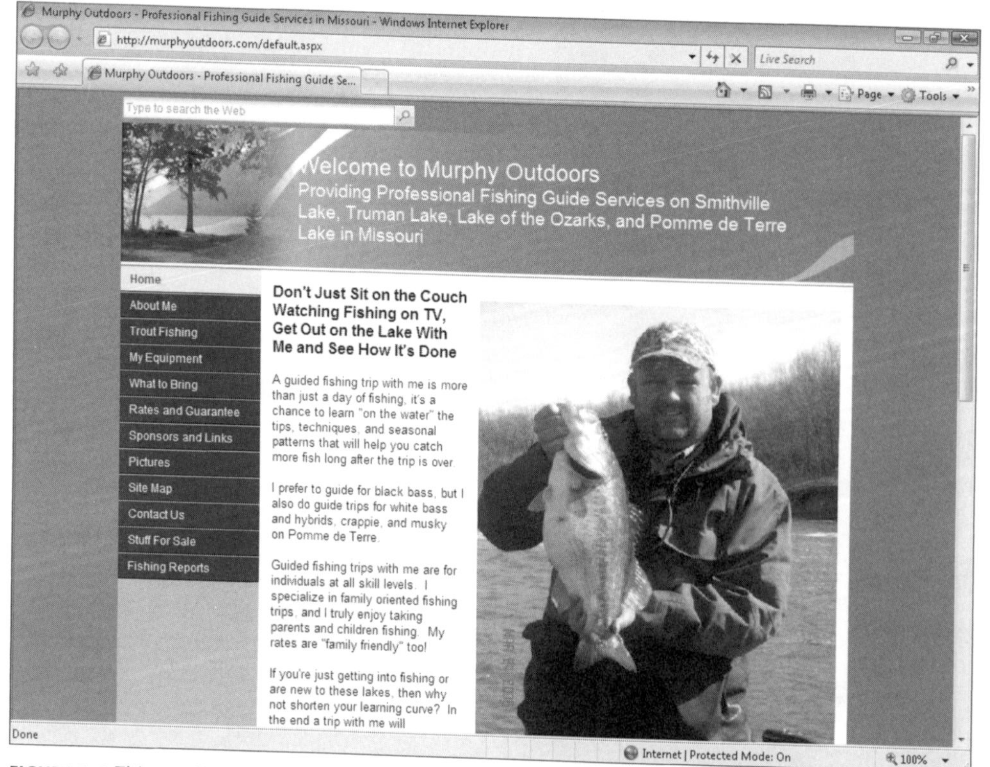

FIGURE 1-4 This small business makes it easy for visitors to find what they need on the site.

Searching and Finding

Think back to business-as-usual in the years before the Web. In the pre-Internet world, building a business meant face-to-face visiting, canvassing, and cold-calling. It meant investing a lot of money in colorful marketing materials. It meant hiring people to help you spread the word. And then, chances are that unless you had an "in" somewhere that could help you gain big visibility quickly, you still had to start with a grassroots effort and hope that fortune smiled and your idea—product or service—caught on.

Today, because of the Web, with a much smaller investment (perhaps simply your own creativity, time, and effort), you can create a site, post information about your business, and see how the world reacts. By learning to work with keywords and search engines, you can help make sure your site pops up when potential customers search for what they want on the Web. It's a great way to get your business in front of people—whether you draw your customers from a local area or can sell to anyone in the world (see Figure 1-5).

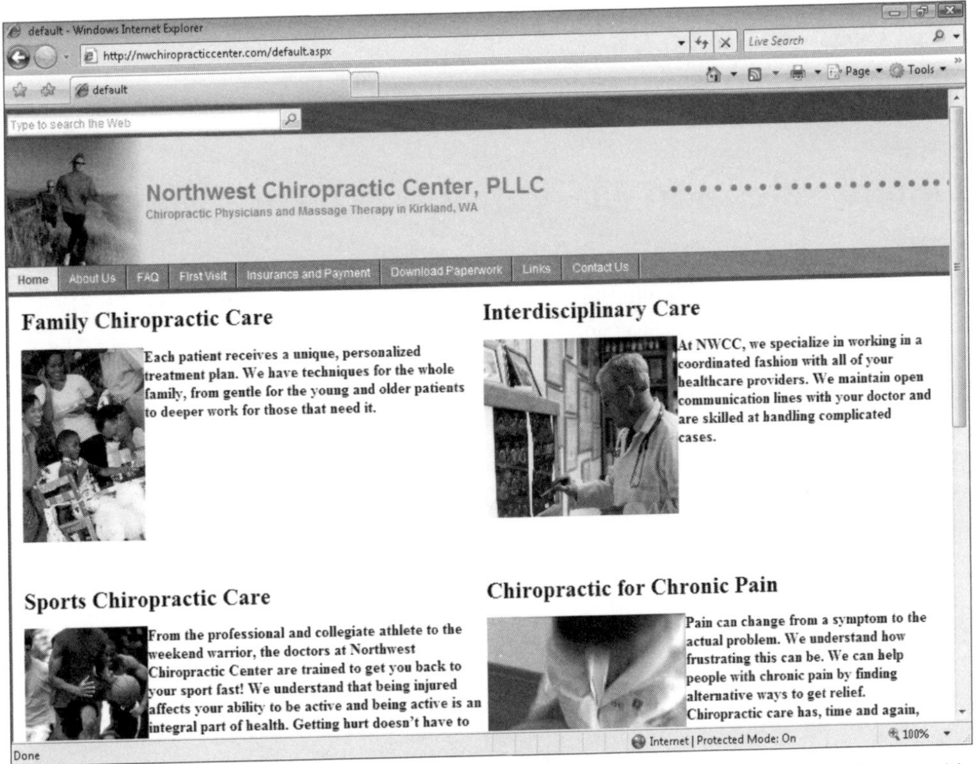

FIGURE 1-5 This chiropractic practice serves customers in a limited geographical area, but offers a wealth of support materials for visitors in any locale.

THEY KNOW WHAT YOU'RE LOOKING FOR

What are people searching for? One fascinating technique to determine which ideas are captivating public attention is to see what people are searching for online. Various sites online provide this kind of up-to-the-minute capability, but some are more helpful than others. Test a few and see what you think:

- **Google Trends** (*www.google.com/trends/hottrends*) presents the latest searches happening now.
- **dogpile SearchSpy** (*www.dogpile.com*) gives you the option of viewing filtered or nonfiltered searches to see what other people are looking for.
- **Lycos 50** (*50.lycos.com*) offers a weekly list of the top pop culture searches on the Web.
- **Yahoo Buzz** (*buzz.yahoo.com*) provides not only the top searches but also a bit of commentary and context as well.

Online Sales and Marketing—It's Your World

2007 was a banner year for Black Friday in the United States. (Black Friday is the day after Thanksgiving, traditionally the biggest shopping day of the year.) In recent years, a new tradition has emerged for online shoppers—Cyber Monday, which occurs when consumers fire up their home or work computers and take advantage of great online deals, reduced shipping charges, and more. (And even better, you get to skip the mall traffic!) In 2007, Cyber Monday sales were up by a full 10 percent over 2006, and they surpassed Black Friday purchases by 13 percent, for a total of 32.5 million unique Web visits on that one day! Web watchers expect the trend to continue at a similar or increased rate.

Popular Sites and Categories

So what are consumers buying online? What brands are they responding to? Which ads work best? And, most importantly, is your business one of the lucky ones that online shoppers will be hoping to find next year? Table 1-2 shows the latest online retailing data from Nielsen Ratings and Table 1-3 shows the categories that had the greatest jump in site visits during October 2007.

TABLE 1-2 Top 10 Online Retailers on Cyber Monday 2007[4]

RANK	RETAILER	USERS (IN MILLIONS)
1	eBay	10,799
2	Amazon	7,225
3	Wal-Mart	5,165
4	AT&T	3,879
5	Target	3,393
6	Circuit City	2,824
7	Dell	2,673
8	Best Buy	2,363
9	Overstock.com	2,154
10	Sears	1,698

TABLE 1-3 Highest Growth in Online Visits[5]

RANK	CATEGORY	VISITORS (IN MILLIONS) OCT 07	PERCENTAGE INCREASE OVER SEPT 07
1	E-cards	33,829	23
2	Flowers/gifts/greetings	35,631	22
3	Online trading	12,434	21
4	Taxes	7,435	17
5	Mall	30,806	13
6	Toys	23,618	12
7	Retail–food	14,791	8
8	Consumer electronics	50,131	8
9	Genealogy	8,892	8
10	Jewelry/luxury goods/ accessories	16,462	8

4 Nielsen NetRatings. *Nielsen Online Reports Cyber Monday Traffic Increased 10% Over 2006.*
5 comScore.com. *comScore Media Metrix Releases Top 50 Web Rankings for October.* Available online at *www.comscore.com/press/release.asp?press=1902.*

Marketing for Success

It's not likely that your business will make it into the top 10 by the next holiday season, but who's to say where your creativity and intention can take you? With the right tools and support for getting your message out to the world, you can begin to give consumers what they want in a focused, effective, and ultimately successful way.

You can use cost-effective Web marketing techniques to create a marketing strategy that takes advantage of the best the Web has to offer. Here are just a few of the techniques you can use to promote your business online:

- Research and choose keywords that get your site ranked high in the search engines.
- Find and join affiliate networks to share links and make customer connections.
- Use Web advertising (banners and links) to spread your message online.
- Use online auctions (such as eBay) to gain visibility for your products.
- Participate in forums and newsgroups in your industry.
- Publish and distribute online publications to increase your audience base.

Marketing Challenges for the Small Business

Having a knack for marketing is a bit like being a talented dancer—it can be taught, but it helps if you have some talent to start with. Not all of us start our businesses with a ready-made marketing sense; in fact, most of us don't. Luckily, you can learn to market your wares by standing on the shoulders of those who have gone before you. Some of the challenges you will face as you begin to learn how to market your business include

- Knowing how to reach your specific audience or customer base.
- Learning which marketing techniques are likely to work best with your specific customers.
- Knowing where your customers shop, what they are interested in, and how you can find them.
- Learning which marketing tools work and which don't.
- Learning to identify sticking points in your marketing campaign.
- Producing marketing programs that work cost-effectively and consistently.

Again, as a small-business owner, you might be trying to do it all yourself—running the business, offering the services, creating the product, responding to customers, and marketing your wares. It's hard—if not impossible—to do everything well. Often, even companies that have the resources and staffing for a marketing department still struggle with the best way to reach potential customers. In fact, the report of a survey published by the Chief Marketing Officer (CMO) Council says,

> *"Thirty-six percent of firms in the survey have no formal system for tracking marketing's role in customer acquisition, retention, and value creation. One quarter say they have a good degree of grading, scoring, and prioritizing, and 21.6 percent maintain a database for channel and sales access. Churn and retention rates are monitored by 44.8 percent of marketers, while 42.4 percent don't and 12.8 percent aren't sure what their company does to monitor such activities."*[6]

SEE ALSO Office Live Small Business includes a number of features designed to help small-business users create and use effective, low-cost marketing strategies to promote their businesses online. Read more about these marketing features in Chapter 2, "Introducing Microsoft Office Live Small Business."

KEEP AN EYE ON THE WEB

There are a number of sites online you can consult to stay on top of the latest Web trends. Here are a few of my favorite eye-on-the-Internet sites:

- ClickZ: *www.clickz.com*
- Nielsen NetRatings: *www.nielsen-netratings.com*
- Computer Industry Almanac: *www.c-i-a.com*
- TrendWatching: *www.trendwatching.com*
- FastCompany: *www.fastcompany.com*
- Pew Internet & American Life Project: *www.pewinternet.org*

6 CMO Council report. Available online at *www.cmocouncil.org*.

Managing Your Business Information

Over the last couple of years, the Web has been gaining a reputation for document hosting, archiving, and retrieval. Businesses are beginning to use server space to house collaborative documents, share workspaces, and more. This functionality often is used by large organizations with a global workforce, but online document storage has practical benefits for our small businesses as well.

Office Live Small Business includes several online galleries—a Document Gallery, an Image Gallery, and a Template Gallery—all of which you can use to upload and store documents related to your business. You can also use Microsoft Office Live Workspaces to collaborate with others in real time; track your marketing campaigns and contacts by using Contact Manager; and keep an eye on your Web statistics, marketing results, and more.

SEE ALSO Office Live Workspace is a new, free, Web-based program that you can use to collaborate easily online with your employees, vendors, or customers. See Chapter 11, "Working with Microsoft Office Live Workspace," for more information about Office Live Workspace.

What's Next

This chapter has given you a picture of what's happening on the Web today and suggested ways your business can benefit by joining in. The next chapter gives you a whirlwind tour of the tools Office Live Small Business gives you for getting your business online, marketing your products and services, and managing all your business information and relationships in a smart, affordable, and streamlined way.

Introducing Microsoft Office Live Small Business

IN THIS CHAPTER, YOU WILL

- Think through your site preferences.
- Stay in touch with Microsoft Office Live Mail.
- Get organized online with calendars and contacts.
- Sell products on your site.
- Advertise online with search marketing.
- Create e-mail marketing campaigns.
- Know your Web traffic.
- Manage your business data.
- Cultivate your client relationships.
- Tailor your account to meet your needs.

ONE OF the biggest challenges of starting and running a successful business involves keeping everything moving along at a good pace. If everything depends on you, it's hard to care for all the important things equally. You've probably heard the phrase "lots of irons in the fire"—that phrase might have been used to describe you! But, at least in the early stages of your business, you need all the irons to be in the fire at the same time—they are important. You need to create your product *and* promote it. You need to find new customers *and* cultivate the relationships you already have. You need to do the practical tasks your business requires—getting funding, doing the bookkeeping, managing your data—and still be able to move effectively into the future, creating the systems and communication channels that ultimately get your business moving smoothly on a successful path.

This chapter gives you a bird's-eye view of ways you can use the different features of Microsoft Office Live Small Business to bring together your important business tasks and manage them effectively. The support built into the program helps you accomplish three huge things: get your business online, promote your business, and manage your business data and relationships. What's more, you get to benefit from the creativity and vision of others—you don't have to spend your time reinventing the wheel.

That's good news, right? Let's take a look at some of the ways Office Live Small Business can begin lightening your load right away.

Your Web Site, Your Way

Web sites, done well, require time and effort. And some creativity, too. A good Web site meets some basic communication goals that your customers and potential customers appreciate (and they'll reward you by coming back to your site, again and again, and hopefully buy something!). Think of the sites you visit regularly, as well as those you don't. What frustrates you on certain sites? What do you like about the sites you consider top-notch?

Although our preferences for things such as colors, fonts, and media (how much and what kind) differ, there are basic guidelines that apply to sites that care enough to create a good browsing experience for consumers. A good Web site

- Knows why you are visiting and what you want to see.
- Makes it clear how to find what you need.
- Provides something of value.
- Gives you an option to send feedback.
- Builds trust by presenting a professional, competent look and feel.

Getting on the Web is a great thing for your business, but it also presents challenges. For example, who is going to design your site? Where will you find the server space? How will you find time to learn the software? And how in the world do you get a domain name?

Your Web site is the hub of all your activity in Office Live Small Business. Designed to make creating a site as simple as possible, Office Live Small Business includes an easy-to-use design tool that provides ready-made templates to work with but still gives you the flexibility to make the site look the way you want it. With the Web site features in Office Live Small Business, you can

- Find and register a domain name for your business.
- Choose from a collection of professionally designed themes for your site.
- Select a style that fits the look and feel you want.
- Customize the colors and fonts.
- Choose the navigation style you want to use.

- Create and add pages.
- Choose and change your page layout.
- Add images, modules, and tables.
- Insert horizontal lines and hyperlinks.
- Ensure the security and stability of your site.

The Site Designer in Office Live Small Business, shown in Figure 2-1, gives you everything you need to choose the look and feel—and navigation style—of your site. Using one simple interface, you can choose from a variety of themes that offer designs created for different industries. You can add your own touches, modules, images, and more by using the options on the Page Editor tab.

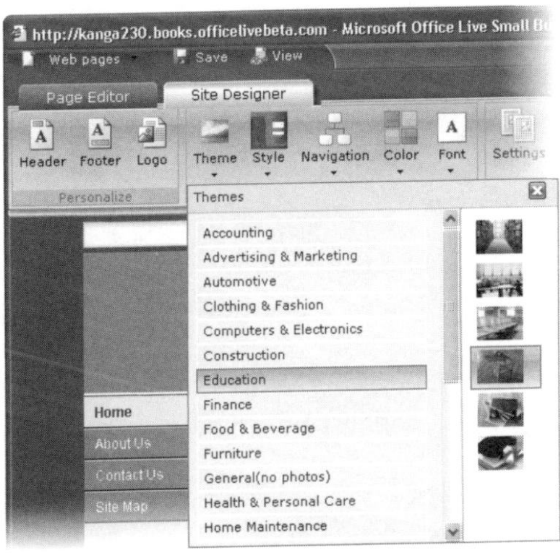

FIGURE 2-1 Use the Site Designer to choose a professionally designed theme for your Web site.

TIP

The themes available in the Site Designer are offered as great starting points for your own ideas. Don't feel locked in to a specific theme—if you are launching a small restaurant and want to use the Education theme, feel free!

SEE ALSO

Chapter 4, "Designing Your Site," is all about designing your site, working with pages, and adding content.

Stay in Touch with Office Live Mail

In addition to your Web site, you need e-mail to present a unified, professional image for your clients. E-mail is an important part of your overall business communications strategy. The domain name you use in Office Live Small Business includes up to 100 company-branded e-mail addresses that you can use to provide a consistent communications front.

Being more than a temporary, fly-by-night Web business is important. Even—or especially—if you are a new business, customers will want to know you're going to be around after they order your products. By using Office Live Small Business's e-mail accounts, you can set up e-mail addresses that match your domain for the other people in your business (or different roles that you manage yourself for now). Plus you have the added benefit of being able to receive and manage your e-mail without buying Web server space.

Because your Office Live Small Business account is available anywhere you have Web access, you can read and respond to your e-mail anytime you want. This flexibility is perfect for home-based businesses and gives you the credibility and the professionalism you need to inspire confidence in clients, vendors, and more.

You check your e-mail by clicking E-Mail in the navigation panel on the left side of the Office Live Small Business window. The Tools To Manage Your E-Mail page offers a variety of ways you can connect with your customers and staff (see Figure 2-2). You can also use Microsoft Office Outlook Connector to synchronize your Office Live Mail with Microsoft Office Outlook 2003 or 2007 so that you can work with it offline if you choose.

SEE ALSO

What does your e-mail address say about you? For a closer look at setting up your e-mail, managing contacts, and reducing spam, see Chapter 7, "Staying in Sync with Microsoft Office Live Small Business Mail."

TIP

Being accessible to your customers is an important part of building relationships. If you count on instant messaging to provide your clients with quick answers to their product questions, you can use Windows Live Messenger in Office Live Small Business to chat online with your clients in real time, using text, voice, and even video. You can download the software directly from your e-mail page.

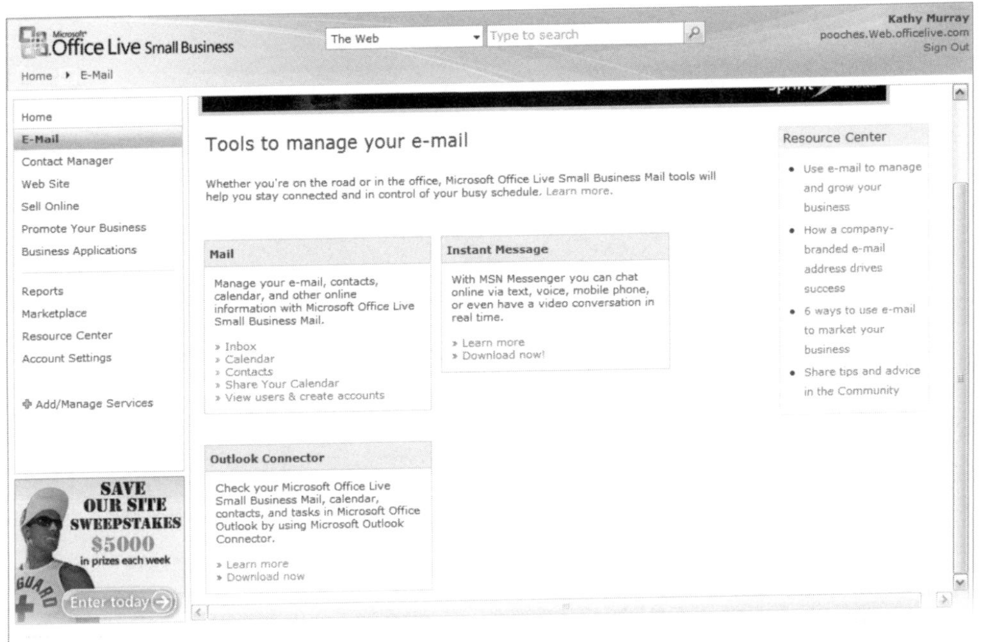

FIGURE 2-2 Office Live Small Business provides you with a number of ways to connect to customers, vendors, and more.

Get Organized Online with Calendars and Contacts

Scheduling and contact management might be two of the big unsung features of online organizing—how do you keep everyone in sync about upcoming meetings, events, demonstrations, and more? How do you know whether anyone has followed up on the pending customer service issues? In a traditional office, you might use company e-mail or send and receive invitations by using Outlook to schedule your meetings. Perhaps you have contact management software in which you log the times you contact clients for proposals, follow-ups, and more.

If you are always on the go, out visiting clients—or running your business from your porch overlooking Hanalei Bay on the island of Kauai—you might want a more solid way of making sure everyone important is notified about upcoming events and important contact issues. You can use the scheduling and contact features within Office Live Mail to create, manage, and alert people about upcoming meetings (see Figure 2-3). You can also share your calendar so that everyone involved can easily see the schedule for the day, week, month, or even the year.

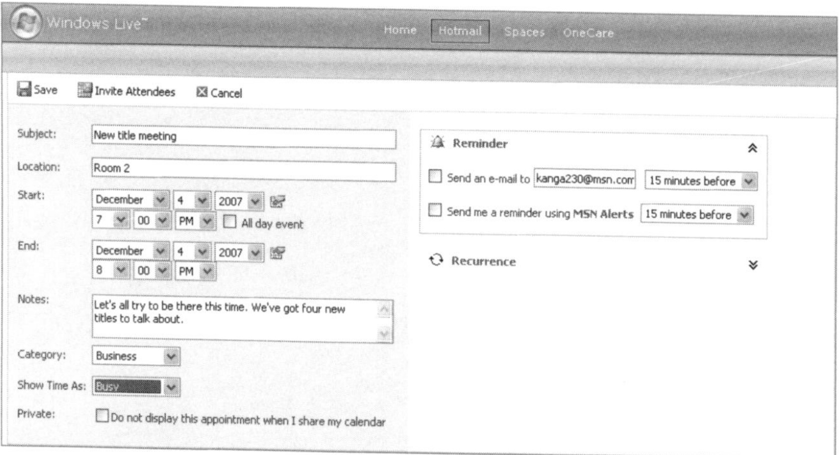

FIGURE 2-3 Office Live Mail, accessible within Office Live Small Business, provides scheduling and contact capabilities.

Sell Products on Your Site

Office Live Small Business offers a complete, secure e-commerce solution you can use to add an online store to your own site and create product listings for eBay auctions. By adding a shopping cart feature to your Office Live Small Business site, you can sell your own products, process order fulfillment online, and view reports that keep you current on your site's sales statistics.

An easy-to-use e-commerce template walks you through the process of setting up your products and getting started with orders and payments. The result is a professional looking e-commerce site that provides a secure, simple checkout experience for your customers. Click Sell Online in the Office Live Small Business navigation bar to start the process (see Figure 2-4).

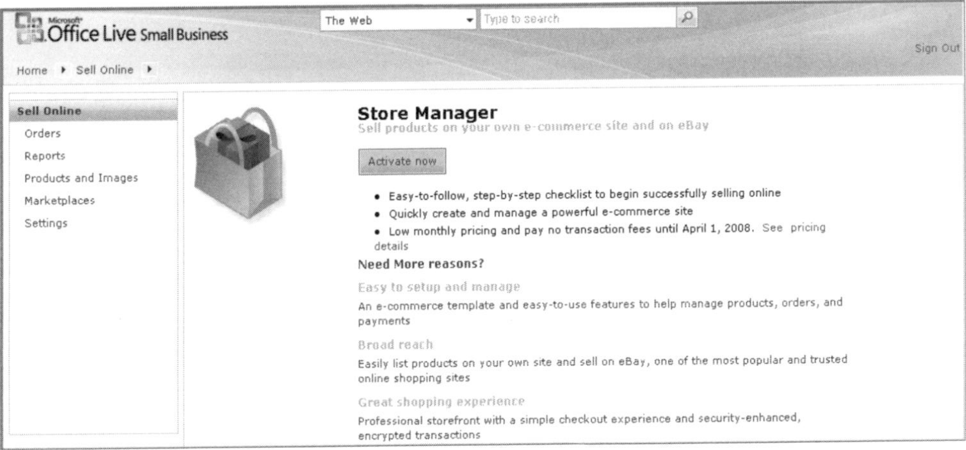

FIGURE 2-4 Get started setting up the Store Manager by choosing Sell Online.

Advertise Online with Search Marketing

Getting your site online is only the first step in getting visibility for your business and bringing customers to your site. As you learn in Chapter 9, "Promoting Your Business," adManager in Office Live Small Business can help you spread the word about the products and services you offer. When you purchase search advertising by using adManager, your site title, description, and URL appear at the top of results pages on MSN, Live.com, or Ask.com, set off with other sponsored sites. You specify whether you want the ads displayed to a nationwide or local audience, and you also choose the search engines you want to use.

When potential customers search for an item listed as one of your keywords, the name, description, and URL of your site appear in the Sponsored Sites box. The user can click the link to move directly to your site.

Search advertising is affordable and manageable—you set the budget for your advertising (for example, $50 per month), and your account is charged only when a user clicks the link to your site in a displayed ad.

With adManager, you can

- Advertise effectively and affordably by choosing, purchasing, and tracking your keywords.
- Create and manage a monthly keyword budget so you know exactly what you're spending.

- Avoid huge advertising expenses by doing it yourself.
- Create reports that show your keyword results for different search engines.

Create E-Mail Marketing Campaigns

How many e-mail newsletters do you currently receive? If you're like most of us, you probably get a few from sites you visit regularly—and some that seem to appear out of the blue. When you sign up for a newsletter, generally it's because the company offers something you're interested in. You want to know when the organic cotton sweaters go on sale. Or you want to know about upcoming dates for a triathlon. Or you're waiting for that end-of-year closeout announcement on high-definition televisions. (Who isn't?)

When you sign up, or opt in, to receive a company's newsletter or other ongoing e-mail communication, you are giving the site permission to send you things. This permission is important, if you're concerned about happy customers. Otherwise, your newsletters and e-mail fliers will go directly into the customer's Junk Mail folder, and what's worse, you might get earmarked as a spammer, which could have longer-term ramifications (such as causing your site to be blocked by search engines).

Office Live Small Business includes an e-mail marketing feature that helps you design, create, send, and track responses to e-mail campaigns you create for customers and prospects (see Figure 2-5).

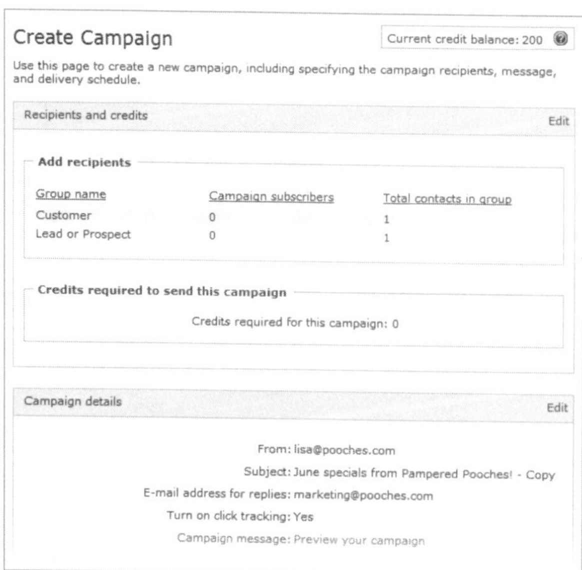

FIGURE 2-5 Create and track e-mail marketing campaigns to invite new and existing customers to your site.

HOW WILL YOU USE E-MAIL MARKETING?

Office Live Small Business makes it easy for you to reach customers who opt in to receive communications from your company. You might want to put an e-mail signup field on your Home page or include a check box at the bottom of an order page. (This makes the most of customer information you've already gathered.) After you have permission, you can send a variety of e-mail communications, which might include

- A product announcement with links to reviews.
- A newsletter providing tips, suggestions, and news from your industry.
- A flier promoting a special Web offer.
- A product fact sheet.
- An invitation to an online event.
- A press release sharing company news.

Know Your Web Traffic

Part of managing your Web site effectively involves knowing who is visiting your site, where they come from, and which marketing events helped bring them to you. That way, you can do more of what works (and yes, less of what doesn't).

Office Live Small Business gives you a whole slew of reports you can use to view your site statistics in different ways:

- The Visitors report displays information about the number of unique visitors per month and average time spent on your site.
- The Site Usage report shows you overall site visit statistics for the entire site.
- The Referring Sources report lets you know where your visitors are coming from.
- The Keywords report tracks the results of the keywords you've purchased.
- The Page Usage report shows you which pages in your site are getting the most attention.

- The System Statistics report lets you know about the systems (operating system, browser, and monitor resolution) your visitors are using when they view your site.
- The Administration reports enable you to manage the functionality of your overall site by managing the pages users see after they complete an action, getting tracking codes (for any sites you might operate independent of Office Live Small Business), and downloading specific reports.

Sometimes, Web statistics just jump and you're not really sure why. Perhaps a blogger mentioned one of your products and caused a (happy) ripple effect that brought people to your site. At other times, you can see a surge of hits after sending out a marketing communication. With Office Live Small Business, you can add marketing events to your reports so that you can view your Web results in light of influencing factors.

NOTE Marketing events include newspaper ads, phone book ads, seminars, site map submissions, coupons, Web site changes, and press releases.

Manage Your Business Data

Office Live Small Business includes two primary business applications you can use to manage the documents and other files you use in day-to-day business. With the first application, Team Workspace, you can create a workspace that your staff can use to share information, post announcements, and work with documents (see Figure 2-6). You can also create a calendar, assign tasks to members of your team, and even host online team discussions.

Document Manager is another business application included free with Office Live Small Business. Use Document Manager to upload, post, store, and share documents and pictures that are important to your business operations. You can easily create a document library with all the documents, pictures, logos, and more you use for correspondence, sales letters, newsletters, annual reports, and presentations (see Figure 2-7).

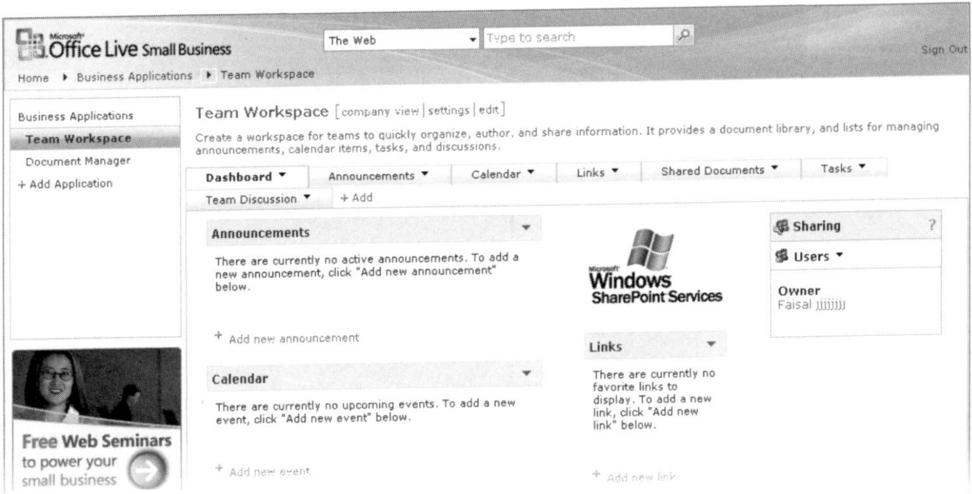

FIGURE 2-6 With the Team Workspace application, you can organize your business data and keep everyone in sync.

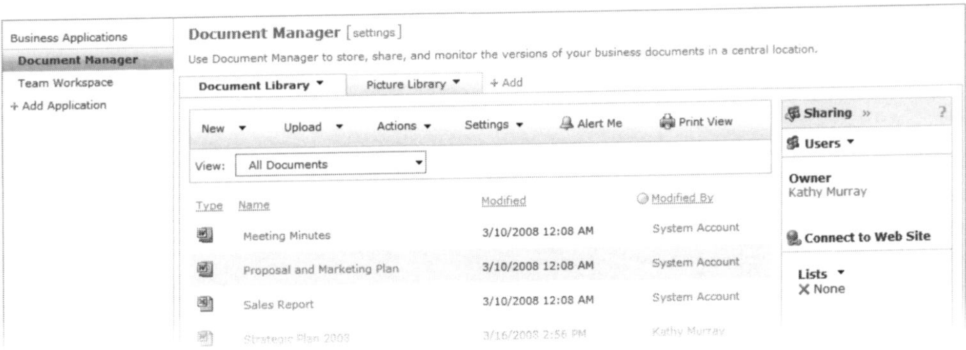

FIGURE 2-7 Document Manager provides you with an easy-to-use document library for business files you use often.

In addition to the Team Workspace and Document Manager applications, you can choose from a number of applications in specific areas. For example, when you click Add/Manage Services in the Business Applications navigation bar, the Select An Application window appears (see Figure 2-8). Click a category to display the list of applications available for that selection.

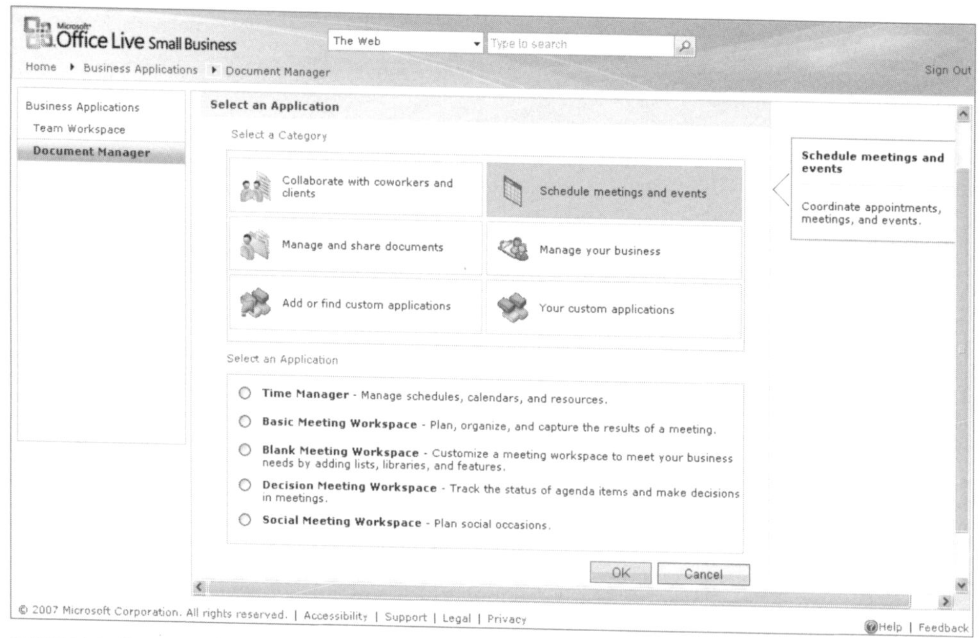

FIGURE 2-8 You can add several applications to help you better manage your business, develop custom applications, manage your time, and collaborate effectively.

Cultivate Your Client Relationships

Few things in your business can be considered as important as your customers. Yes, you need a great product or service. Definitely, you need good management, terrific staff, and great customer service. But knowing your clients and being consistent, reliable, and timely in your communication with them goes a long way toward building credibility for your business and ensuring you have long-term, happy customers (who will return to your company and bring their friends).

Office Live Small Business recognizes the key role relationships play in your day-to-day business life. Your clients aren't the only people who matter—cultivating good relationships with your vendors, partners, employees, and prospective customers is important, too. For that reason, Contact Manager is built right into the program so that you can create client and company accounts; synchronize your contacts seamlessly with Outlook; and track companies, opportunities, products, and more (see Figure 2-9). You'll never again have to cross your fingers and hope that someone followed up with the person who was interested in a huge special order last week. Now you can simply look it up in Office Live Small Business and see when the follow-up contact was made—and by whom.

In addition to tracking all this important business contact information, you can also create and share Web forms and lists, and enable alerts so that you receive notification when the contact information changes on your site. Used effectively, Contact Manager can help you streamline your contact management in a smart way that saves you time and trouble and helps you avoid the heartache of unhappy customers.

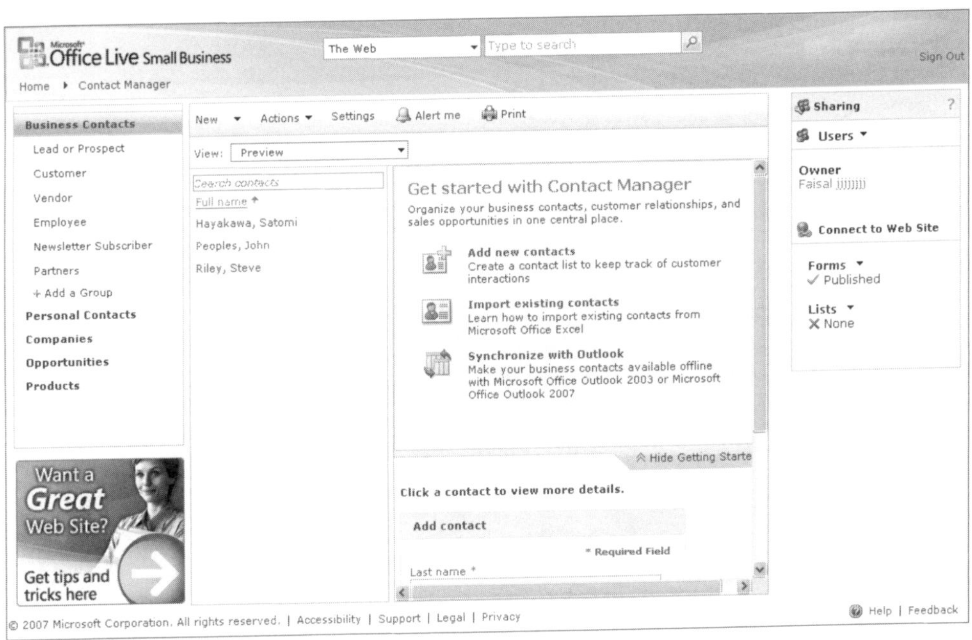

FIGURE 2-9 Contact Manager helps you organize, track, and manage important business contacts.

Your Account, Your Way

Even though Office Live Small Business takes care of a lot of things for you, setting up your account the way you want it is totally your call. You can use the Account Settings feature in Office Live Small Business to set the permission level for your site, manage your Office Live billing, add users and e-mail accounts, manage your domain names, and purchase additional services (see Figure 2-10). In addition, you can add alerts so that you receive e-mail prompts when changes are made on the site.

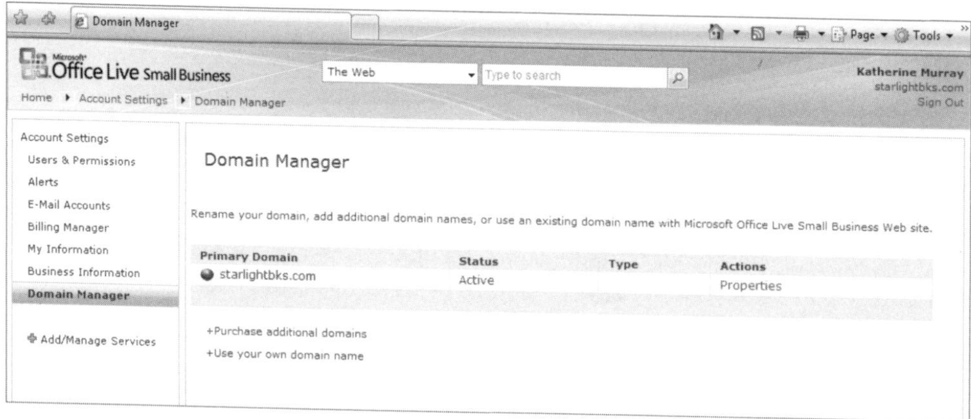

FIGURE 2-10 Use Account Settings to set up your business information and add users, permissions, e-mail accounts, and more.

YOUR BUSINESS ONLINE: Q&A INTERVIEW

Jay Harper, Managing Director and CTO
Planet Earth Friendly: *www.planetearthfriendly.com*

Q *What are your favorite features in Office Live Small Business?*

A Two big things have been the most helpful. The first is the ease of use and a complete out-of-the-box experience. Click, point and shoot, and your Web site is on the air. The second would be the helpful community within Office Live. I am at no means a Web designer or code writer, but I did not have to be with the friendly and helpful experts in the Office Live community. Any question or help I needed to embed Java, run live streams, install banners and other creature comforts to my Web site and pages all came from my Live community of smart, family members. Their LPE (lots of practical experience) made my first shot at Web design a home run, way out of the park!

Q *How does having a Web site help your business?*

A Shakespeare said that all the world is a stage, and if that is true, then the Internet is the theater everyone is sitting in. Paperless way of doing business is what we champion, and e-marketing/e-commerce is the way of the present and the future. The response has been overwhelming from our client base and the industry. We have experienced 'instant credibility' by having a site that gives greater insight to our commitments and services.

Q *How do you use the marketing and management features in Office Live Small Business?*

A adManager and beta words have improved our search engine responses with Google, Yahoo, Excite, and many others. Best of all was that it did not cost a whole lot. Just a simple ad account set at a certain amount per month, and it is that simple. Management of the site is extremely easy and adaptable. I have never had issues adding and deleting user and content to the site, and site reports make Office Live a real-time monitoring entity. Office Live gives the end user a way to track visits and hits with accurate signatures and history data.

Q *What do you want to do next with your site?*

A Re-launch the company as a nonprofit appealing to schools, retirement communities, and hospitals to go with green initiatives.

Q *What advice would you pass along to a small business owner trying Office Live for the first time?*

A Quit thinking small. With Office Live, big thinking is encouraged, and big performances are only a few mouse clicks away. Launch with great flair with minimum design time. No one got big by being small!

GETTING STARTED IN BUSINESS: A STARTUP TOOLKIT

If you're just getting started in business, you're probably in that falling-in-love period with an idea that is just burning to be acted on. You've developed a new product the market needs or you have a service you think will really fly. Knowing the how-to's is an important part of putting down a good foundation and taking steps toward realizing your dream.

Although having specific tools—computers, software, and more—will be an important part of your success, the most important tools you have to work with when you're first starting out are thoughts. Your thoughts will help you plot your course and stay on it. Your thoughts will calm you (or send you running for the hills!) when the doubts and challenges begin to pop up. Here are some important ideas to put in your startup toolkit and pull out as you need them:

- **Clarify your vision.** As an entrepreneur, a lot rides on your talent, your passion, and your energy. Chances are that if you are starting a business now, you are an idea person and have quite a bit of courage (and an independent streak, too). Before you begin investing money, time, and energy in creating your business, spend some "seasoning" time testing, expanding, and getting to know your idea from all directions. Know what you think—and feel—about your idea. Resist the temptation to get caught up in the wave of your own enthusiasm and believe your own marketing spin. Do the work to put all the financial projections together, ask yourself whether the business matches the "real" goals you have in life, and test the image of the business thoroughly. (Startup Nation, at *www.startupnation.com*, has a number of great tools for developing a life plan and establishing your business in the context of a life well lived.) Once you've gone through this clarifying stage, you'll be able to start building on your idea with confidence.
- **Identify your resources.** Nobody does this alone. You might bootstrap your business through its first few months, but soon you will need resources to help manage and build on your success. Business resources such as Office Live Small Business help you manage business data and relationships effectively and flexibly; resource roles—such as finding the right accountant, banker, attorney, and insurance agent—are invaluable. As you begin to pull together the pieces of your business, count your resources as a huge part of your overall assets and be intentional about the way you include them during your startup stage.

- **Gather your supports (and use them!).** Having business advisers is an invaluable part of navigating a small business, whether you're a sole proprietor working at your kitchen table or part of a progressive team that spans the globe. Early on, identify four or five friends, peers, or professionals who understand the nature of your industry, the challenges you are likely to face, and the various responsibilities you are balancing. If someone you respect agrees to mentor you, even better. Look for examples of people who have been successful in the area you aspire to and set up a planned meeting schedule (for example, once a month for lunch) so that you can regularly check in and get feedback.
- **Create (and work) your systems.** We tend to spend a lot of time doing things we've already done—worrying about this particular problem, bumping up against that personality type, freaking out over a specific deadline that rolls around at the same time every month. Save yourself a lot of time and psychic energy by setting up systems to help manage things for you. Do your marketing on Mondays; end the work week on Fridays with follow-up thank yous to new clients. Pay your bills on a specific day; plan presentations for Wednesdays. Thinking of your work in month-long blocks of time helps you release the stress of wondering when you'll get to something. Once something is scheduled, you'll know it is being taken care of and you can free your mind to be creative in this moment. And that makes room for the great ideas you need in order to grow your business today.
- **Keep the inspiration flowing.** Entrepreneurial exhaustion is the downside of passion—it's that moment when you flop into the recliner, feeling worn out and used up, knowing that you've done as much as is humanly possible in a single day. This state of mind is not unusual, even for high-energy, high-output people. When you feel an energy crash coming on, relax into it and take it as just another form of inspiration—the type that's inspiring you to rest and rejuvenate. Allow your mind to get quiet; do something you enjoy; take an evening or weekend off; let your mind, body, and spirit rejuvenate. Having a startup business is a lot like having a newborn in your household—it needs almost all your attention and energy at first. Like a new parent, enjoy moments of quiet (yes, your business will nap once in a while) and look for opportunities to talk with others who understand and support what you're dealing with. If you build time and opportunity for inspiration into your business right from the start, it can blossom in creative ways as your business begins to grow.

What's Next

This chapter introduced you to many of the features included in Office Live Small Business that can support you as you get your business online, promote your business, and manage your data and relationships. The next chapter launches into the practical pieces: you'll find out how to sign up, set up your account, choose the business services you want, and begin using Office Live Small Business to introduce your business to the world and position it for growth.

Getting Started with Microsoft Office Live Small Business

IN THIS CHAPTER, YOU WILL

- Learn the system requirements for Microsoft Office Live Small Business.
- Create your Office Live Small Business account.
- Take a look around the Office Live Small Business window.
- Get to know the Office Live Small Business services.
- Set up your Web site account.
- Work with domains.
- Create e-mail accounts.
- Work with Account Settings.
- Find out where to go for help.

IT SEEMS like every big decision we make involves some kind of a leap of faith. You had a good idea for a business. Then what? Perhaps you talked to a few people or did a little daydreaming. You may have done a thorough analysis of the marketing and developed a strategy for carving out your niche. Or you may—like many of us—have been so excited, so pumped up with creative energy that you simply gathered your ideas and jumped in with both feet.

Starting a new business is an exciting, hopeful endeavor, and, as you no doubt have discovered by now, it has its challenges of doubt and worry. Getting the right supports set firmly underneath your new enterprise is an important part of ensuring its long-term success. This chapter shows you how to add a major player to your support team by signing up for Microsoft Office Live Small Business and getting Web space and e-mail accounts established. And the best part is that using Office Live Small Business doesn't require a big leap or an investment of time and resources that you don't have. You can get started easily—right now—for free.

WANT TO UPGRADE YOUR WEB EXPERIENCE?

If you spend a lot of time online and have a clunky, slow dinosaur of a computer, you may want to consider upgrading your system to enable you to work more efficiently and reliably (and be less crabby with your co-workers and spouse). Today's Web is lightning fast compared with the early days of the Internet (think late '80s). But because many entrepreneurs live by the adage, "Time is money," sitting and waiting on a Web page is agonizing—and for some, unthinkable. You can easily increase the speed and capacity of your computer by doing the following:

- **Add to your computer's Random-Access Memory (RAM).** Memory prices fluctuate (like the price of gasoline), so search online to find the best deals. Be sure to do the research to find exactly the type of memory you need for your particular system, because "close matches" won't work. If you're not sure how to find the memory you need for your particular system, start with the Web site of your computer manufacturer. Dell, for example, offers memory modules for the systems it sells, and you can be sure you're purchasing the right memory for your system. (And the memory arrives with instructions for installation; it's much easier than you might think.)
- **Upgrade to a larger hard drive.** The amount of storage you have available might not directly impact your Web experience, but if you are searching for, selecting, and uploading files to your site, the whole computer can begin to run like molasses when you are running out of disk storage. To keep things running as fast as possible, make sure that you have plenty of available disk space. (And don't forget to back up your system regularly—you never know when you're going to need those saved files.)
- **Upgrade your modem or your Internet connection.** The type of Internet connection may depend largely on what's available in your area, but for users who have a choice, making the decision about the type of connection they want to invest in may mean a larger monthly expense. If broadband (also referred to as DSL) is available in your area and fits your budget, it's worth considering, because the connection speed is infinitely faster than dial-up and is more reliable.

System Requirements for Office Live

First things first. What type of system do you need to run Office Live Small Business?

Part of the beauty of this online service is that it provides a huge amount of support without requiring a lot from you. (And for most of us who run small businesses, that's good news!) You don't need to add memory, storage space, hardware devices, or fancy gadgetry. Because the program is Web based, the processes that impact whether or not the system works effectively are all housed online, along with your data files, contacts, and more.

You will need the following items to access and work with Office Live Small Business (but, hopefully, these are things you've already got in place):

- A computer (desktop PC, laptop, or mobile device) with Internet access
- Windows Internet Explorer 6.0, Windows XP or Windows Vista, or Mozilla Firefox

NOTE The Market Share report published in November 2007 by Net Applications, a market research group, says that 78.3 percent of all Web browsing in the United States is done from Windows XP. Windows Mobile devices accounted for a 0.6 percent share, although with the growing adoption of Windows Vista and improved access for mobile devices, those percentages are sure to change.[1]

1 Net Applications. Market Share, November 2007. Available online at *marketshare.hitslink.com/report.aspx?qprid=10&qptimeframe=M&qpsp=106&qpmr=14&qpdt=1&qpct=0&sample=4*.

Creating Your Office Live Small Business Account

Office Live Small Business is a comprehensive set of Web-based tools that helps you get your business online, attract customers, and manage your business. The service is set up to provide all the basics in a free, easy-to-use format that you can access anyplace you have Web access. The program is designed so that you can begin with a set of core services and then add on services à la carte—so you can tailor the program to fit just the needs of your particular business. That way you're not paying for services you don't use, and you can change your subscriptions—by adding new services or removing ones you want—at any time.

The first step involves signing up for Office Live Small Business. Here's how to do that:

1. Connect to the Internet and open your Web browser.
2. Go to *smallbusiness.officelive.com/*.
3. Click Sign Up Free.
4. Enter your Windows Live ID and password.

NOTE If you don't have a Windows Live ID, click Register Now and fill in the requested information to get one. Then enter your new Windows Live ID and password in the blanks on the Office Live Small Business Sign In page.

5. Fill in the blanks to provide your name, business name, and organization size, and click Save and Continue.

NOTE In the previous version of Office Live, users selected from one of three Office Live programs: Office Live Basics, Office Live Essentials, and Office Live Premium. Each of the different programs offered different services. (Basics was free, and Essentials and Premium had additional services included in a monthly subscription fee.) In response to user feedback, the Office Live team has changed the subscription strategy so that small-business owners can simply choose only the services that serve their needs at a particular time. This makes the program even more flexible for you and enables you to invest in the areas that will really help your business grow.

A Look Around the Office Live Small Business Window

As soon as you sign up for Office Live Small Business, you will see a Home page similar to the one shown in Figure 3-1. This page provides you with links to all the pages and features in Office Live Small Business, along with a series of how-to articles in the Getting Started section and a quick summary of your Web statistics.

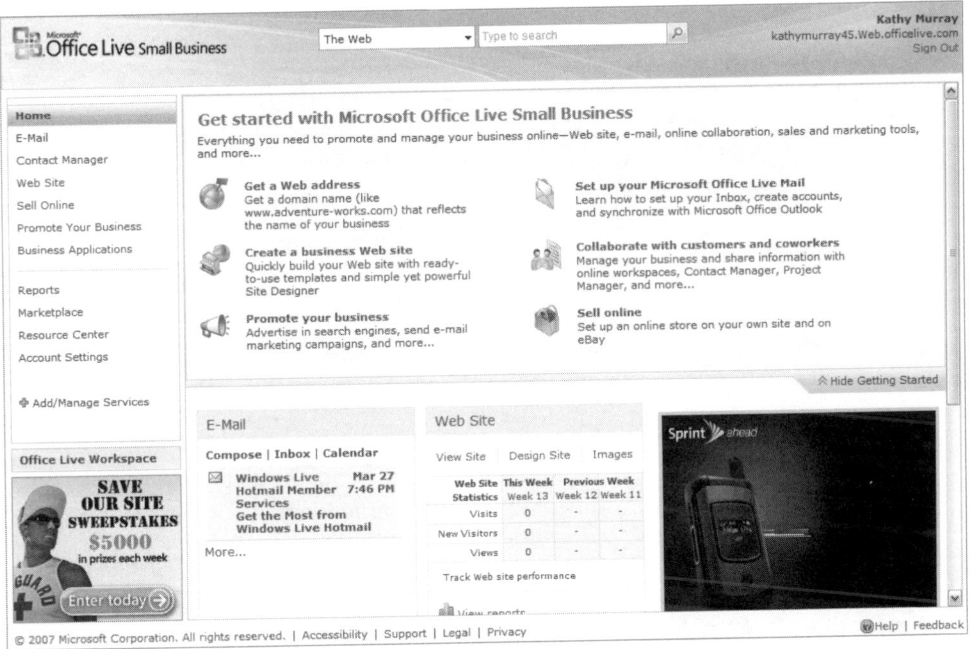

FIGURE 3-1 Your Office Live Small Business Home page offers everything you need to begin creating your Web site and managing your business information effectively.

Links for Success

The navigation bar, along the left side of the Home page, provides the path into various features of Office Live Small Business:

- E-Mail displays tools you can use to create e-mail accounts and check your e-mail, work with your personal calendar, and work with Windows Live Messenger to chat—via text, voice, or even video—in real time with customers, peers, vendors, and more.

- Contact Manager takes you to a powerful contact management tool that enables you to collect all information, leads, opportunities, and projects that relate to specific contacts in your database. Contact Manager works seamlessly with other business applications in Office Live Small Business as well as with Office Live Small Business Mail.
- Web Site gives you the doorway into all things Web. Here you can design, publish, revise, and work with your Web pages.
- Sell Online takes you into the e-commerce area of Office Live Small Business. Here you can set up your account to enable you to sell online, either directly on your Office Live Small Business site or in tandem with sales on eBay.
- Promote Your Business gives you the ability to reach customers in smart, low-cost ways. Using adManager, you can set a budget and easily create pay-per-click ads that reach the areas you want them to reach; using the e-mail marketing feature, you can create, launch, and track e-mail marketing campaigns that reach potential customers and help increase visibility for your business.
- Business Applications takes you into the area of Office Live Small Business in which you can manage the information, projects, and relationships that are such an important part of your day-to-day work.
- Reports enables you to produce reports on various activities in your business. From Web statistics to keyword usage to referring sources and more, you can see at a glance what's working and what's not in your marketing and online efforts.
- Marketplace takes you to a rich resource in Office Live Small Business, in which you can find partners and third-party vendors offering add-ons and services that might be just what you need to fill a much-needed gap in your team.
- Resource Center provides you with all sorts of links to articles, tutorials, webcasts, and more that show you how to get the most out of Office Live Small Business and grow your business online.
- Account Settings enables you to view and modify your Office Live Small Business account settings. Here you assign the necessary permissions for other users to work with your Office Live Small Business site, set alerts, establish e-mail accounts, update your business information, work with your domain settings, and more.

In addition, you can use Add/Manage Services, at the bottom of the navigation bar, to add, modify, or remove add-on services to your Office Live account. The next section tells you more about the various services that you can add to the core features in Office Live Small Business.

Getting Started

The Getting Started area appears at the top of the Home page and at the top of the page that appears when you click each of the choices in the navigation bar, providing links to the next steps in the selected process. For example, when you click Business Applications, the set of Getting Started links helps you upload documents to the Document Manager, add an application, find custom applications, use the Team Workspace, and sync your calendar with Microsoft Office Outlook 2007 (see Figure 3-2).

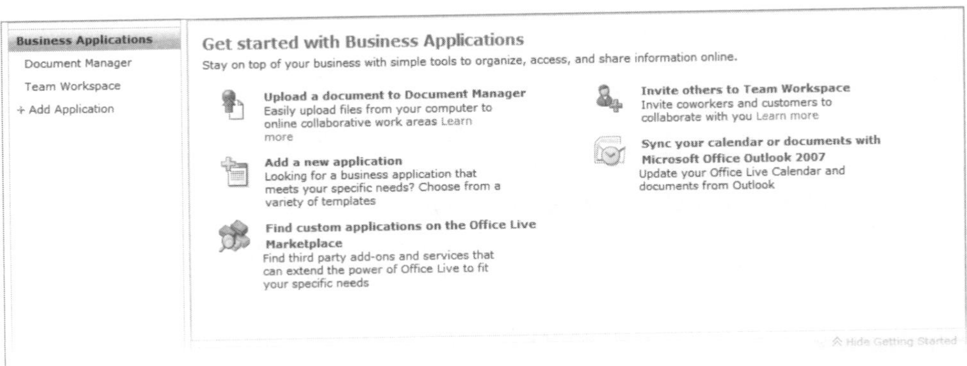

FIGURE 3-2 The Getting Started area provides links to information on next steps in the different services.

The Resource Center sidebar on each page in Office Live Small Business provides you with additional links to articles, demonstrations, overviews, and more.

Once you get comfortable finding your way around Office Live Small Business, you can hide the Getting Started area and maximize your workspace on screen by clicking Hide Getting Started. You can redisplay the tips and links at any time by clicking the Getting Started tab at the top of the work area.

Introducing Office Live Small Business Services

Office Live Small Business is designed to be a key member of the support team for small business owners like you—someone who is running or working in a small business, who has a limited amount of time and resources, and who often has many irons in the fire at once. You need to see results for your investment, and you don't have a lot of time to spend researching and trying things that don't work. Office Live understands that. For that reason, Office Live offers the basic core services for free—that way, getting on the Web isn't an obstacle for anyone—and provides low-cost services for features you may need as you expand your business online.

For example, consider a small pet grooming business. When the owner first started in business, she simply wanted to post a Web site with her logo, contact information, and a few photos of happy four-legged clients. As her business started to grow, she wanted to enhance her site and begin to do some local pay-per-click advertising. Later, when her business really started taking off, she added a pet boutique to her site and sold the natural products she used in her grooming service. Each step of the way, Office Live Small Business was able to keep pace with her and offer just the services she needed for where she was in the growth cycle of her business. Free services enabled her to create her site, get a domain (free for the first year), add photos and content, and get e-mail accounts (see Figure 3-3). When she was ready to do some search advertising, she signed up for a low-cost add-on that enabled her to set a budget for the advertising and track her results. When she was interested in adding a boutique to her site, she subscribed to another low-cost feature to take care of the e-commerce transactions and create a simple purchasing experience for her customers.

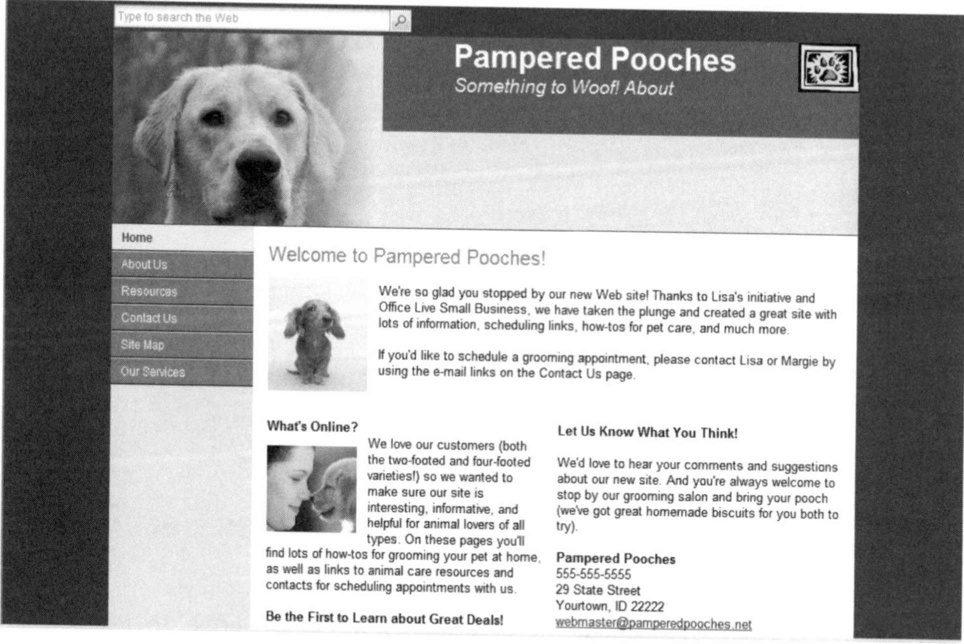

FIGURE 3-3 Adding a professional site is easy—and free—in Office Live Small Business.

The Free Stuff: Core Services

Office Live Small Business breaks down the no-Web-site barrier that often gets in the way of small and struggling enterprises. By making Web site tools, server space, and selected business applications freely available, Office Live Small Business ensures that every small business that wants a place on the Web can find one. The core services offered free of charge in Office Live Small Business are these:

- Web site design, hosting, and management
- E-mail, calendar, and instant messaging
- Contact and project management tools

Get on the Web—Today

When signing up for Office Live Small Business, your most pressing need may be to get your business on the Web. Office Live Small Business comes with a number of free, easy-to-use, but powerful tools you can use to create, publish, and enhance a Web site for your business. The Page Manager enables you to work effectively with all the pages you create; the Site Designer helps you give your pages a professional look; the Image, Document, and Template Galleries provide you with the means to collect and organize the files you use on your site; and the Page Editor gives you the tools to customize the layout and content of your page in a way that meets industry standards.

SEE ALSO For a full discussion of using all the Office Live Small Business Web tools to create a professional quality Web site, see Chapter 4, "Designing Your Site."

In addition to professionally designed templates and effective Web tools, you receive a generous amount of server space (500 MB) and bandwidth (10 GB, monthly) to support even the largest and most sophisticated of sites.

TIP

Not enough space or bandwidth for you? You can easily add storage in blocks of 100 MB for $4.95 per month or bandwidth in 24 GB increments for $1.95 per month.

Stay in Sync with E-Mail and Scheduling

In addition to the free Web design and hosting tools, Office Live Small Business offers a Web-based e-mail service that is based on Windows Live Mail. You can create up to 100 e-mail accounts for use with your Office Live Small Business site, as well as set up and use instant messaging with customers, vendors, staff members, and peers.

TIP

If you want the e-mail without the ads, you can upgrade your 100 free e-mail accounts to a premium account, which gives you ad-free e-mail for $9.95 per month.

SEE ALSO

Chapter 7, "Staying in Sync with Microsoft Office Live Small Business Mail," gives you all the specifics on working with Office Live Small Business Mail to keep in touch with co-workers, customers, vendors, and prospective clients.

Office Live Small Business Mail also includes a calendar feature that you can use to set appointments, schedule meetings, set up tasks and events, and more. Using the calendar feature can help you share your information, let team members know when you're available, and leave notes and reminders you can follow up on at a later time.

Finally, if you want to provide instant access to clients and vendors, you can use the free instant messaging feature based on Windows Live Messenger. Not only does this provide nearly seamless communication with others, but it also helps reinforce the brand of your business when you use your business logo as the image that appears in the IM window.

TIP

You can use Outlook Connector to make it possible to download e-mail messages and contacts from Office Live Small Business Mail to Outlook 2007. Outlook Connector is available as a free download from the Microsoft Download Center (*www.microsoft.com/downloads*).

Manage Business Information Effectively

Office Live Small Business also includes a number of business applications that help you manage information, projects, and business relationships effectively. As part of the free core services, Office Live Small Business includes Contact Manager, a full-featured contact management program that enables you to track contacts, opportunities, businesses, and more as you build relationships through e-mail, marketing campaigns, phone calls, face-to-face meetings, and other interactions. The Project Manager helps you organize and track the various phases and tasks in various projects, and the Team Workspace provides you with secure online space where your teams (including staff, vendors, client groups, and more) can gather, post announcements and events, use document libraries, and discuss projects.

SEE ALSO In addition to these three robust applications, you can choose from among 20 additional business applications in several different categories. Chapter 10, "Working with Business Applications," walks you through using, adding, and customizing business applications.

TIP If you don't find the business application you want, you can click Add Or Find Custom Applications and search for custom applications developed by third-party vendors and made available through Office Live Marketplace.

Growing Your Business: Add-On Services

Once the basics are in place, you're ready to spread the word about your business. Office Live Small Business offers a set of affordable, professional add-on services that make it easy for you to expand into new areas through online marketing, adding e-commerce features, and getting the word out via search advertising.

TIP One of the great things about Office Live Small Business is that you can select the services that fit your needs and skip the ones that don't. You can choose to use any or all of the add-on services, depending on the needs of your particular business.

Store Manager is an easy-to-use e-commerce feature that adds a shopping cart to your site with just a few simple clicks of the mouse. Because the utility uses the template you've selected for your site design, the e-commerce area of your site will match the look of your overall site. In addition to adding online sales capability to your own site, you can easily produce product listings and sell your products on eBay, dramatically increasing your sales capabilities. Using Store Manager, you'll be able to sell products online and accept credit card payments. You'll also be able to create invoices and confirmation e-mail messages seamlessly, which helps you provide a professional purchasing experience for your customers.

Store Manager is easy to set up and use, and Office Live Small Business walks you through the process. Store Manager offers two different ways to sell your products online: You can add sales capability to your site only, or add it to both your site and eBay. The integration with eBay is a useful feature—you can easily create product listings (see Figure 3-4); add images; and track, report, and regularly download transaction information. The cost for using Store Manager for your site alone is $19.95 per month, plus a 1 percent transaction fee; when you add the eBay functionality, the cost is $39.95 per month, plus the 1 percent transaction fee.

SEE ALSO For more information on how to add Store Manager, set up your e-commerce features, and create product listings for eBay, see Chapter 8, "Selling Products Online."

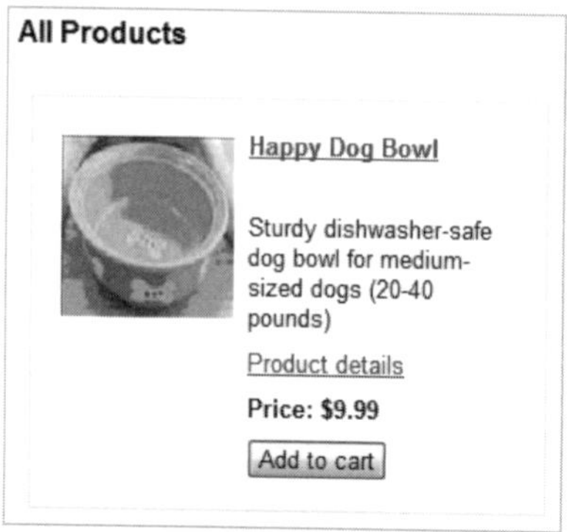

FIGURE 3-4 List products on your site and on eBay.

E-mail marketing is a smart, cost-effective, and earth-friendly way to share information, offers, and links with your growing customer base. Using the E-Mail Marketing service in Office Live Small Business, you can create, send, and track e-mail marketing campaigns that match the look and feel of your site (see Figure 3-5). You can also produce reports that show the results of your e-mail marketing campaigns and identify what works—so you can do more of it.

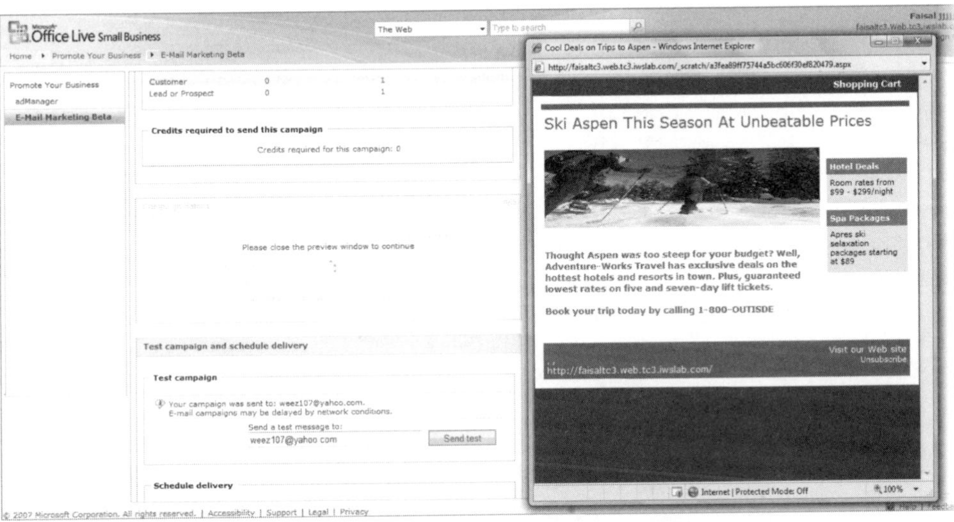

FIGURE 3-5 E-Mail Marketing enables you to reach customers with newsletters, special offers, and more, with messages that match the design of your site.

Another way to reach customers and prospective customers is through search advertising with adManager. When people search for a product or service that is similar to yours, what words do they type in the search box? If the words they enter are identified as your keywords and you have signed up for search advertising, your site could be one of the top results listed in their search results. With search advertising, you can advertise locally or globally, reaching the customers that are most likely to be interested in your products or services. Office Live Small Business helps you get the most from your search ads by enabling you to set a budget for your search advertising and set the rate you want to pay for the pay-per-click advertising. Whether you want to spend $30 or $3,000 per month in search advertising, spreading the word with adManager can bring great results. You simply enter the text you want to appear in the search ad, insert your Web address, choose your keywords, set your budget, and you're ready to go!

SEE ALSO To learn how to set up and work with E-Mail Marketing and adManager, see Chapter 9, "Promoting Your Business."

Setting Up Your Web Site Account

Okay, that's it! You're in! Now you know the whole range of services at your disposal, and you're probably eager to get started on your site. The rest of this chapter shows you how to set up the basics so that you can get this show on the road.

With the previous version of Office Live Small Business, new users needed to choose a domain name and enter a credit card right off the bat as they created a new site. Now sign-up and setup are easier than ever, and there's no pressure to decide on a domain name until you're ready.

Office Live Small Business makes it as easy as possible for you to begin working on your site right away. Once you have your Windows Live ID and have created an Office Live Small Business account, you can access the Web tools by clicking Web Site on the left navigation bar. The screen shown in Figure 3-6 appears.

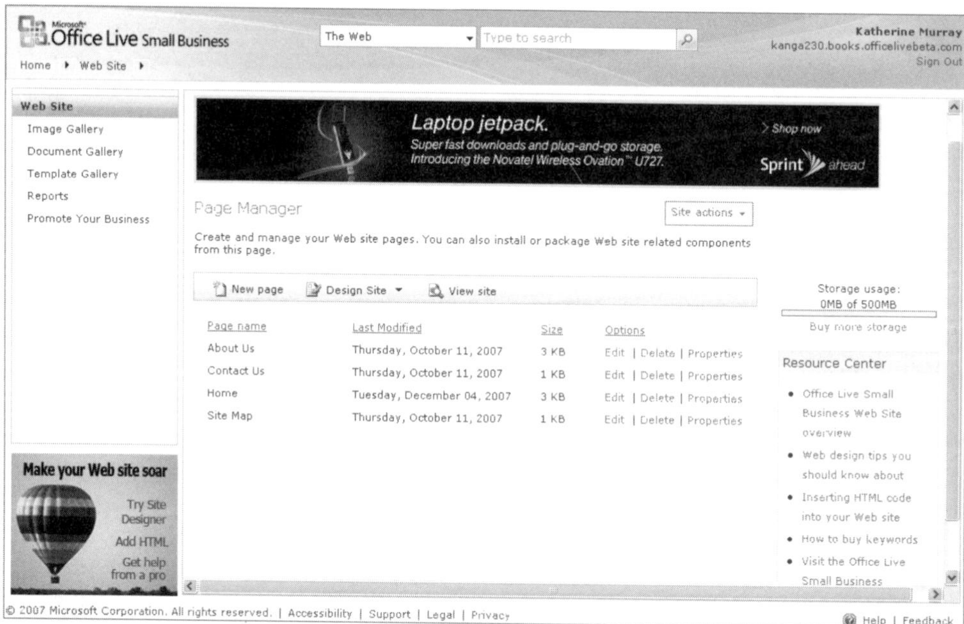

FIGURE 3-6 The Web Site page displays the Page Manager, with four basic pages you can customize right away.

NOTE In the preceding figure, note that the Getting Started area has been hidden to allow more room on the screen.

Perks and Benefits—and How It All Works

If you've looked into the possibility of having a Web site before, you know that it can be expensive and time-consuming—a resource drain for a small business. Professional design costs for your site will range from $1,500 (on the low end) to thousands of dollars. One recent online article showed an estimated cost of $8,500 for a 10-page site.[2] In addition to the design costs, you've got hosting fees (monthly or annual); site registration fees; and the work hours spent updating, maintaining, and improving the site.

Office Live Small Business gives you the following things as part of the core Web services:

- 500 MB of server space (and you can add more, if you choose, in 100-MB increments).
- A custom domain (free for the first year; then $14.95 per year after that).
- 100 e-mail addresses you can use to brand your business (upgradable to ad-free e-mail for $9.95 per month).
- 24-hour customer support 7 days per week, including free phone support for the first 30 days for all users, and continuing free phone customer support for users who purchase the add-on services (Store Manager, adManager, and E-Mail Marketing). But even if you use only the free services, customer support is available to you via e-mail 24 hours a day, every day. You never need to feel you're in over your head when support is always within reach. The Office Live Small Business team averages four hours or less in responding to customer e-mail messages.

Everything you use to create, design, update, and manage your Web site; reach customers; and manage your business information is stored in the server space assigned to your account. This means that you can access your site and business information anywhere you have Web access, and that the information is always stored securely within Microsoft's advanced network firewall services (using a daily backup system) so that you know that even if you experience computer trouble, your information and your site are always safe.

TIP

The daily secure backups of all customer business data also means that if you inadvertently damage your site or files, you can recover your data from the backups stored on the Microsoft servers.

2 Source: *bajooter.com/archives/how-much-does-a-10-page-website-cost*

Getting Started on Your Site

When you're first preparing to create your site, you probably have the following questions:

- **How many people will be working on this site?** You'll need to create the necessary permissions for those users to have access to the Web tools.
- **What do we want our site to do?** If you want to create a simple site that gives prospective customers and existing clients information about your business, you can start out with the basic pages included in the Web templates by default. If you have additional needs or want to add e-commerce or lead generation features, you will want to add on the necessary services (Store Manager, adManager, and E-Mail Marketing) as you begin creating your site.
- **Where will we get the text and images?** The Document and Picture libraries available in the Web tools are a great way to gather, organize, use, and manage the content you use on your site. As you get ready to add items to your pages, think through the various elements—articles, logos, photos, and more—you may want to include on your site pages.

Setting Site Permissions

Many owners of small businesses tend to do everything possible themselves (present company included!), which means that you may be the sole proprietor of your business and your site. If you work with a team, however, one of your first tasks in setting up your site will be to give others the permission they need to work on the Web site. Here's how to do that.

To set the necessary permissions for others to work on the site, follow these steps:

1. On your Office Live Small Business Home page, in the left navigation bar, click Web Site.
2. Click the Site Actions arrow and choose Site Administration (see Figure 3-7).
3. The Permissions page lists the users you have set up for your Office Live Small Business account. Click Edit in the Options column to display the existing permissions for a specific user.
4. In the Edit User Information dialog box (see Figure 3-8), click the Role arrow and click the level of permissions you want the user to have.

FIGURE 3-7 Change user permissions so others can work on your site, by clicking Site Administration in the Site Actions menu.

NOTE You will see an Edit item in the Options column only for users you have added in addition to the Owner of the account. There is no Edit or Delete option for the primary account holder.

FIGURE 3-8 Change permissions in the Edit User Information dialog box.

SEE ALSO For information about adding users to your account, see "Adding User Accounts" in the "Working with Account Settings" section later in this chapter.

UNDERSTANDING PERMISSIONS

Office Live Small Business offers three levels of permissions for those who have the ability to access the Office Live account:

- In the Administrator role, users have full access to the site and can view, modify, delete, or add to the information on the site (including creating and deleting user accounts) without any restrictions.
- In the Editor role, users can make changes or add comments to the site, but do not have the ability to work with the administration tools used for setting permissions, adding or removing user accounts, working with domains, and more.
- In the Reader role, users can see all content and comments, but cannot make any changes to what they see.

Working with Domains

The domain you choose for your site is an important part of the overall identity of your business. If you create a domain that closely matches your business name or captures part (or all!) of your major product or brand, each time a potential customer sees your URL, he or she will be reminded of your product or service. That's great marketing!

Office Live Small Business makes it easy for you to create your own custom domain, redirect a domain you already have so that you can use it with Office Live, or manage multiple domains. This section gives you the basics of each of these three domain activities.

Registering Your Domain Name

Version 2 of Office Live Small Business makes getting your own domain name easier than ever. And what's more, you don't have to make that decision right off the bat. If you want to start working on your site and think carefully about the name you choose for your domain (which is a very good idea), you can delay purchasing the domain until a later time. When you first begin working with Office Live Small Business, the service creates a private address for you that uses your Windows Live ID as part of the Web address. You can create your site and begin to use the other services in Office Live Small Business and then sign up for the domain when you've had a chance to think about it a bit.

CHOOSING A GOOD URL

Aaron Goldman is a self-described "URL-aholic" who publishes a site (*www.GoodURLBadURL.com*) that tracks both good and bad URLs (along with photos). Here is his list of Do's and Don'ts for naming your site in a way that will ultimately help you get your message out (in a positive way):

Do's

1. Capitalize The First Letter Of Each Word.
2. Use different colors or bold to help each word stand out.
3. Whenever possible, use YourBrandName.com.
4. If .com is not available, use YourBrandName.net.
5. If .com and .net are taken, find a new brand name. Seriously.
6. Use YourSlogan.com when running an integrated media campaign.
7. Use subdomains when driving people deeper than your home page—e.g., Product.YourBrandName.com.

Don'ts

1. Don't include www. We know to go to the World Wide Web to find you.
2. Don't include http://. If your audience isn't Web-savvy enough to know where to type the URL, you shouldn't have a Web site.
3. don'tusealllowercase (canyoureallytellwhereonewordendsandthenextbegins?)
4. DITTOFORALLUPPERCASE.
5. No-hyphens/or slashes.
6. Don't use acronyms, abbreviations, or numbers unless your brand is widely known as such.
7. Don't bury your URL at the bottom of a billboard. I'm the only nerd driving around with a 4x zoom lens to find URLs.[3]

3 This information has been included by permission of Aaron Goldman.

TIP

Office Live Small Business provides you with up to 100 e-mail accounts you can use along with your Office Live account. If you intend to register a domain name for your Web site, consider waiting to set up your e-mail accounts until the domain is purchased. This way you can be sure that when you start assigning e-mail accounts they will have the correct domain as part of the e-mail address. E-mail addresses are an important part of branding (building the identity of) your business.

When you're ready to register a domain name for your Office Live Small Business site, follow these steps:

1. Click Web Site in the navigation bar on the left.
2. Click Register A Domain Name in Getting Started.
3. In the Add/Manage Services window, click the Web Site And E-Mail category.
4. In Domains, click Sign Up. The screen shown in Figure 3-9 appears.

TIP

Now Office Live Small Business uses private domain name registration to help keep your contact information off the lists people use to send spam and phishing e-mail messages.

5. Type the domain you want in the Domain Name box and click Check Availability. If the domain is available, you will see a message similar to the one shown in Figure 3-10. If the domain is not available, you will be prompted to enter a new domain name.

TIP

It's not unusual for users to have to try a few times before coming up with a domain name that fits their business and is available. Don't get discouraged if you can't get the names you were hoping for—just spend a little extra time thinking about possibilities and then try again.

6. When you find the domain you want, click Confirm.
7. Office Live Small Business will review your contact information and then prompt you for a credit card. The first year of your domain registration is free, but your credit card will be charged at the beginning of the second year. After you enter your information, click OK.

8. Click Complete My Order to finish the process.

Office Live Small Business

Faisal jjjjjjj
Sign Out

Add/Manage Services

Cancel changes and go back

Your selection

change selection

Add: Domains

Add a domain

Your current purchased domains

Primary domain: faisaltc3.Web.tc3.iwslab.com

Secondary domains: blarblarbblarbultrasuperms.com

Type the domain name that you want to register

* Domain name: .com $14.95/year

Private Registration (included in cost)

Check availability

Already have a domain? Redirect it to Microsoft Office Live Small Business.

Complete signing up

FIGURE 3-9 When you're ready, you can register for a custom domain to help build the brand of your business.

Register a new domain name
Congratulations. The domain name pamperedpooches.com is available.
Click Confirm to continue registering pamperedpooches.com.
Click Back to try a different domain name.
Confirm
Back

FIGURE 3-10 A message lets you know that the domain you entered is available.

Congratulations! You've just registered your first domain name using Office Live Small Business.

TIP

There's no law limiting you to one domain. If your business takes off—or you have other Web ideas you want to try—you can get additional domains by clicking Purchase Additional Domains on the Domain Manager page.

Using Your Existing Domain

If you've already created a Web site using another provider, you can easily redirect your site to Office Live Small Business so that you can enjoy the full benefit of the site design, promotion, and management services available to you. The process involves two parts. First, you tell Office Live Small Business which site you want to include in the service, and then you change the name server settings in your existing site's hosting software so the host knows where your site is being stored. The following steps walk you through the process:

1. In the Office Live Small Business Home page, click Account Settings.
2. Click Domain Manager.
3. Click Use Your Own Domain Name (see Figure 3-11). If prompted, enter your Windows Live ID and password.
4. In the Bring Your Domain To Office Live area, type your existing site domain in the Domain To Redirect box. Then select the identifier (.com, .net, .biz, and so on) in the box to the left of the Confirm button (see Figure 3-12).
5. Choose whether you want to redirect only the Web site or both the site and associated e-mail addresses.
6. Click Confirm.
7. Next, go to the site where your existing site is currently hosted and log in using your account ID and password.
8. Find the place on the site where you can edit server information for your site. The option may look something like Edit DNS, Name Server Settings, or DNS Server Settings.
9. For the primary and secondary name servers, enter **NS1.officelive.com** and **NS2.officelive.com**. Save your changes.
10. Sign in to your Office Live Small Business account and first click Account Settings and then Domain Manager. When the process is complete, the existing domain will appear in the Additional Domain Names area on the Domain Manager screen.

TIP If you don't see the option you need, contact your host's customer service for help.

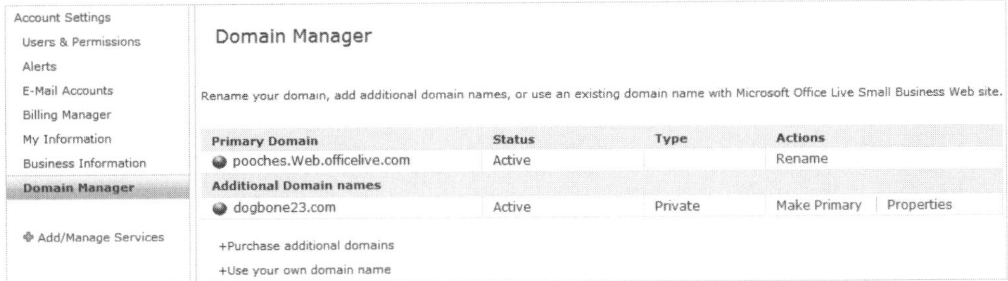

FIGURE 3-11 Redirecting an existing site takes just a few clicks.

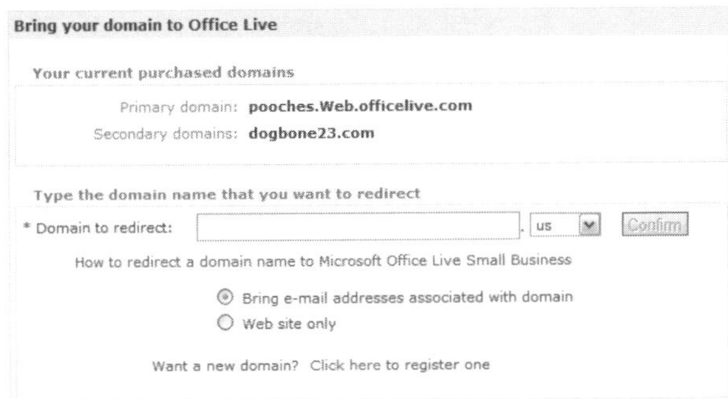

FIGURE 3-12 Enter the domain you want to redirect and indicate whether you want to move associated e-mail accounts as well.

Managing Your Domains

After you've purchased and/or redirected domains to your Office Live Small Business account, you can manage your domains by assigning or renaming them or changing site properties.

Choose a Primary Domain

When you add more than one domain to your Office Live Small Business account, you need to let the program know which site is the primary site for the account. By default, the site you created first will be listed as the primary site, but you can change this easily by following these steps:

1. On the Office Live Small Business Home page, click Account Settings.
2. Click Domain Manager.

3. On the Domain Manager screen, locate the domain you'd like to make the primary site (refer to Figure 3-11).
4. Click Make Primary.

Office Live Small Business changes the sites according to your selection, and the new site will be used as the primary site for your account.

Rename a Domain

If you decide your domain isn't working for you—or you come up with something you like better—you can easily rename your domain using the Domain Manager. To rename a domain, follow these steps:

1. On the Office Live Small Business Home page, click Account Settings.
2. Click Domain Manager.
3. Click Rename in the Actions column.

> **NOTE** Changing the name of your domain may affect your placement in search results and will have an impact on account and e-mail settings. Rename domains only when the change is necessary.

Change Domain Properties

The Domain Manager also gives you the option of editing the properties that are part of an existing domain. To see the properties for a selected domain, display the Domain Manager and click the Properties link in the far right side of a domain row.

> **NOTE** The Properties link appears only when you have registered more than one domain with Office Live Small Business.

In the Domain Properties screen, review the information that appears and click Edit Properties if you want to make a change. The information becomes editable so that you can change the data recorded for that domain. Make your changes and click Save when you're done.

Creating E-Mail Accounts

As you learned earlier in this chapter, Office Live Small Business gives you 100 e-mail accounts—for free—when you first create your account. These e-mail accounts are advertising-supported, which means that you will see ads displayed as you are creating, sending, and organizing your mail.

If you'd rather have the e-mail accounts without the display ads, you can upgrade your e-mail to a premium account for $9.95 per month.

To create and set up e-mail accounts so that others in your business will have their own business-branded e-mail accounts, follow these steps:

1. On the Office Live Small Business Home page, click Account Settings.
2. Click E-Mail Accounts. The E-mail Accounts window shows you the e-mail accounts currently configured for your account (see Figure 3-13).
3. Click Create New E-Mail account. The dialog box shown in Figure 3-14 appears.
4. Enter the user e-mail you want to use for the account and press Tab.
5. Type a password for the account (and retype it to confirm).
6. Enter a first name and last name for the user account.
7. Click Next. Office Live Small Business creates the account.
8. Click Finish.

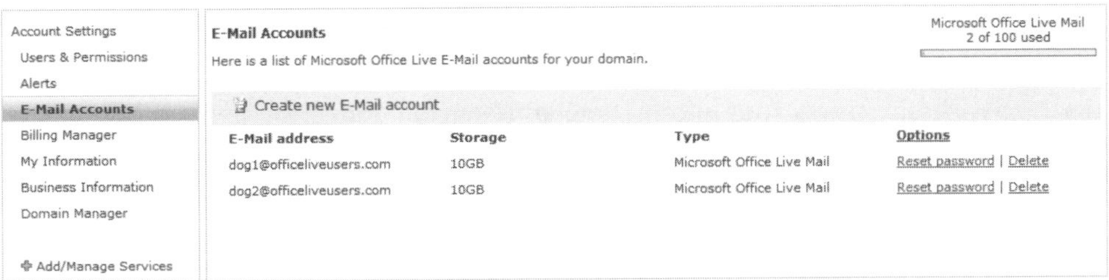

FIGURE 3-13 The E-Mail Accounts page shows you the e-mail accounts currently set up for your account.

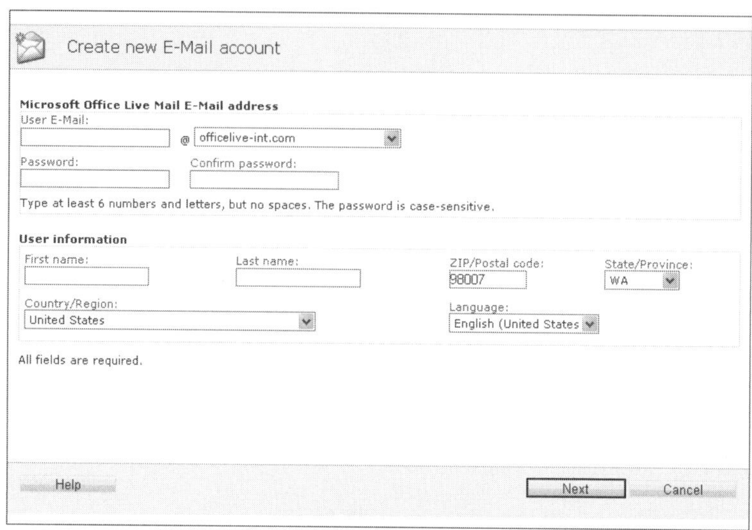

FIGURE 3-14 Fill in the blanks to add your first e-mail account.

SEE ALSO For more about working with e-mail, including using spam filters, adding calendar items, and using instant messaging, see Chapter 7, "Staying in Sync with Microsoft Office Live Small Business Mail."

Working with Account Settings

The Account Settings area of Office Live Small Business enables you to make decisions about the way you want your services to work. Specifically, in Account Settings, you'll add user accounts and set permissions, set up alerts (so you are notified when something is changed or added to the site), create and manage e-mail accounts, set up billing specifications, add your information, and manage domains.

Adding User Accounts

Earlier in this chapter, you learned that in order to give users the permissions they need to work on your Web pages, you need to first create their user accounts. You add new users to your Office Live Small Business account by choosing Account Settings in the left navigation bar. To add a user account to your Office Live Small Business account, follow these steps:

1. Click Users & Permissions.
2. Click Add User.
3. In the Add User dialog box, shown in Figure 3-15, enter the e-mail address of the person you want to create the account for.
4. Click in the Display Name box and type the name you want to appear as the user name.
5. Click Next, and click the arrow to the right of the role setting for each of the four features listed (see Figure 3-16). You can choose Administrator, Editor, or Reader roles.
6. Click Next, and then enter a brief message for the recipient of the e-mail notification, as shown in Figure 3-17.
7. Click Send to send the new account notification.

Add user

Type the e-mail address and name
If you want to use an existing e-mail address, type the user's e-mail address and name. If you want to use a new Microsoft Office Live Small Business e-mail address, create an Office Live Small Business e-mail account for the user.

E-mail address:

Display name:

All fields are required.

Help | < Previous | Next > | Cancel

FIGURE 3-15 Begin the process of adding a new user by entering the e-mail address and user name.

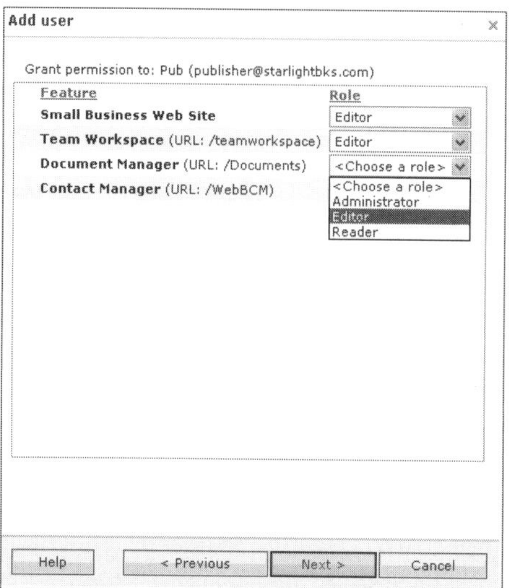

FIGURE 3-16 Choose the role you want to assign to the new user.

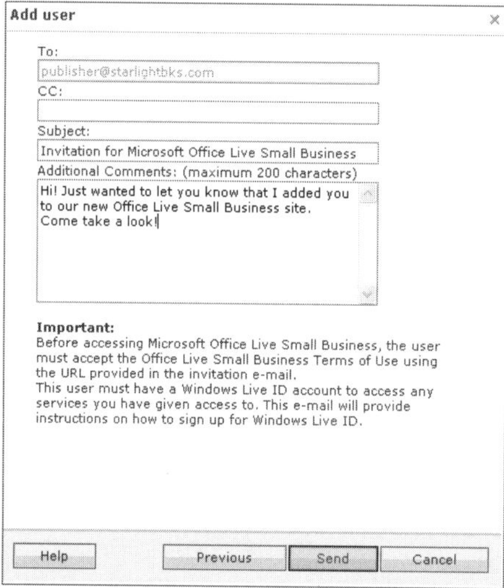

FIGURE 3-17 Send a note to the new user to finish adding the new account.

After you click Send, a Congratulations! page appears, letting you know that the message has been sent and showing the roles you've selected for the new user. Click Finish to complete the process.

TIP

You can change roles and permission levels at any time by choosing Account Settings, clicking Users & Permissions, and clicking the Edit link to the right of the user name in the Permissions list. When the Edit User Information page appears, click the arrow to the right of the role you want to modify, select the new role, and click Save.

Setting Up Site Alerts

When you work with multiple users on your site, it's nice to know when new items are added, changed, or removed. Additionally, you'll want to know when content is changed, files are uploaded, and so forth. You can set up Alerts in Office Live Small Business so that you are automatically notified whenever one of the events you select occurs on the site. Here's how to do that:

1. On the Home page, click Account Settings.
2. Click Alerts. The My Alerts page appears (see Figure 3-18).
3. Click Create Alert. In the Alert Area section, click the arrow and choose the business application you want to be alerted about (Accounting Sharing, Contact Manager, Document Manager, or Team Workspace).
4. Next, select the list or document library item you want to be alerted about. This list displays options related to your first selection. So for the Contact Manager, the document library list will include the choices Business Contacts, Companies, Opportunities, and Products (see Figure 3-19). Click the item you want to create the alert for.
5. You can further customize the alert on the next page by entering an alert title, selecting the person you want to receive the alert, changing the type of events that trigger the alert, and setting the frequency for the alert notifications. For example, you might want to choose to receive a daily summary of changes that occur when people modify a picture in the Picture Library of your site.
6. Click OK to save the new alert.

NOTE

Alerts are available only for Business Applications and Document Library features.

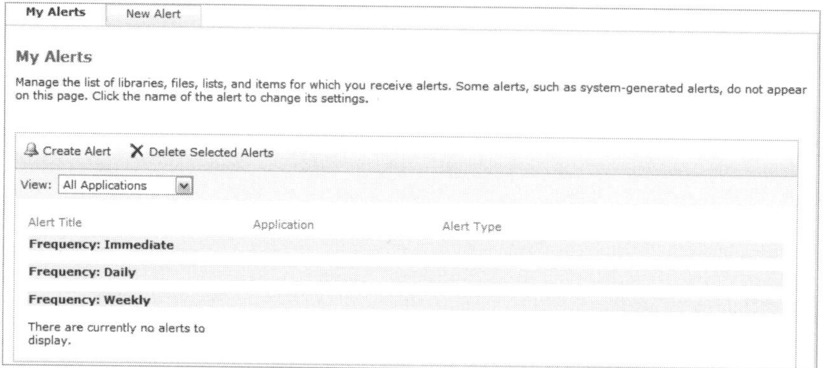

FIGURE 3-18 Set alerts to get notifications when changes are made in business applications or document libraries.

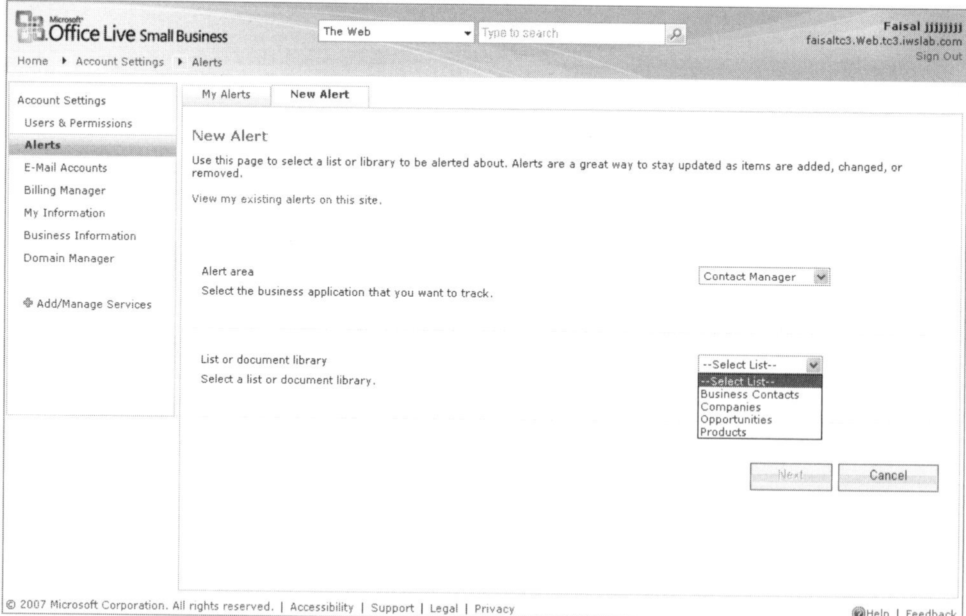

FIGURE 3-19 Choose the event about which you want to be alerted.

TIP

To see a list of all existing alerts for your Office Live Small Business site, click View My Existing Alerts On This Site.

USE THE BILLING MANAGER

The Billing Manager enables you to check the status of the add-on services you sign up for with Office Live Small Business. You can review your service subscriptions, check recent payments, get information on payment methods, and more. Click Account Manager in the left navigation bar, and then click Billing Manager. Review your subscription services and payment method, and make any desired changes on this page.

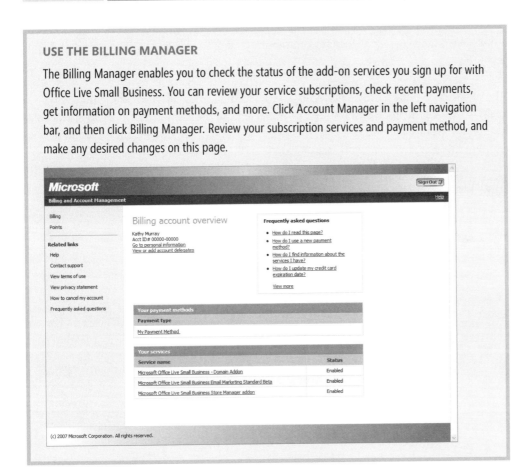

Where to Go for Help

Even though Office Live Small Business is designed to be easy to learn and use; and to be a low-risk and low-cost way to get your business online, reach customers, and manage your business information, it's possible you will have a question or two as you go through the process of creating your new site. For this reason, Office Live Small Business includes a comprehensive help system that is designed to support you in various ways, with

- An online help system.
- The Resource Center.
- The Office Live Small Business community.
- 24-hour, 7-days-per-week telephone support.

The online help system provides step-by-step information on all the major features and tasks in Office Live Small Business and provides links to more information. Help is available on literally every page—simply click the small Help icon in the lower-right corner of any screen to display the Help window (see Figure 3-20).

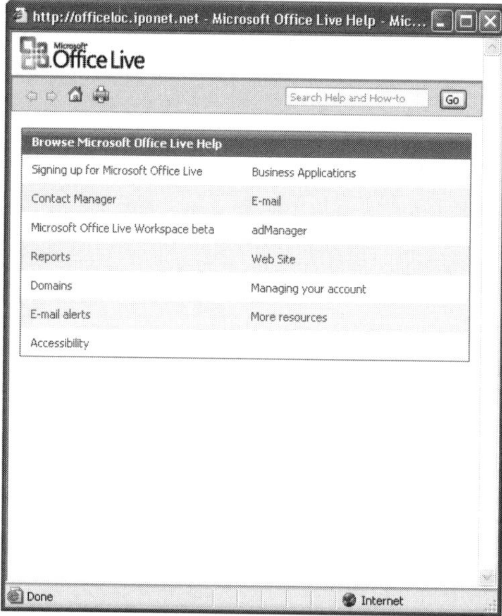

FIGURE 3-20 Office Live Small Business offers a comprehensive help system with step-by-step instructions for all services and features.

The Resource Center is available in the left navigation panel on the Home page of Office Live Small Business. You'll find how-to articles, videos, and business articles designed to help you make the most of the program services and increase the effectiveness and reach of your business (see Figure 3-21).

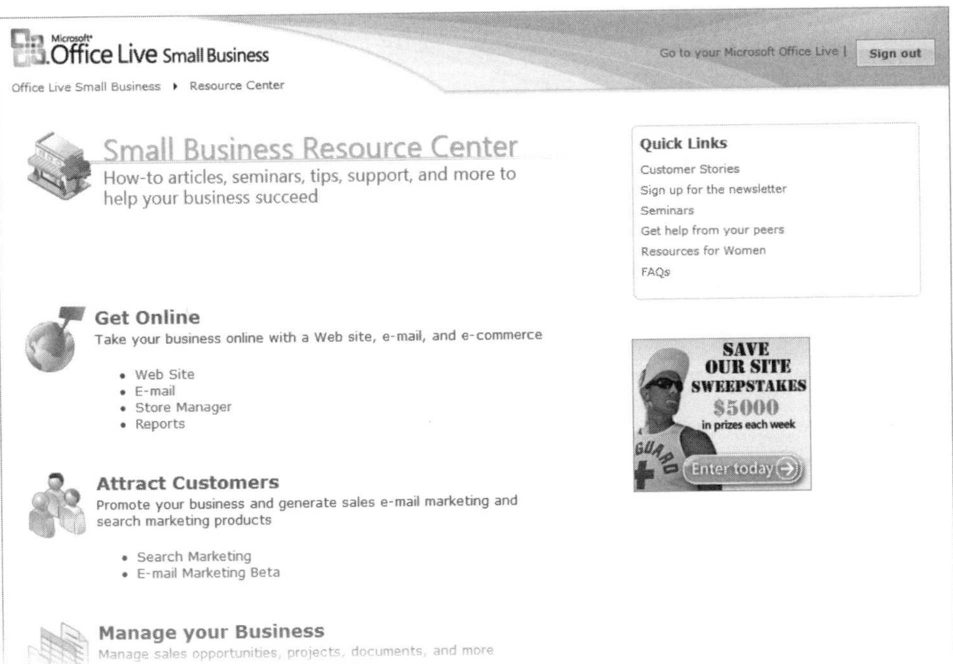

FIGURE 3-21 The Resource Center offers a variety of articles and videos to help you get the most out of Office Live Small Business.

The Office Live Small Business Community is an active forum in which users of all experience levels come together to ask and answer questions, share tips, and learn how to use features together. This is a moderated board, meaning that members of the Office Live Small Business team frequently particulate, so it's a great place to get your questions answered!

Finally, 24/7 phone support is something that no other Web service offers small business owners—and for people just starting out on the Web, it's a big relief. Free phone support is available around the clock, every day of the week, for the first 30 days after you create your Office Live Small Business account. If you sign up for one of the subscription add-on services (Store Manager, adManager, or E-Mail Marketing), free phone support continues for the life of your subscription. If you choose to stick with the free core services, phone support won't be available beyond the 30-day timeframe, but you will have access to 24-hour e-mail support, and the Office Live team tries to respond to all e-mail messages within four hours.

KEY SUPPORTS FOR NEW BUSINESSES

You've probably heard the saying that starting a new business is about 10 percent inspiration and 90 percent perspiration. If you've been dreaming your idea into reality for a long time, you know that in addition to a good idea, you need support—and lots of it—to make your dream a reality. Identifying key resources—and using them regularly—will go a long way toward giving your new business a healthy start.

You can think of a good support system as the four corners of your business foundation. Getting sound advice in these four primary business areas will give you a good start:

- A financial advisor to help you find, manage, and—yes, spend—your money
- A legal advisor who can help you make decisions about the type of business you want to start, what form your business will take, and how you need to legally set it up
- An insurance advisor who can tell you what your risks are, what you need to do to minimize them, and which programs will work best given your type of business and resources
- A business advisor who can give you tested-and-true insight about growth strategy, long-range planning, personnel issues, leadership, and more

Where will you find these valuable support people? For short-term answers and quick solutions, you can find lots of information online (in the United States, check out the Small Business Administration site at *sba.gov*), but also consider finding professionals you can visit in the three-dimensional world as well. A long-term relationship with an accountant you trust will go a long way when you're breaking out in a cold sweat over the new equipment you just purchased.

To find great support people, start by asking other business owners who they go to and why. Gather recommendations from others, and then schedule an appointment with the person you've identified or ask to get together over coffee. (Be sure to find out whether the professional charges for the initial meeting—you don't want to pay what might be a hefty dollar amount for a person you don't click with.) Before you meet, of course, do your homework online—see what kind of Web site the professional has; check out the number of links to his or her site; try to get a feel for the style and professionalism of the firm. (Remember that these are the same kinds of things your customers are wondering about you when they visit your site.)

You might want to check out community forums such as Startup Nation (*www.startupnation.com*) and ask other business owners where they found the reliable professionals they go to for various things. You'll no doubt get lots of good ideas—and probably some real clunkers. Be sure to sift through all the advice and discern what fits for your business—and what feels right to you—before you make that initial call.

YOUR BUSINESS ONLINE: Q&A INTERVIEW

Arafua Anim, Owner
Amelia's Cakes: *www.ameliascakes.com*
Chocolate Juice: *www.chocolatjuice.com*

Q *What are your favorite features in Office Live Small Business?*

A Site Reports and Site Designer.

Q *How does having a Web site help your business?*

A It has given us local and international exposure.

Q *How do you use the marketing and management features in Office Live?*

A We use search keywords in metatags.

Q *What do you want to do next with your site?*

A Add more products to sell online.

Q *What advice would you pass along to a small business owner trying Office Live for the first time?*

A Office Live is the best product out there for a small business needing a Web site. It is very affordable, easy to use, and a great resource tool for tracking customer traffic and search keywords, and offers you the ability to modify your site listings in real time.

Arafua Anim is the owner of Amelia's Cakes (www.ameliascakes.com), a boutique bakery business "started by one mom with a sweet tooth and her friends in the Washington D.C. area," and Chocolate Juice (www.chocolatjuice.com), a maker of hand-crafted, fine chocolates. Thanks for taking the time to answer our questions, Arafua!

What's Next

Now that you've signed up for Office Live Small Business and have your e-mail accounts and user permissions, you're ready for the next big step: designing your site. The next chapter walks you through the process of choosing a site template, selecting layouts, and adding text and pictures to your site pages.

Designing Your Site

IN THIS CHAPTER, YOU WILL

- Get to know the Web tools.
- Choose a theme and header style.
- Work with colors and fonts.
- Set page headers and footers.
- Add text to your site.
- Format and edit text.
- Upload your images.
- Add hyperlinks.
- Add a logo to your site.
- Add pages.
- Select a navigation style.
- Add keyword and description metatags.
- Preview your site.
- Organize site resources.

WHAT'S THE first thing you do now when you hear about new products or services that capture your interest? You look them up on the Web. Chances are, a well-ordered Web site, with professional images, a good color scheme, and well-written text (with no typos) makes a good impression. *These folks seem to know what they're doing*, you think. And maybe you'll click the link and take a look at the products they are selling online.

Similarly, when people come to your site, they want to know a few things about you. First, what's your company all about? Next, what is the quality of the items or services you're selling? Finally, can they trust you to follow through on your promises?

It may seem strange that a few colors, photos, and words on a page can begin to give customers answers to those kinds of questions—but they do. When your Web site meets or surpasses their expectations, your prospective customers will feel good about you, your company, and your product. When your site is disorganized, looks amateurish, or lacks important pieces of information, customers are likely to wonder whether you've got your act together. Instead of clicking your product sales page, they are likely to click away from your site.

This chapter introduces you to the easy-to-use Web tools available in Microsoft Office Live Small Business. You'll learn to choose a Web template, select a header style, add text and pictures, and work with the layout of your pages. Along the way, you'll think about what your customer expects to see, and learn how to convey the look and feel you're hoping for.

Introducing the Web Tools

Your introduction to the Web tools in Office Live Small Business begins on the Home page. If you haven't already, go ahead and sign in to your account. On the Home page, you'll see the Web Site gadget directly below the Getting Started area. This gadget gives you Web stats at a glance, so that once you get your site up and running, each time you sign in to Office Live Small Business, you'll be able to see how many visits, visitors, and unique views your site is getting (see Figure 4-1).

Web Site

View Site | Design Site | Images

Web Site Statistics	This Week Week 15	Previous Week Week 14	Week 13
Visits	0	1 ↓	2
Sale	0	0	0
Views	0	1 ↓	11

View reports

Increase visits to your Web site now

Using your own tools to design your Web site? No problem. See what you need to know.

FIGURE 4-1 Each time you sign in to Office Live Small Business, the Web Site gadget gives you an overview of your Web traffic.

Click Web Site in the left navigation bar to begin your tour of the Web tools. The Getting Started area lists the first steps in the process. The sections on the following pages introduce you to the three main Web tools you'll use as you create, update, and maintain your site: Page Manager, Site Designer, and Page Editor.

> **NOTE** These three main tools cover all the basic tasks you'll want to accomplish as you create your site, but there are other tools as well. Later in this chapter, you'll learn about the Image Gallery, Document Gallery, and Template Gallery. You'll use the Reports feature to gather all kinds of information about your site visits. (See Chapter 6, "Tracking Your Web Statistics," for more details.) You'll use the Store Manager to add e-commerce capability to your site. (Check out Chapter 8, "Selling Products Online," for the step-by-step on adding a shopping cart to your site.)

Page Manager

The Page Manager (see Figure 4-2), located on the Web Site main page, is the tool you will use to work with the existing pages in your site, add new pages, choose a design for the site, and change page properties. By default, Office Live Small Business creates four sample pages for you to use or customize. You can add new pages to your site by clicking New Page.

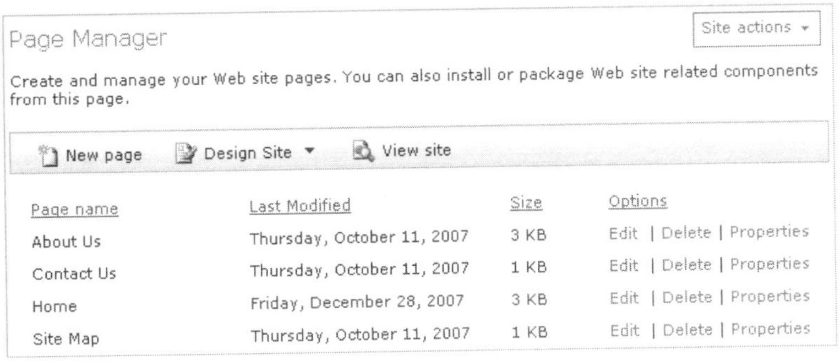

Page Manager

Site actions

Create and manage your Web site pages. You can also install or package Web site related components from this page.

New page | Design Site | View site

Page name	Last Modified	Size	Options
About Us	Thursday, October 11, 2007	3 KB	Edit | Delete | Properties
Contact Us	Thursday, October 11, 2007	1 KB	Edit | Delete | Properties
Home	Friday, December 28, 2007	3 KB	Edit | Delete | Properties
Site Map	Thursday, October 11, 2007	1 KB	Edit | Delete | Properties

FIGURE 4-2 The Page Manager appears on the Web Site page. You can use it to work with the various pages in your site.

Site Designer

When you click Design Site in the Page Manager, a list appears. Click Design Site, and the Site Designer window opens. The Site Designer (see Figure 4-3) is an easy-to-use Web design tool that presents you with a number of templates and styles you can easily apply to the pages you modify or create. With the Site Designer, you'll make design choices that affect the overall look and feel of your site—colors, fonts, themes, header styles, and more.

Page Editor

The Page Editor (see Figure 4-4) appears as a tab in the Site Designer window, providing you with tools you will use to work with the individual pages in your site. The Page Editor includes tool groups that you can use to add content, format text, change the page layout, and add tables and links.

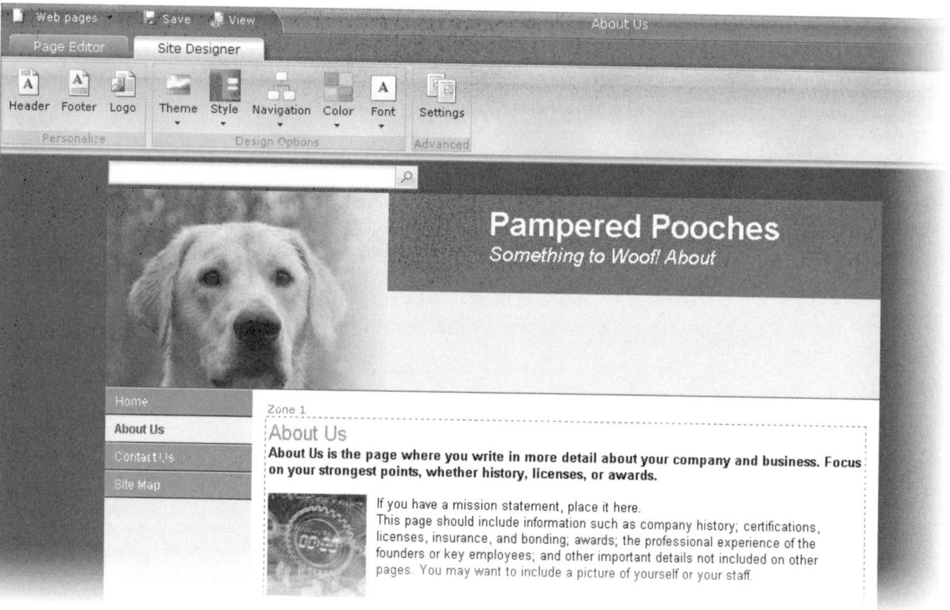

FIGURE 4-3 The Site Designer is where you choose the overall look for your site, including the design template, navigation style, and header.

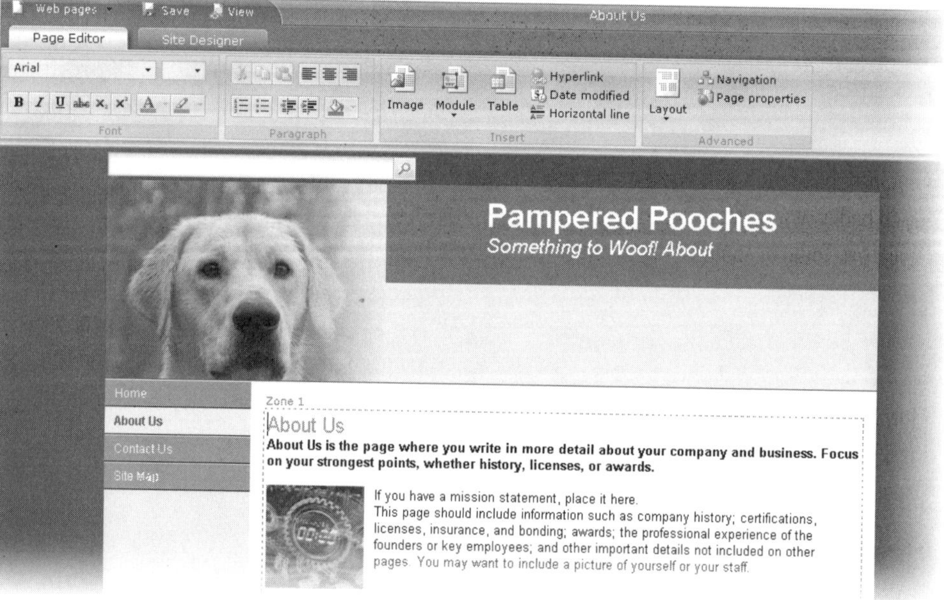

FIGURE 4-4 The Page Editor gives you the tools to work on the content of individual pages: text, images, layouts, and more.

Choosing a Theme and a Header Style

The first choices you make about your site will likely have to do with the overall way you want the site to look. The color scheme you select, the layout style, and the arrangement of the text on the pages all say something about your business.

Office Live Small Business presents you with a huge range of theme choices that are designed to correspond with the type of business you run. There's no hard-and-fast rule to this—you can choose a Lawn & Garden theme, for example, if you have a pet-sitting business—but take a look at all the different categories before you make your decision. You can choose from themes designed specifically for the following business areas:

- Accounting
- Advertising & Marketing
- Automotive
- Clothing & Fashion
- Computers & Electronics
- Construction
- Education
- Finance
- Food & Beverage
- Furniture
- General (no photos)
- Health & Personal Care
- Home Maintenance
- Insurance
- Lawn & Garden
- Legal Services
- Manufacturing
- Medical & Dental
- Pet Supplies & Services
- Real Estate
- Retail Store
- Salon & Spa
- Sports & Recreation
- Transportation
- Travel & Leisure

TIP Remember that your Web site speaks for you—around the clock—until you can meet the customer and speak to him or her yourself (or show your professionalism through phone contact or via e-mail), so invest some thought in your choice of the best theme that fits the style of your particular business.

Look through the various themes and select one for your site by following these steps:

1. Click Web Site on the Office Live Small Business Home page.
2. In the Page Manager, click Design Site to display the list, and click Design Site a second time to open the Site Designer.
3. Click Theme to display a list of design templates (see Figure 4-5).
4. Scroll through the categories and click the one that fits your business.
5. In the column on the right, click the image that you want to use as the graphic image in your site header. The list closes, and the changes are applied dynamically to your site.

FIGURE 4-5 The theme you choose determines the overall look of your site.

If you don't like the effect, you can change the theme and experiment with many different looks. Just remember to keep your customer in mind and consider not only your personal color preferences but also the overall sense of the site design and how well (or not) it matches the message you want your visitors to receive.

NOTE	The site header is the area at the top of your Web pages that gives a consistent look and feel to your site. The header will be repeated from page to page so that site visitors recognize the continuity throughout your site.

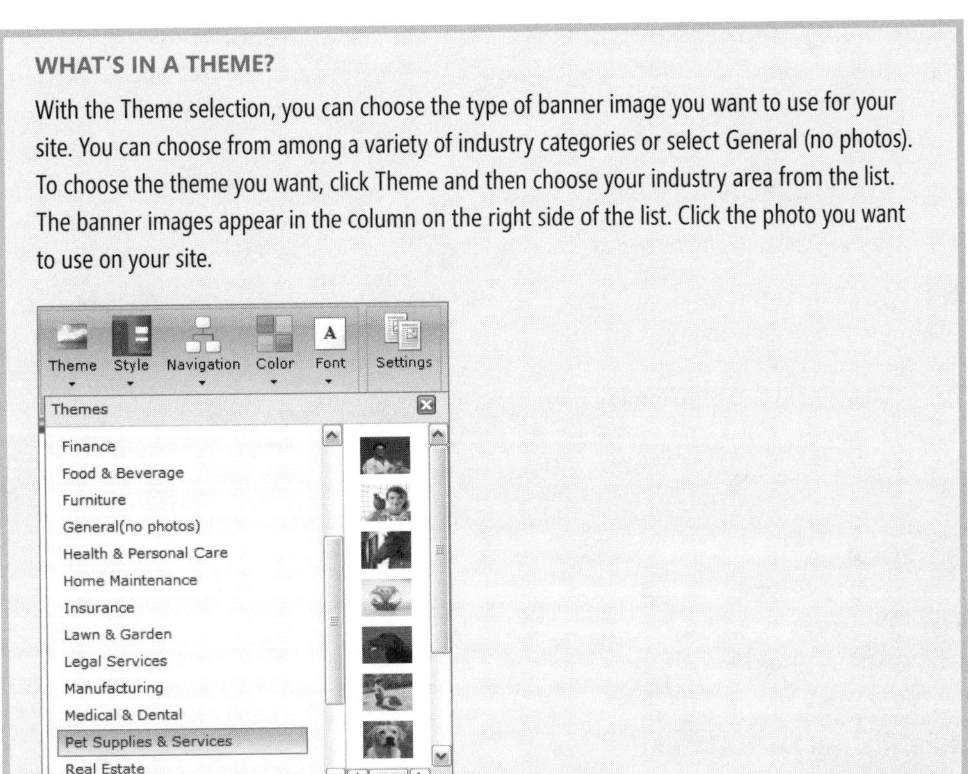

WHAT'S IN A THEME?

With the Theme selection, you can choose the type of banner image you want to use for your site. You can choose from among a variety of industry categories or select General (no photos). To choose the theme you want, click Theme and then choose your industry area from the list. The banner images appear in the column on the right side of the list. Click the photo you want to use on your site.

Working with Colors and Fonts

A color is a color is a color, right? Not exactly. A color can influence whether you read a page. A color can make you hungry (it's true). A color can suppress your appetite. A color can help you feel confident or encourage you to trust what you're reading. Colors have a great influence on the visitors coming to your site—and that's a great reason to pay careful attention to the colors you select for your site. Red is a high-energy color; blue is passive; green is relaxing; yellow is stimulating (be careful about how much yellow you use because a little goes a long way). Take a look at your favorite sites and see how they use color. What are the predominant hues? How do they make you feel?

When you begin to explore color possibilities for your site, you'll discover that Office Live Small Business offers you a wide range of professionally designed palettes (coordinated colors) that you can use for the various elements in your site (see Figure 4-6). To try on a new color scheme, follow these steps:

1. Click the Site Designer tab.
2. In the Design Options group, click the Color arrow to display a list of color palettes.
3. Scroll through the list and click the color group you like. The colors are applied to the theme you selected, overriding any theme colors in use.

FIGURE 4-6 Color palettes offer complementary color sets that coordinate the page background, header, navigation bar colors, and more.

TIP Interested in what causes our color response? Want to find out more about the effects of colors on purchasing, learning, and more? Check out the site *www.colormatters.com* to read a variety of interesting articles on the subject.

Choosing Fonts

Your choice of font also communicates something important about the overall tone and feel of your business. Some fonts (such as Tahoma and Trebuchet) are more relaxed than others. Times New Roman is all business. Courier New is a geeky programming (or typewriting) font. The look of the letters on your page will send a signal about your company's personality—so choose carefully. And also consider the readability of the text—a whole page full of Courier New, for example, is likely to annoy your visitors (and they will click away to an easier-to-read page). When you have lots of text on a page, choose an easy-to-read font such as Arial or Verdana. These fonts are easy to read, even in small sizes (so you can fit more text on the page for the visitor to view).

When you're ready to choose a font for your page, follow these steps:

1. Click the Font arrow in the Design Options group.
2. Click the font family you want to use for your site (see Figure 4-7).

FIGURE 4-7 Choose a font that is easy to read so that your site visitors will want to hang around awhile.

FONT CONSIDERATIONS

Even though you probably have a number of interesting fonts on your computer, only a few will be effective on your Web site. Why is that? In order for text to be displayed properly on the screen, any font you use on your Web page must also reside on the visitor's computer. If the visitor doesn't have a particular font, the screen display will default to another font, which may wreak havoc on the appearance of your text. Office Live Small Business offers seven basic font choices that are found on all Windows computers:

- Arial
- Courier New
- Georgia
- Tahoma
- Times New Roman
- Trebuchet MS
- Verdana

To find out more about fonts on the Web, you can visit *www.ampsoft.net/webdesign-l/WindowsMacFonts.html*, which offers a comparison of fonts available on Windows and Macintosh systems. Additionally, this site includes links to a number of different displays so that you can see how fonts appear in different browsers.

Setting Page Headers and Footers

The page header is likely to be the first thing most of your site visitors notice. It offers your site a title (which may be your company name), a tag line, and a Web search area (if you choose to display it). The page footer probably won't get as much attention. (We know statistically that most site visitors—unless they are really interested in your content—will read whatever they find in the first screenful of information and infrequently scroll down to the bottom of the page.)

You can customize your site header by clicking Header in the Personalize group in the Site Designer. The Customize Header dialog box appears, as you see in Figure 4-8. Click in the Site Title box and type the new title for your site. If you want to change the style, color, font, or size of the text, use the formatting controls above the text box.

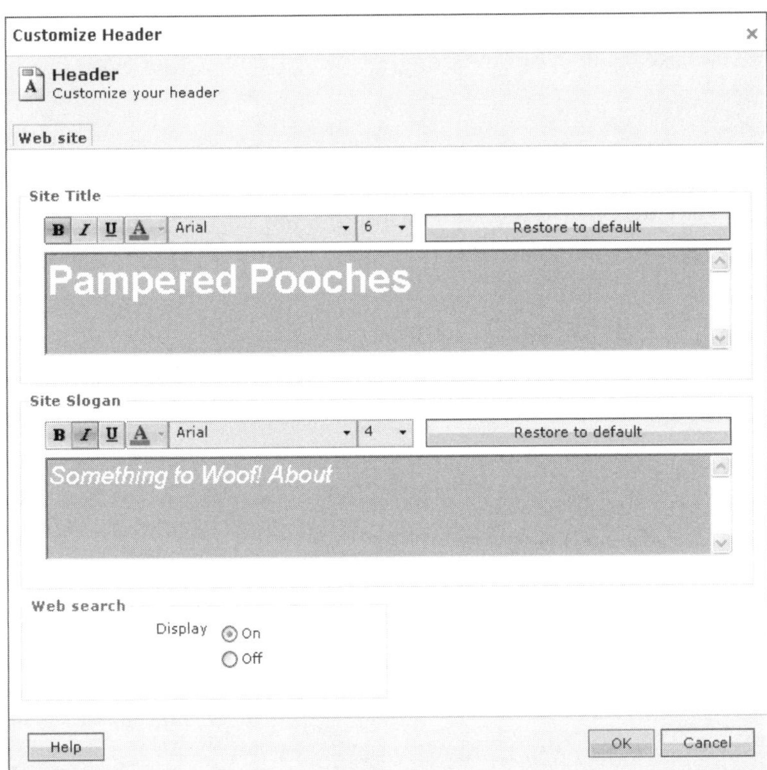

FIGURE 4-8 Add a title, slogan, and search box to your page header in the Customize Header dialog box.

Typically, your site slogan, or tag line, will be smaller so that the site title stands out predominantly. If you want to enter a slogan, type the text in the Site Slogan text box and format it using the controls above the box.

Finally, you can choose whether to include a Web search box above and to the left of your site header. This search box provides a way for visitors to search the entire Web and is a service that adds a professional touch to your site. If you want to display the Web search box, leave Display set to On. If you want to hide the Web search box, click Off. Save the header changes and update the site by clicking OK.

TIP

You add an image to the header by clicking the Theme arrow in the Design Options group of the Site Designer. The image in the header comes from the selection you made when you click an item in the right panel of the list.

Adding a footer is a similar process, although you have a few more options. When you click Footer in the Personalize group in the Site Designer, the Customize Your Footer dialog box appears (see Figure 4-9).

If you want to include links to other sites (perhaps other sites you have on Office Live Small Business), you can add them in the List Of Links box at the top of the Customize Your Footer dialog box. Click Add Link and enter the link you want to add. Repeat as needed for as many links as you want to include.

NOTE If you have a long list of links, avoid the temptation to insert them in the footer of your page—adding them to a Links or Resources page will help visitors find them more easily.

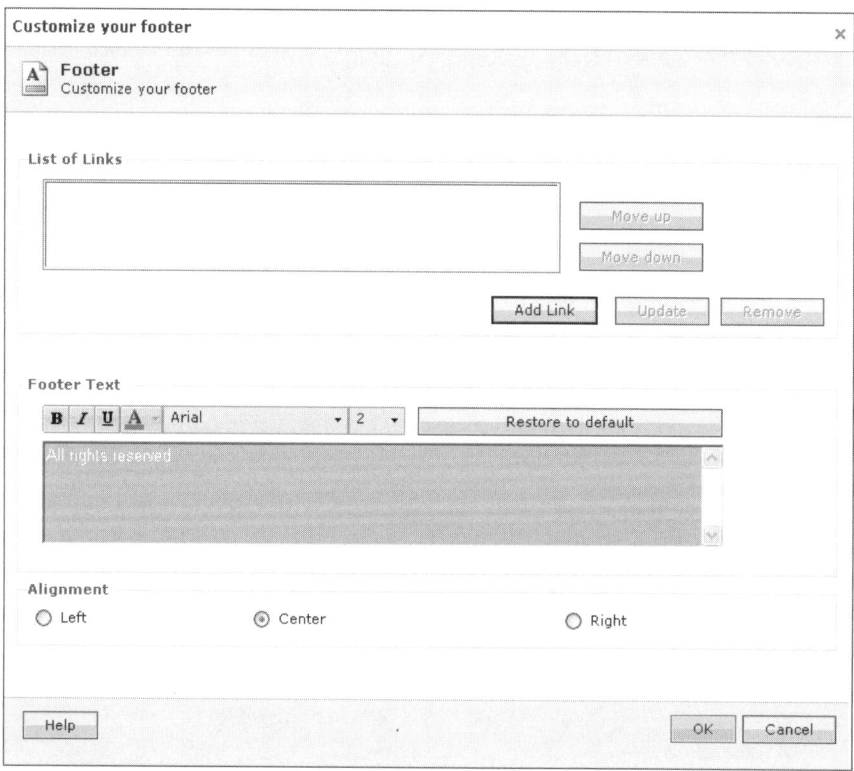

FIGURE 4-9 Add links or text to the page footer and choose the alignment in the Customize Your Footer dialog box.

By default, *All rights reserved* appears centered in the footer of your Web site. You can change the text to whatever you want (although including copyright information is a good idea). Format the text as you like, using the text tools immediately above the Footer Text box.

Choose the position for the text by clicking Left, Center, or Right. Finally, click OK to save the footer changes.

Adding Text to Your Site

Once upon a time, Web sites were almost all text. The earliest days of the Web were mostly about posting information and not so much about creating an experience. Today, few Web visitors would be happy landing on your site and finding a page of black (or blue) text on a white (or gray) background. We expect color, images, entertainment—and not as much text as we used to see.

Even though other elements on a Web page have become increasingly important, nothing replaces the text you use to tell potential customers who you are, what you do, and why they can trust you to do what you promise. Your text gives visitors a sense of the overall tone of your business—are you relaxed and friendly, serious and detail-minded, or welcoming and helpful (or all of the above)? The way in which you communicate—through the written word—will give your site visitors an insight into how you do business. The way in which you display the text will help reinforce (or contradict) that impression as well.

WHAT DO YOU WANT TO SAY?

It's worth spending a little time thinking carefully about the type of text you want to include on your site. Do you want to tell the story of your business, or get right down to selling your products? Is it important to you to give potential customers a little behind-the-scenes information, or do you just want to show them what you have to offer? There's no hard-and-fast rule to this—let your own business be your guide. Think about who your potential customers are and what they are likely to want to see when they get to your site. What will they want to know about you?

If you're not sure about the answer to that question, take a few moments and make a few phone calls. Ask some of your favorite clients for their opinions. What would they most like to see on your Web page? Most customers won't mind a brief conversation like that if you're careful with their time and use their input. And besides, inviting them to help recognizes them as valued customers, which helps reinforce their relationship with you—and their good feeling about your company.

When you're ready to add text to your page, follow these steps:

1. In the Page Manager, click the Edit link for the page you want to change.
2. In the Page Editor, highlight the text you want to replace and press Delete.
3. Type the text you want to include (see Figure 4-10).

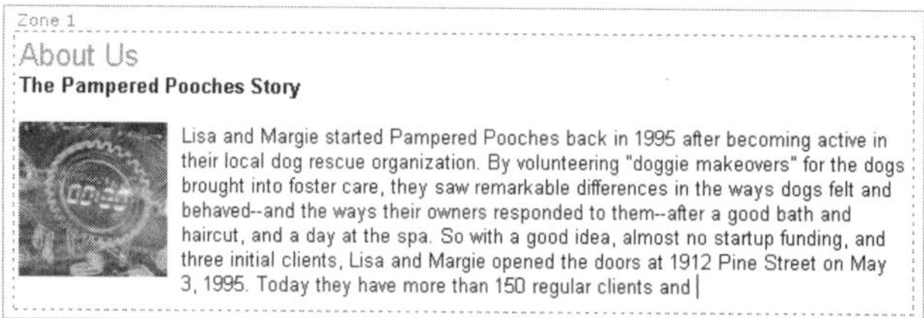

FIGURE 4-10 Entering text on the page is a simple matter of typing to replace the placeholder text already on the page.

> **TIP** You can easily save time and effort by copying text you've composed in a word processing document and pasting it into your page in Office Live Small Business.

Formatting and Editing Text

After you get the text on the page, you may want to make a few changes. With the tools in the Font and Paragraph groups (which you may recognize from other applications, such as Microsoft Office Word 2007), you can change the look, color, format, and alignment of the text.

> **NOTE** What is a *zone*? The Page Editor displays each area of the page within a dotted red rectangle. Each rectangle is named and numbered as Zone 1, Zone 2, or Zone 3. You'll learn more about zones and modules in Chapter 5, "Taking Your Site to the Next Level," when you work with some of the more advanced Web features in Office Live Small Business.

Changing the Look of Headings

Office Live Small Business includes placeholder text in each of the zones on the pages you work with. You can choose to preserve the format or change it to suit your own needs. Here's how to change the look of the zone headings on your page:

1. Display the page you want to change.
2. Highlight the text you want to use as a heading.
3. Click the Font arrow and choose a font from the list.
4. Click Bold, Italic, or Underline as desired.
5. Click the Font Size arrow and choose a size from the list (see Figure 4-11).
6. Click the Font Color arrow and choose a color from the palette.

TIP

If you change the color of the heading on your page, be sure to choose a color that complements the colors that are already part of your site theme.

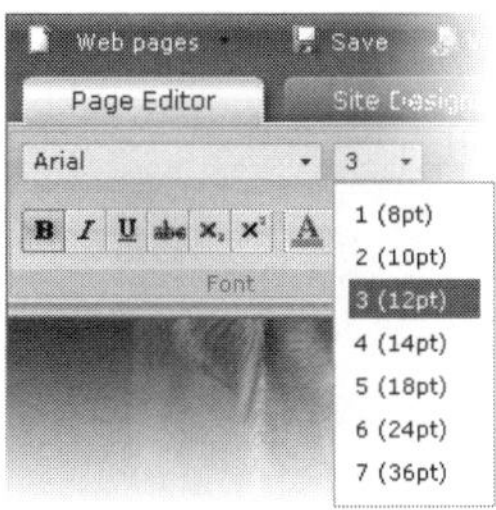

FIGURE 4-11 The font sizes in the Font Size list show both the HTML sizes and the more familiar point sizes for the text.

NOTE

Text sizes in HTML are shown in size levels ranging from 1 to 7, with 1 being the smallest and 7 being the largest. In print documents, text size is generally shown in *points*, a typographical term used to indicate the height of a character on a printed line. On the printed page, 72 points equals 1 inch, so a 72-point letter will be 1 inch tall.

Creating a Bulleted List

Bulleted lists sometimes get a bad rap because everybody uses them—sometimes *ad nauseum*. But on the Web, when people are looking for information quickly, bulleted lists can be convenient, helpful, and efficient. What's more, adding them is super easy. Here's how to do it:

1. Select the text you want to turn into a bulleted list.
2. Click the Bulleted List tool in the Paragraph group.

Bullet characters are inserted automatically and the text is indented and aligned (see Figure 4-12).

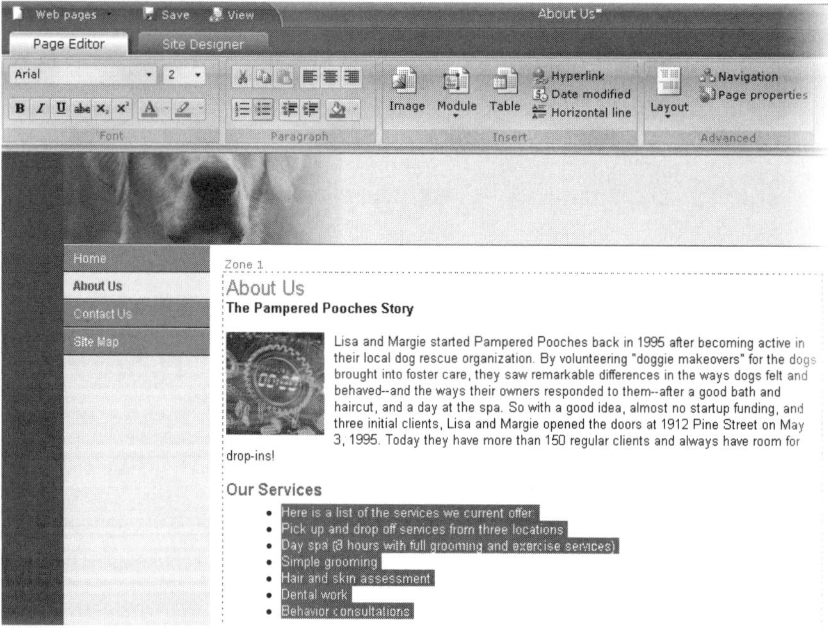

FIGURE 4-12 Select text and click Bulleted List to create an instant unordered list.

> **TIP** You can increase the indention of the bulleted list by clicking Indent.

TIP

In HTML, a bulleted list is coded as <UL>, which stands for *unordered list.* The list gets its name from the fact that the items in the list can appear in any order. In contrast, an *ordered list,* or <OL>, is the designation used for a list that must appear in a particular order. In Office Live Small Business, an ordered list is called a *numbered list.*

Uploading Your Images

Now that you've added some text to your site, how about adding images? Site visitors will expect to see some kind of visuals on your site, something that gives them a sense of the products and services you're offering. You might include images like these on your site:

- Product photos
- Staff photos
- Service-related images
- A photo of your facility
- A map to your office

Office Live Small Business provides an Image Uploader tool you can use to automate the process of adding images to your site. In addition to the Image Uploader tool, you can also add art to the Image Gallery.

Preparing to Upload Images

When you first click Images in the Insert group of the Page Editor, the pop-up message shown in Figure 4-13 appears. When you click Upload, you are prompted to download the Image Uploader so that you can use the photos and art files already stored on your computer system. Click Download, and the Image Uploader Setup Wizard begins, as you see in Figure 4-14. Follow the prompts on the screen to complete the installation of the Image Uploader.

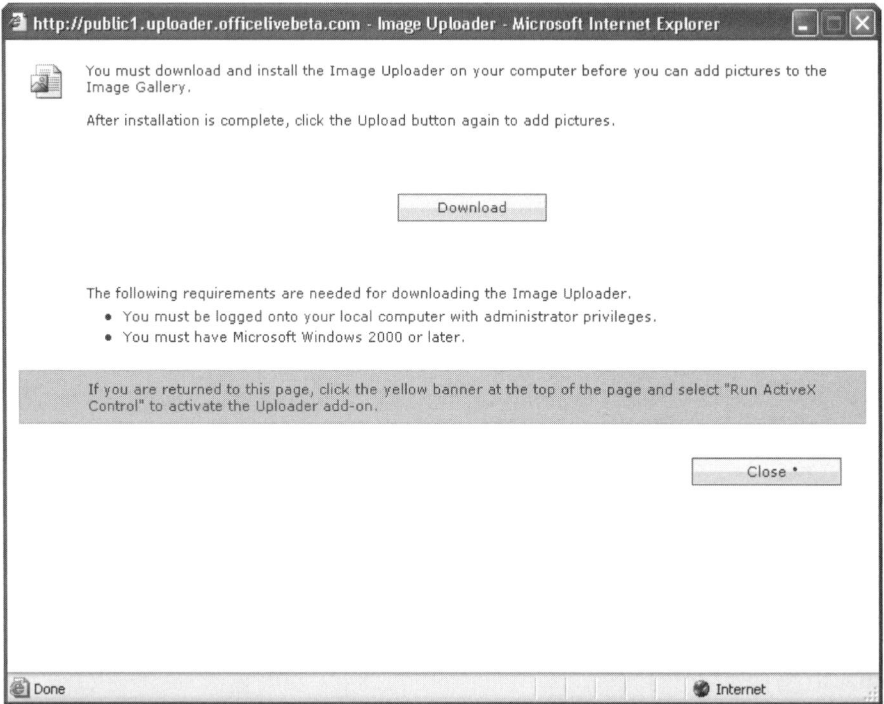

FIGURE 4-13 When you add images for the first time, Office Live Small Business prompts you to install the Image Uploader.

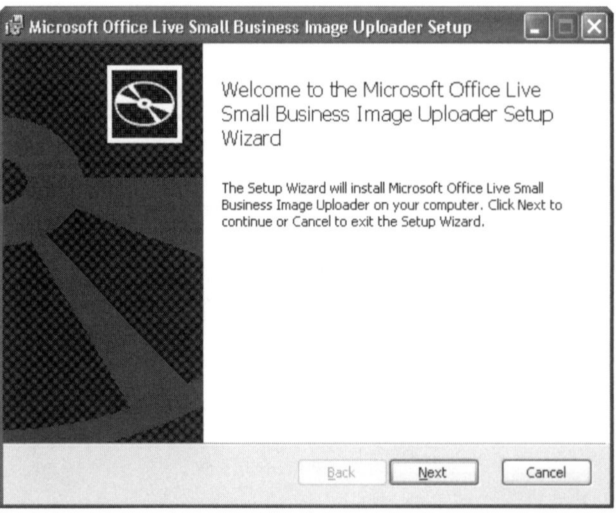

FIGURE 4-14 The Image Uploader Setup Wizard launches and walks you through the process of installing the utility.

Adding Art to the Image Uploader

After the Image Uploader Setup Wizard finishes, you are ready to add photos to the Image Uploader so they'll be ready when you need them. Here's the process:

1. Click Image in the Insert group.
2. In the Insert An Image dialog box, click Upload Images. The Image Uploader launches.
3. In the left panel, select the folder containing the images you want to add.
4. In the right panel, select the check box in the upper-left corner of each image you want to upload (see Figure 4-15).
5. Click Upload Now, and click OK.

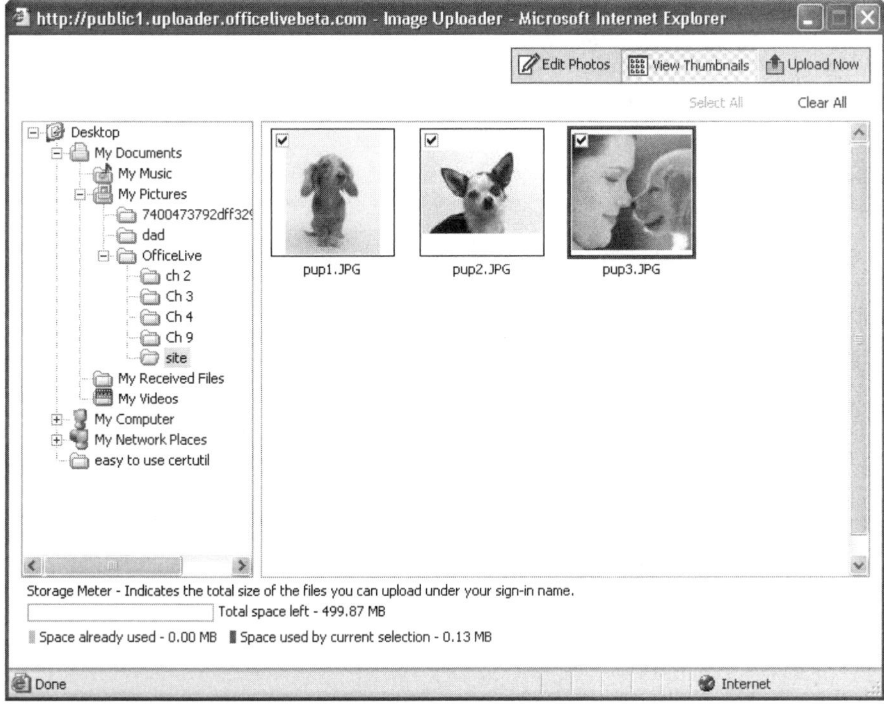

FIGURE 4-15 Choose the images you want to add to your site in the Image Uploader.

The Image Uploader also includes an Edit Photos feature you can use to do simple corrections on the images you upload to your site. This is a great feature that you can use to correct lighting and brightness problems, do simple color corrections, crop the images, and more before you add them to your Image Library. This same utility is part of Windows Live Spaces and makes touching up your photos simple and quick.

Adding Images to the Web Page

After you've added some images to the Image Uploader, you can easily insert them in the placeholder objects on your Web pages. (You can also insert images where there are no placeholder graphics—an image you add to the page will be positioned at the cursor position.) To add a photo or clip art item to your page, follow these steps:

1. On the Web page, select the image you want to replace.
2. Click Image in the Insert group.
3. In the Insert An Image dialog box, click the image you want to add and click OK (see Figure 4-16).
4. You may need to resize the newly added image by clicking one corner of the photo and dragging it in the direction you want to resize it.
5. When the photo is the size you want, click outside the image.

You can also add images directly to the Image Gallery, available on the Web Site main page. To find out how to use the Image Gallery, Document Gallery, and Template Gallery, see "Organizing Site Resources," later in this chapter.

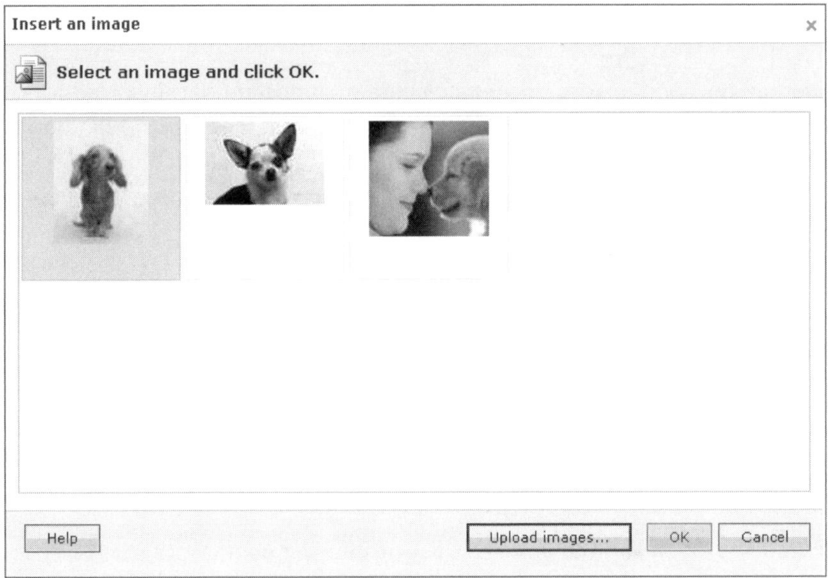

FIGURE 4-16 Add an image to your page by using the Insert An Image dialog box.

Setting Text Wrap Around Images

Once you add the image to the page, you may need to do a little tweaking to get everything to fit the way you want it to. When you change the text wrap setting for a picture, you modify the way in which the text flows around the photo or art image. Here's how to change the text wrap for a picture you've added:

1. Right-click the image you want to wrap text around.
2. Click Float Left or Float Right (see Figure 4-17).

FIGURE 4-17 Control the text wrap by right-clicking an image and choosing Float Left or Float Right.

Adding Hyperlinks

Although the design, text, and images on your site play an important part in introducing your business to potential clients by communicating just the right message, nothing on the Web would work without the hyperlinks. The links are what makes the World Wide Web a web—they bring visitors to your site and lead them to various pages within it.

Creating a hyperlink is a very simple thing. Here are the steps:

1. In the Page Manager, click Edit for the page you want to change.
2. In the Page Editor, highlight the text to which you want to apply the link.
3. Click Hyperlink in the Insert group (see Figure 4-18).
4. In the Insert Link dialog box, click the type of link you want to create (see Figure 4-19):
   - Click Web Site if you want to link to a site outside your own.
   - Click A Page On My Web Site if you want to link to one of the other pages in your Office Live Small Business site.
   - Click E-mail if you want to create a link that opens an e-mail window.
   - Click Document if you want to create a link that enables a user to open or save a document.
   - Click Other if you want to create a type of link that doesn't fit any of those previously listed.
5. Click in the Link box and type the Web address of the page, file, or document you want to use as the target of the link.

NOTE The Link option changes depending on the type of link you select. If you click A Page On My Web Site, the Select Page button appears to the right of the Link box so that you can select the page in your site you want to use. If you click Document, the Select Document button appears so you can choose the document you want to link to.

6. If you want the target of the link (another site, a page in your own site, an e-mail window, or a document) to open in a new window on top of your Web site window, select the Open Link In A New Window check box.
7. Click OK to save your changes and create the link.

It's a good idea to open the target of the link in a new window if the link leads visitors either off your site or to a page where they are likely to jump to another site. When you click Open Link in a New Window, your Web site stays open on the user's screen while the new window opens on top of it. When the user is finished viewing the target of the link, your site is still displayed.

FIGURE 4-18 To add a link to your page, select the text you want to link and click Hyperlink.

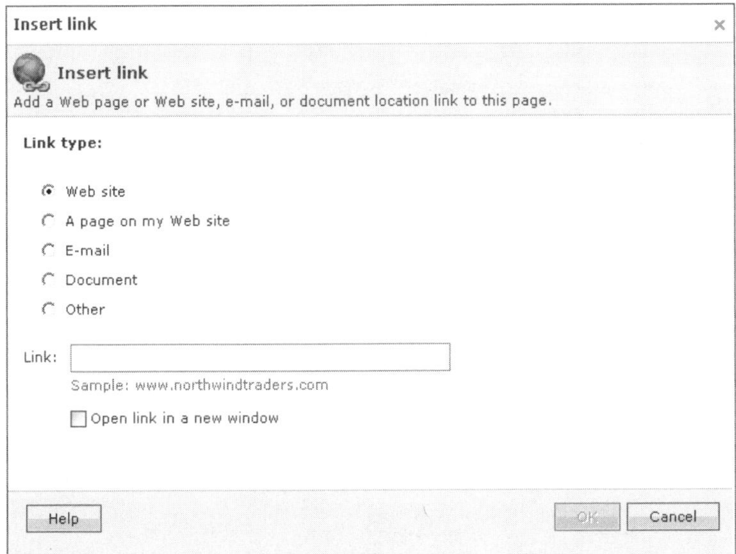

FIGURE 4-19 Choose the type of link you want to create, enter the address, and click OK.

Adding a Logo to Your Site

If you have a customized logo saved as a .jpg or .bmp file, you can easily add it to your site in Office Live Small Business. The process is simple—very similar to adding a photo or piece of clip art to your pages. The steps for this process are on the following page.

1. Click Site Designer.
2. Click Logo in the Personalize group.
3. In the Change Your Logo dialog box, click Upload Pictures if you need to add the image to the dialog box.
4. Click the image you want to use as the logo. (If you decide you want to forgo the logo altogether, click No Logo.)
5. In the Display Options area, select whether you want the logo to appear at the top of each page of the site or beside the page title.
6. In the Size area, choose Small, Medium, or Large for the size of the logo (see Figure 4-20).
7. Click OK to save your changes.

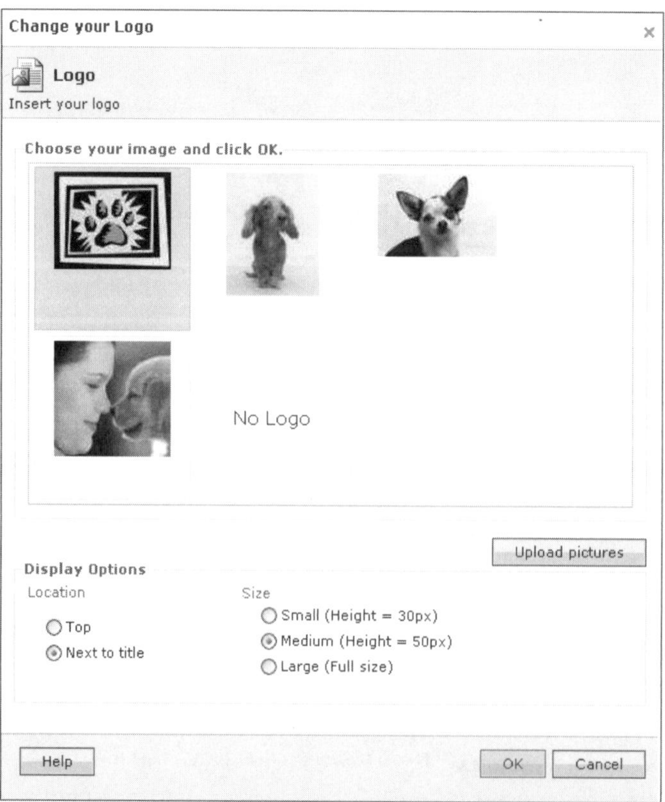

FIGURE 4-20 Add a logo by using the Change Your Logo dialog box.

Figure 4-21 shows a medium logo added next to the title on the Pampered Pooches site.

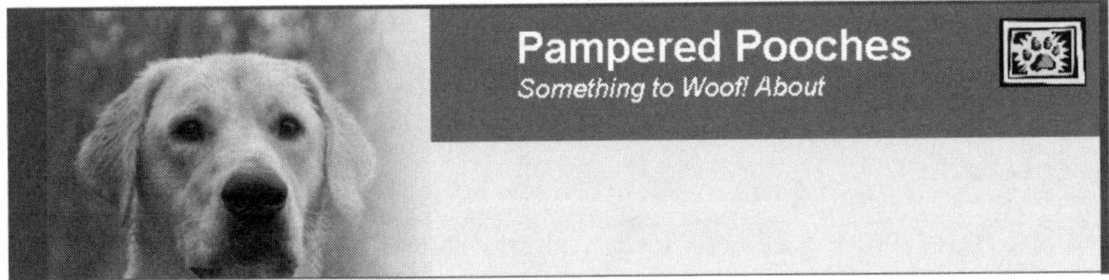

FIGURE 4-21 A medium logo is added beside the title.

WHAT MAKES A GOOD LOGO GOOD?

Are there some characteristics that "good" logos have that other logos don't? Think of the logos you are most likely to recognize. Chances are that you see them everywhere—Coke, IBM, Nike, Dell. What do they all have in common? Colors we remember. Simple, strong design. Bold characters. They make an impression and they are easy to remember.

As you design a logo for your business, brainstorm about logos that have caught your attention and identify the elements that made the logo memorable. Then consider ways in which a bold, memorable logo can fit in with your mission, products, and services.

And for one designer's take on the four key characteristics in logo design, you may want to check out this article: *www.webdesignfromscratch.com/logos.cfm*.

Adding Pages

When you're first starting out with a brand new Web page, four pages may seem like a lot of space to fill. As you begin adding content and photos, you'll discover that those pages quickly fill up and you'll need to add more. You add pages by using the Page Manager. Here's how to do it:

1. In the Web Site main page, click New Page in the upper-left corner of the Page Manager.
2. The Create Web Page dialog box appears (see Figure 4-22). This is the first page of a wizard that will walk you through the process of adding a new page. Click through the templates and find the one with the type of layout you need for your new page.
3. Click Next.

TIP

The various page templates available in the Create Web Page dialog box each creates a specific type of page for a particular kind of information. If you are unsure about which template you need—or don't yet know what you want to put on the site—click General. This template creates a generic page you can customize later when you know what type of content and layout you want to add.

4. On the Choose Page Properties page, enter a title for the new page (see Figure 4-23).
5. Type the Web address for the new page.

TIP

If you are creating a new page that will replace an existing one, you can enter an existing page name and select the Overwrite Existing Page check box to replace the old page with the new one.

6. Leave the check box selected in the Navigation area if you want the page to appear in the navigation bar.
7. Type the title you want to appear in the navigation bar and, if the page will be a subpage of an existing page, click the Select Parent arrow and choose the page from the list.

8. Click Finish to add the page to your site.

The page is displayed so that you can add text and images and customize the page as needed.

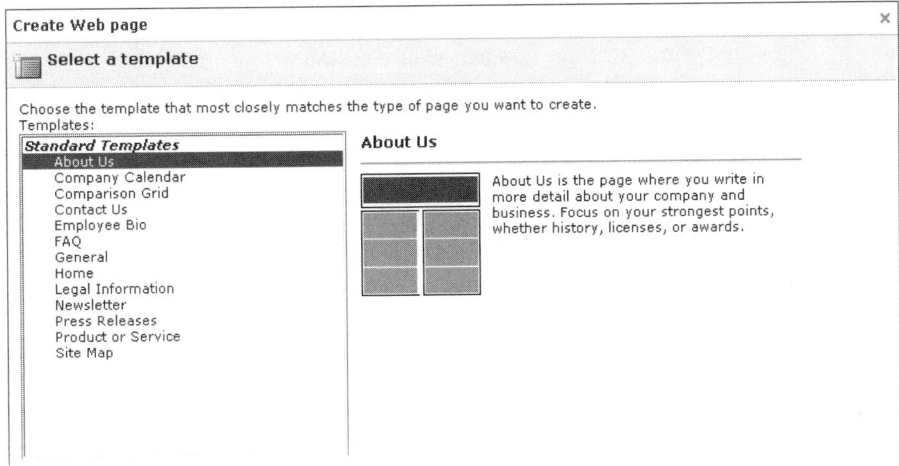

FIGURE 4-22 Choose a page template to use as the basis for the new Web page.

Create Web page

Choose page properties

Users can navigate to your site by typing the Web site address into a browser. Type only the last part of the address that you are creating, keeping it short and easy to remember.

Page information

*Page title: customerfaq

*Web address: http://kanga230.books.officelivebeta.com/ faq.html

Overwrite existing page:

Navigation

Show this page in the Navigation bar.

Navigation title: FAQ

Select parent: About Us

FIGURE 4-23 Enter page information and navigation choices on the Choose Page Properties page.

PLANNING YOUR SITE

It's easy to add pages to your site, but it's a good idea to have an overall plan that involves how much information you want to provide in different areas of your site. That way, you can get an idea of how many product pages you want to create—for example, how many informational pages and the number of article pages. (This also helps you get a sense of whether you need to take advantage of the additional storage or bandwidth options that Office Live Small Business offers.) These questions can help you think through the types of pages you want to add to your site:

What are the primary pages you want to include?
Example: Home, Our Services, Scheduling, What Our Customers Say, and About Us

Will you have subpages available that are linked to the primary pages? (If so, list them)
Example: Three subpages under Our Services: Grooming, Day Spa, and Behavior Consultation

Do you plan to expand your site over time? How many pages do you estimate including in the finished site?
Example: Shopping Cart to be added in 2008. Estimated site page total: 20

TIP

You can also create a new page quickly while you're working in the Page Editor Web window by clicking Web Pages in the upper-right corner of the window and choosing New Page.

Selecting a Navigation Style

Office Live Small Business gives you three different navigation styles to choose from for your site. The default navigation is the Left navigation style, in which the links to the pages on your site appear in a vertical bar along the left side of your page.

The Top & Left navigation option displays areas along the left and top of the page area that can be used for navigation. This enables you to give site visitors a choice of the navigation style that they're most comfortable with. (This seems to be the option of choice for major e-commerce sites as well—see the sidebar "Navigation and E-Commerce" later in this chapter for examples.) The Top navigation choice arranges your page links across the top of the page area, just below the header. This style works well when you want to keep the design as simple as possible while maximizing the amount of page space available for content.

To choose a navigation style for your site, follow these steps:

1. Click the Site Designer tab.
2. In the Design Options group, click the Navigation arrow.
3. Click the Navigation style you like: Left, Top & Left, or Top (see Figure 4-24).

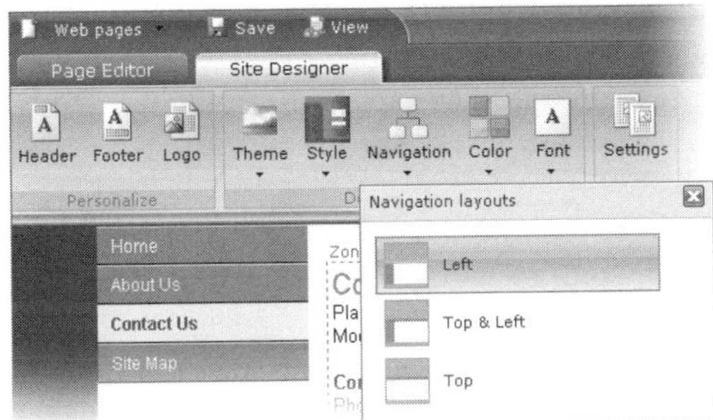

FIGURE 4-24 The navigation style you choose for your site has a big impact on how easily visitors can find what they need on your site.

The current page changes immediately to reflect your new choice (see Figure 4-25). If you aren't happy with the look, simply repeat the steps and choose a different style.

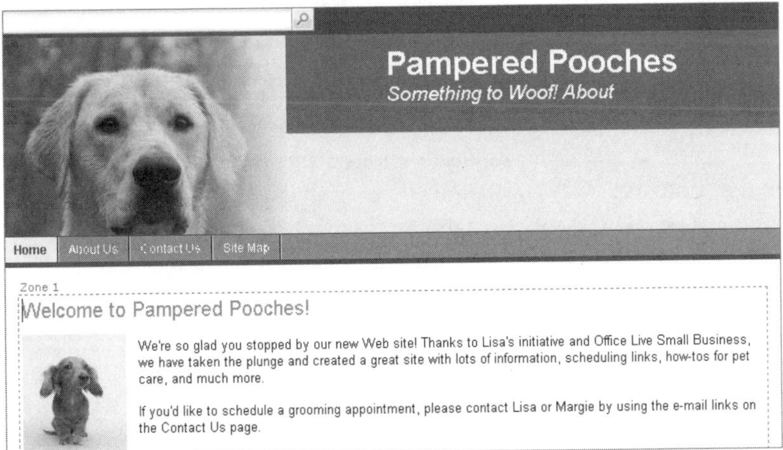

FIGURE 4-25 The Top navigation style positions page links between the page header and the content area.

NAVIGATION AND E-COMMERCE

It's worth the investment to spend a little time surfing the Web and visiting your favorite sites. Which navigation styles do they use? Because different sites have different goals—one site might be designed simply to provide product information, while another site sells products—it will be helpful to research sites that have a goal similar to yours. Do you see a common type of navigation style being used on those sites?

It's interesting to note that all the sites listed in the top 10 online retailers for Cyber Monday 2007 have Top & Left navigation options. Let's take a closer look at a few of them to see what kind of navigation options they offer their visitors:

- Amazon.com was the No. 2 site visited on Cyber Monday 2007. The navigation style on this site gives visitors a variety of options. Not only can visitors choose from the left navigation bar; they can also click from links along the top of the page area. Both the top and left navigation areas offer rollout secondary menus so that users can be specific about what they want to find.
- Dell was seventh out of 10 on the top 10 Cyber Monday sites, attracting a more specialized audience than Amazon.com or eBay might attract. Dell offers a very clean site, with navigation options along the left and a double row of navigation options across the top of the page. The tabs enable you to choose the major department you want to see, and the link bar beneath the tabs change (not unlike the Microsoft Office Fluent Ribbon in some of the 2007 Microsoft Office programs!) depending on the tab you select. Unlike Amazon.com, Dell does not provide users with rollout secondary menus.
- eBay uses yet a different approach. Rated the No. 1 visited site on Cyber Monday 2007, eBay attracts a diverse and Web-experienced audience. eBay offers categories along the left navigation bar and includes a Categories drop-down link in the left-most position of the top navigation bar. When you click the Categories arrow, a gallery of categories opens. This gives users the option of choosing the category from the left navigation panel or the top bar, while limiting the amount of space invested in displaying categories in the drop-down gallery.

Choosing Navigation Pages

Now that you've decided how you want the navigation panel or bar to look, you need to decide what you want to appear within it. Depending on the size of your site, you may have many pages that you don't want to show in the navigation bar. For example, consider the Pampered Pooches site. The owners plan eventually to include different pages for each of the top 20 dog breeds, with tips on grooming, training, and temperament for each breed. Of course, they don't want all 20 of those pages to appear in a navigation bar on the left side of the page. How should they handle it?

Here's how they approach it: First, they consider the different types of resources they want to provide site visitors. They come up with three categories:

- Articles for Owners
- Web Links for Pet Health
- Rescue Associations

To solve the problem of the navigation, the owners create a Resources page that appears in the navigation bar alongside Home, About Us, Contact Us, and Site Map. Then they create three more pages—Articles, Pet Health, and Rescue—as children of the Resources page (which is called the *parent* page). Finally, they will create their breed-specific pages as children of the Articles page. Only the Resources page will appear equal to the other pages in the navigation panel.

TIP

You can add child pages to the navigation bar if you choose. These pages appear in the bar or panel only when that page is selected. In the Pampered Pooches example, this means that the three subpages—Articles, Pet Health, and Rescue—would not be visible on the Home, About Us, or Contact Us pages, but when the user clicks Resources, the three pages appear in the navigation bar. To change whether a subpage appears in the navigation bar, click the page Properties link in the Page Manager and select the Show This Page In The Navigation Bar check box in the Choose Page Properties dialog box.

Making Navigation Changes

You can modify the way you've set up the navigation pages at any point during your Office Live Small Business work session. You can reorder pages and change the way in which the pages relate (perhaps making one page a parent and another a child, for example) from the Page Manager. Here are the steps:

1. In the Page Manager, click Design Site.
2. Choose Modify Navigation from the list (see Figure 4-26).
3. In the Navigation dialog box, click the page you want to change (see Figure 4-27).
4. If you want to place one page under another, click the page in the list on the left and click the Place Page Under arrow to display the list. Click the title of the page under which you want to put the page. Then click the Change Parent button.
5. Repeat as needed for other pages in the list on the left.
6. Use the Move Up and Move Down buttons to arrange the pages in the order in which you want them to appear in the navigation bar.

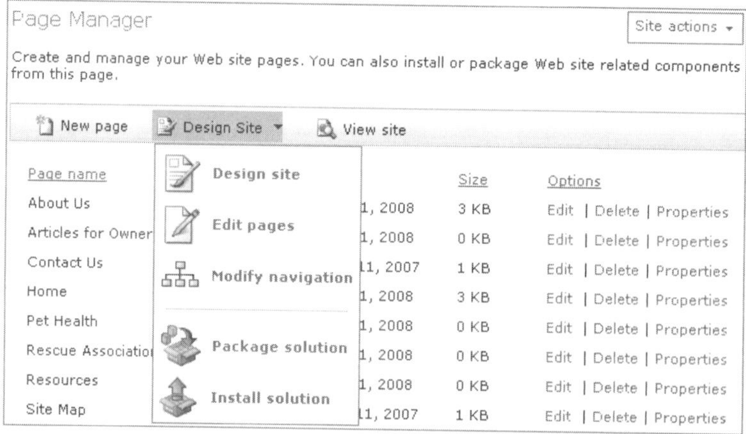

FIGURE 4-26 Choose Modify Navigation in the Page Manager to change the order of items in the navigation bar.

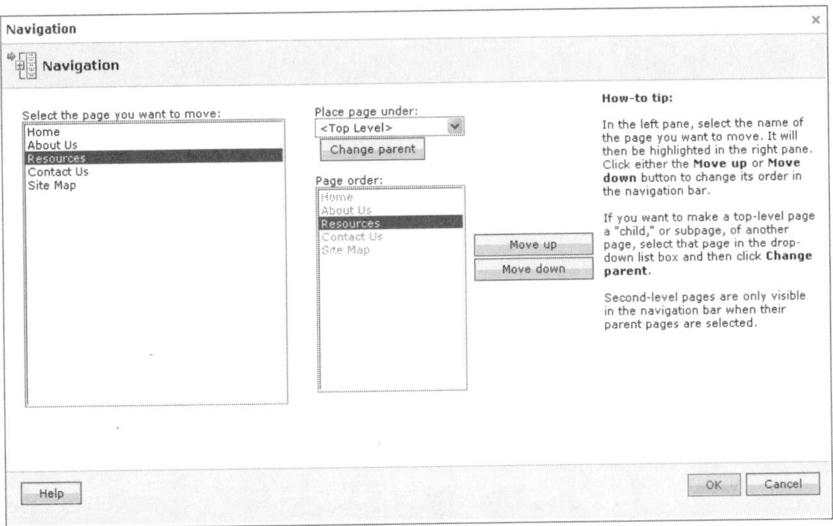

FIGURE 4-27 Reorder navigation pages in the Navigation dialog box.

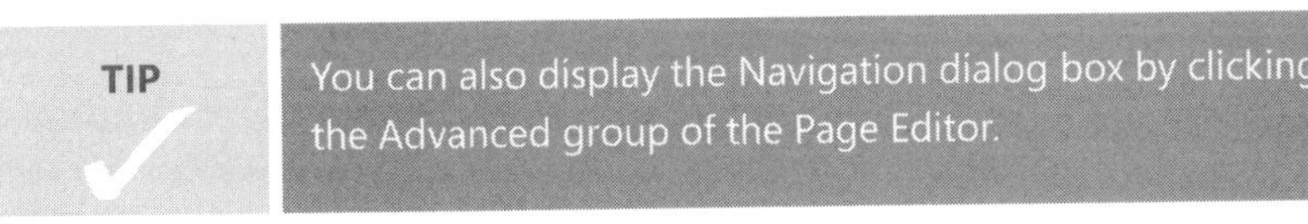
TIP

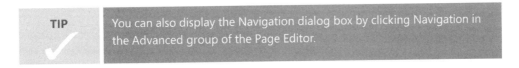

You can also display the Navigation dialog box by clicking Navigation in the Advanced group of the Page Editor.

Adding Keyword and Description Metatags

When you click Properties for a page in the Page Manager, the Choose Page Properties dialog box appears. In this dialog box, you can enter Page Settings, such as Page Title and whether you want to include the page in the navigation list or bar on your site.

On a second tab called Search Engine Optimization, you can enter the keywords and a description for your site. Keywords are important because they are the words that cause your site to be displayed as a search result when a potential customer enters the word in a search engine such as Google, Windows Live Search, or ChaCha. For example, in Figure 4-28, the keywords include *dog grooming, pet spa*, and *animals*. When someone searches for *dog grooming* on Windows Live Search, the search engine will be able to find the site because of the keywords entered.

It's important to enter keywords for each page in your site; it increases your chances of being included in search results.

NOTE

You can raise your visibility in search results by adding pay-per-click search advertising with adManager. You can set a budget that controls how much you want to spend each month and then let adManager submit the ads you create in the sponsored area of search results. To find out more, see Chapter 9, "Promoting Your Business."

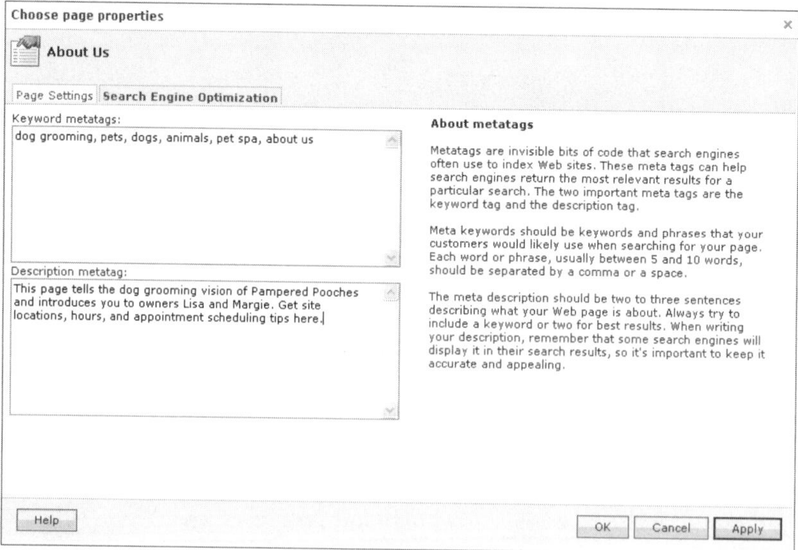

FIGURE 4-28 Enter keywords to help visitors find your site through search engines.

Previewing Your Site

You can easily see how your Web site is shaping up by previewing it. You can preview your site three different ways in Office Live Small Business:

- In the Page Manager, click View Site in the Page Manager toolbar.
- In the Page Editor, click View at the top of the Web window.
- In the Site Designer, click View (also at the top of the Web window).

TIP

When you're working in the Page Editor Web window, you can move from page to page in your site by clicking the Web Pages tool in the upper-left corner of the window and choosing the page you want to see from the displayed list.

The page appears in your default Web browser (see Figure 4-29). Test all links, read through your text, and check your images to make sure they look the way you'd hoped. Make sure your navigation panel or bar works properly, and scan the page to see whether you've left anything out that seems important. After you finish previewing the site, click the browser close box to return to Office Live Small Business.

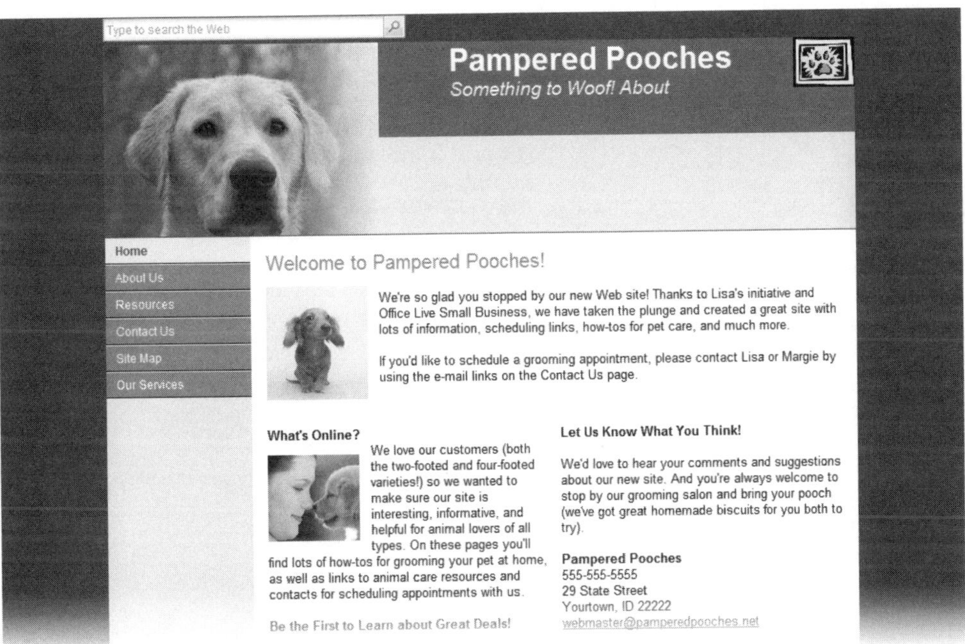

Type to search the Web
Pampered Pooches
Something to Woof! About
Home
About Us
Resources
Contact Us
Site Map
Our Services
Welcome to Pampered Pooches!
We're so glad you stopped by our new Web site! Thanks to Lisa's initiative and Office Live Small Business, we have taken the plunge and created a great site with lots of information, scheduling links, how-tos for pet care, and much more.
If you'd like to schedule a grooming appointment, please contact Lisa or Margie by using the e-mail links on the Contact Us page.
What's Online?
We love our customers (both the two-footed and four-footed varieties!) so we wanted to make sure our site is interesting, informative, and helpful for animal lovers of all types. On these pages you'll find lots of how-tos for grooming your pet at home, as well as links to animal care resources and contacts for scheduling appointments with us.
Be the First to Learn about Great Deals!
Let Us Know What You Think!
We'd love to hear your comments and suggestions about our new site. And you're always welcome to stop by our grooming salon and bring your pooch (we've got great homemade biscuits for you both to try).
Pampered Pooches
555-555-5555
29 State Street
Yourtown, ID 22222
webmaster@pamperedpooches.net

FIGURE 4-29 Preview the page in your browser to check all links, content, and layout.

A WEB PUBLISHING CHECKLIST

Before you begin sending your Web address to potential and existing customers, take a few moments and go over the following things:

- Make sure there are no typos in your content.
- Check all punctuation and capitalization in the text to make sure it is correct.
- Look at the headings on all the pages. Are they the same font, color, and size?
- Pay attention to the spacing in the different zones on your pages. Make sure it is consistent from page to page. If you've added a blank line after the headings on page 1, make sure you also add a line after the headings on page 4.
- Have you used the same font for the text on all your pages?
- Review the images on your site. Are they good quality?
- Do the photos need editing so the color and brightness look professional?
- Are you happy with the way the text wraps around the images?
- How do the headers and footers on the pages look?

Finally, before you circulate the Web address of your new site, ask some trusted friends or coworkers to review the site for you. Ask them to pay special attention to anything that seems confusing or difficult to navigate. Be sure to make any changes your reviewers suggest before you share your new site with prospective customers.

Organizing Site Resources

When you click the Web Site link in the Office Live Small Business navigation bar, a list of resources appears to the left of the page area. These areas provide you with a set of tools you can use to organize the different files you'll use with your site, produce Web reports, and work with promotion opportunities for your site.

In this section, we'll explore the first three resources:

- Image Gallery, the spot for your photos and art files
- Document Gallery, the place for documents, worksheets, and more to use with your site
- Template Gallery, the space for Web pages you save to use as templates for other new Web pages

Image Gallery

The Image Gallery is the place where all your image files are stored when you upload them using the Image Uploader. You can also upload images directly to the gallery by clicking the Image Gallery link. Each time you click Image in the Page Editor and add a photo or art file to your page, you are inserting art that has been included in the Image Gallery (see Figure 4-30).

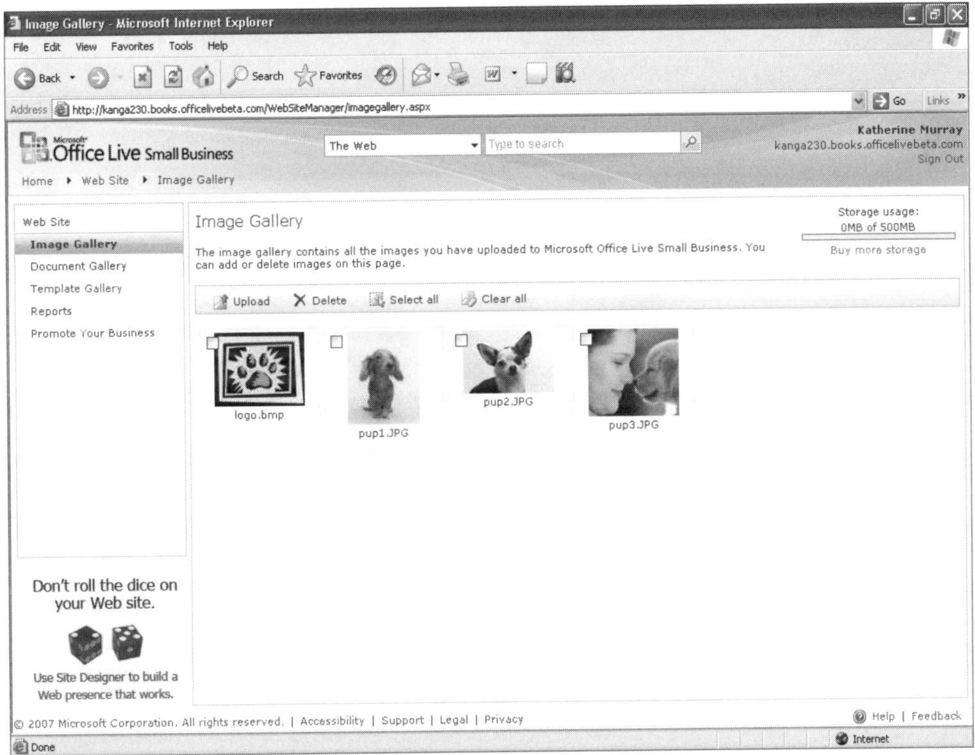

FIGURE 4-30 You can Upload, Delete, Select All, or Clear All images in the Image Gallery.

Document Gallery

With the Document Gallery, you can collect documents that are important to your customers or to the functioning of your site. You might, for example, post a copy of your new brochure, available as a PDF file on the Web. Your customers could download it by clicking the link that connects to the document in the Document Gallery. Or perhaps you'd like to provide a Microsoft Office PowerPoint presentation of your newest products. Upload the presentation to your Document Gallery, and customers will be able to access it when you link it to a page in your site.

PLAN YOUR WEB STRATEGY

Just getting your business online may be your primary objective when you first think about a Web site, but somewhere in the middle of the process you will undoubtedly begin asking yourself important questions like the following:

- What do we really want to show online?
- What do our customers want to see?
- What do we want them to do once they get to our site?

Initially, considering your site from your customer's point of view can help you create the kind of Web experience that will give them what they're looking for (which will keep them coming back). As you begin to think about your long-range goals on the Web, however, you need to consider how your site will help you reach the goals in your company's business plan.

For example, do you intend to eventually have a storefront for your business, or will you run it solely online? Do you want to sell primarily from the Web, or will you have sales reps in the field? As you begin to grow, will you recruit employees on your Web site, or keep it small and family-centered?

Each of these questions speaks to a different aspect of the life of your site. You may find it helpful to get out your business plan and sit down with a big blank sheet of paper so you can draw a Web timeline. On the left end of the timeline, make a big "you are here" mark. Then divide the paper into thirds. The first third will be year 1, the second third is year 2, and the last third—you guessed it—year 3.

Now, with your business plan in one hand and your Web timeline stretched before you, brainstorm about the goals you've established for your business over the next several years and plot out the ways in which the Web can help you meet those goals. Write the goals on the Web timeline and add the features you'd like to include. Suppose that you want to begin publishing a quarterly newsletter in 2008. Office Live Small Business can help you do that easily with the addition of e-mail marketing. Perhaps you want to present your new products to all field sales reps next summer. You can upload a PowerPoint presentation to a Team Workspace in Office Live Small Business and invite the reps to the space to participate.

The point is to think now about what you want to happen in the future for your business and to—creatively and flexibly—get a vision of the way your new Web site can help you reach your planned business goals. You might be surprised how naturally everything fits together!

YOUR BUSINESS ONLINE: Q&A INTERVIEW

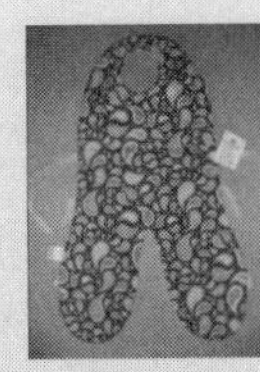

Jeanne Roth and Leslie Smith, owners
Lil Darlins: *www.lildarlins.org*

Q *What are your favorite features in Office Live Small Business?*

A When starting a small business, there are three essential things you need besides whatever it is you're selling. They are: a Web site, an accounting system, and a payment processor. Office Live Small Business provided me with the opportunity and know-how to develop a basic Web site for free—that was a big plus as I had no idea how to create one or the cash to pay for one! Office Live also provided the link to downloading Microsoft Office Accounting Express 2007, which gave me my accounting system free for the first year. I have since upgraded to Microsoft Office Accounting Professional 2008. Lastly, Office Live led me to a payment processor, PayPal's Website Payments Pro, which integrates easily with your accounting system for credit/debit card transactions via a gateway through EmartCart.com, which provides you with a shopping cart on your Web site (also free for basic service). With these three in place, you are now open for business!

Q *How do you use the marketing and management features in Office Live?*

A Our Web site is the cornerstone of our business; without it there is no point of reference that we exist. It allows us to reach customers all over the world, but how we develop and promote it is the key to success. Exposure, exposure, exposure is to our Web site as Location, location, location is to real estate. Everyone wants to see your Web site URL to learn about you and your products, whether it's the editor of a magazine or newspaper who is featuring an article on your business, a hang tag on your products, a friend of a customer, a search engine, a sign on your vehicle, an exhibitor directory at a trade show—all want your Web site URL. Office Live provides Microsoft adCenter as an additional advertising vehicle to your Web site, and site reports show the amount of traffic (hits) on your Web site. And we all know what increased traffic brings—hopefully increased business—but not without a good Web site!

Q *What advice would you pass along to a small business owner trying Office Live for the first time?*

A The Microsoft adCenter provides an advertising vehicle for you to create several campaigns pinpointing keywords that will bring customers to your Web site and hopefully enough to increase your search engine rankings. This is paramount so that your Web site comes up on the first page rather than the 20th page in a Google search. As I mentioned earlier, site reports give you the visibility of what pages your customers are viewing on your Web site, which search engines are performing the best for you, and where the people are from who are visiting your Web site—all this information helps you decide which areas you need to improve to increase traffic to your site.

Jeanne Roth and her daughter, Leslie Smith, started L'il Darlins, LLC in 2006 with a mission of designing children's specialty items that are creatively constructed and will hold up against wear and tear. Thanks to David Roth, Jeanne's husband and "Father, Financier, Treasurer, Accountant, Webmaster, and Go-fer" for taking the time to do this interview.

What's Next

This chapter introduced you to the Web tools and got you started with the basics of Web design and page layout. The next chapter continues our exploration of the Web tools by showing you how to add to the capabilities of your site. Specifically, you'll learn how to customize your site by changing the layout, adding Web modules, and using your own HTML and cascading style sheets (CSS). Additionally, you'll find out about adding video, blogs, and more.

Taking Your Site to the Next Level

IN THIS CHAPTER, YOU WILL

- Change page layout.
- Add tables.
- Enhance your site functionality with Web modules.
- Learn about advanced Web features.

JUST GETTING a professional-looking site up on the Web is a huge accomplishment, so congratulations! After you have the basic design and content situated the way you want it, you might find yourself beginning to wonder what you can do next. People seem to be flipping over video—should you add video clips to your site? Customers really like to see user reviews before they buy a product; perhaps giving your customers the opportunity to share their great experiences with your company will be effective in encouraging others to try your wares.

This chapter shows you how you can take your Web site to the next level by changing the layout of your page, adding tables, inserting Web modules, and (for those of you who are comfortable with Web technologies) work with CSS (cascading style sheets) and HTML on your site. You also learn how to add video clips and even a blog to your site.

> **NOTE** Not all sites need all things, so choose your enhancements carefully. Think about your audience. What will your customers want to see? What will they really use? Remember that your customers will appreciate it if you give them what they are looking for in the easiest possible way. Sometimes bells and whistles actually get in the way of what the user wants to accomplish online.

Changing Page Layout

As you learned in the previous chapter, Microsoft Office Live Small Business makes page design easy for you by providing ready-made pages and Web page templates you can use as is or modify to suit your needs. You can change the layout of your pages at any time and create a totally new look for your site with a few simple clicks of the mouse. Here are the steps for changing the layout of a page:

1. Click Web Site in the left navigation bar.
2. In the Page Manager, click the Edit link for the page you want to change.
3. Click Layout in the Advanced group of the Page Editor (see Figure 5-1).
4. Click the layout you want. Table 5-1 describes the available choices.
5. If necessary, use Cut and Paste in the Paragraph group to move the page content into the appropriate zones.

TABLE 5-1 Choosing a Layout

LAYOUT STYLE	NAME	DESCRIPTION	USE WHEN
	Single area	Entire page is one large content area	You have large blocks of text or want to display a large image.
	Two, side by side	Two vertical columns arranged parallel on the page	You want to display two running columns, similar to newsletter text (with or without images).
	Three, side by side	Three vertical columns arranged side by side on the page	You want to compare a list of product features.
	Three, span bottom	Two vertical columns appear in the upper half of the page, with one horizontal column below	You want to include several different text segments on the page.
	Three, span top	One horizontal area at the top of the page with two vertical areas below	You want to create a page intro followed by a two-column list or content divided into sections.

FIGURE 5-1 You can choose from a gallery of ready-made layouts for your Web pages.

Adding Tables

Tables can serve more than one purpose on your Web site. A well-organized table helps your site visitors find information they're looking for in an easy-to-understand format. A table can also help you arrange your information so that it aligns neatly on the page. One more perk—and it's a big one: you can insert information in a table to ensure that table items will appear the way you want them to, no matter which browser your customer might be using. Here are the steps for adding a table to your Web page:

1. In the Page Manager, click Edit to open the page you want to add the table to.
2. Click to position the cursor at the point where you want to add the table.
3. Click Table in the Insert group. The Create Table dialog box appears (see Figure 5-2).
4. Click the table type you want to create. Table 5-2 describes the table choices.
5. Click the Color Scheme arrow and choose the color that best fits your color scheme.
6. Enter the number of columns and rows you want to create.
7. Click OK to create the table.

TABLE 5-2 Choosing a Table Style

STYLE	NAME	DESCRIPTION
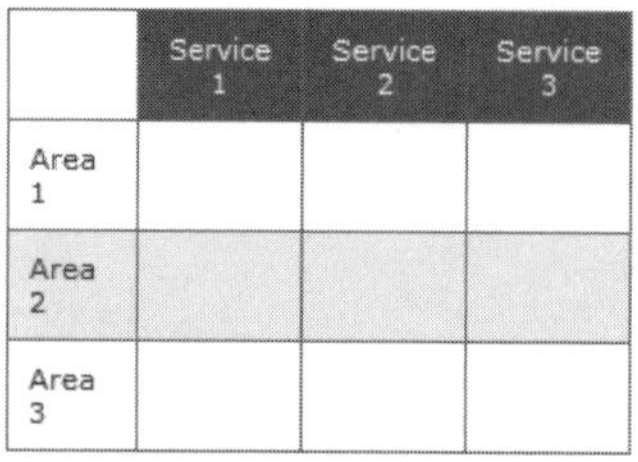 Service 1 | Service 2 | Service 3 Area 1 Area 2 Area 3	Service Comparison	Use this table to compare three services that your company offers.
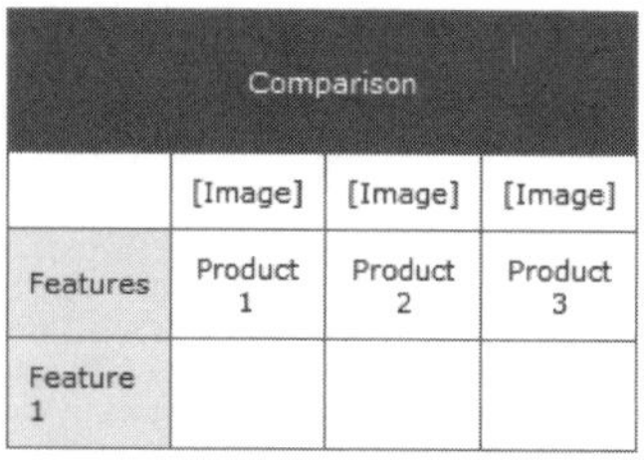 Comparison [Image] | [Image] | [Image] Features | Product 1 | Product 2 | Product 3 Feature 1	Product Comparison	Use this table to compare products by including product photos and feature lists.
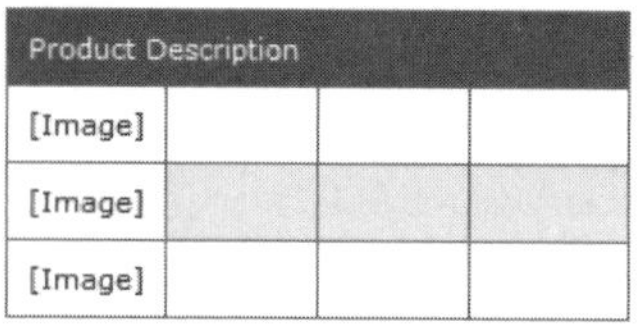 Product Description [Image] [Image] [Image]	Product Description	Use this table to create a listing of your products, with photos in the left column.
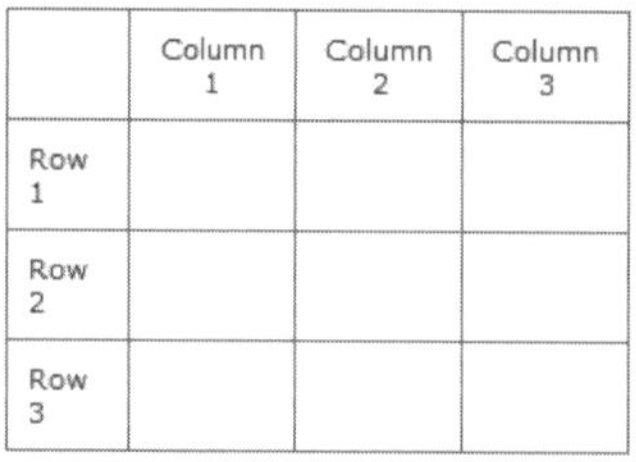 Column 1 | Column 2 | Column 3 Row 1 Row 2 Row 3	Generic Style	Use this table when you want to build a custom table.

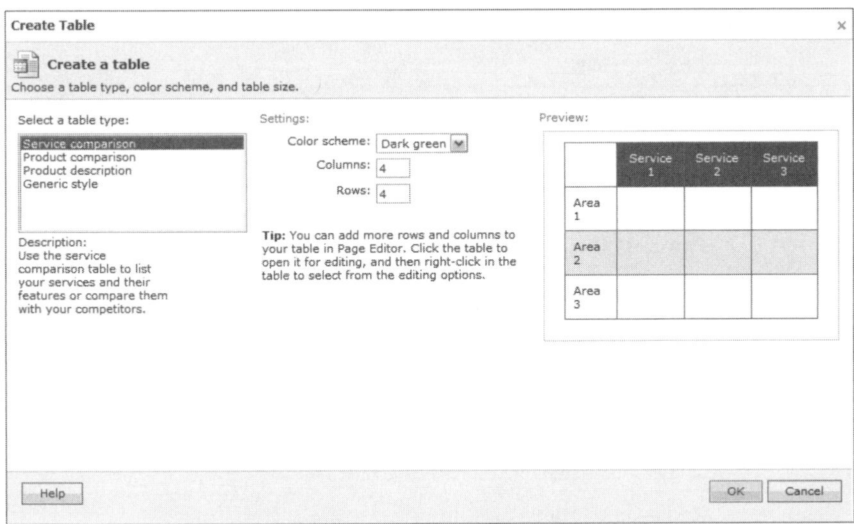

FIGURE 5-2 Use the Create Table dialog box to add a table to your Web page.

TIP

You can format the information in the table to fit your Web page by using the tools in the Font group of the Page Editor. For example, you might want to change the color of the table heading, make it bold, or include a bulleted list in one of the cells of the table.

Modifying Tables

You can easily make changes to a table you've added to your Office Live Small Business page. Simply right-click anywhere on the table; a list of available options appears, as you see in Figure 5-3. Click the command that reflects the action you want to carry out. Table 5-3 explains more about the table-editing options.

TABLE 5-3 Table-Editing Tools

OPTION	DESCRIPTION
Cut	Deletes selected text or images
Copy	Places a copy of selected text or images on the Clipboard
Paste	Pastes a copy of any item on the Clipboard at the cursor position
Delete Column	Removes the column at the cursor position
Delete Row	Removes the row at the cursor position
Insert Column	Inserts a column to the left of the cursor position
Insert Row	Inserts a row above the row at the cursor position
Merge Columns	Merges specified columns into one column
Merge Rows	Merges specified rows into one row
Float Left	Positions the table along the left margin of the zone
Float Right	Enables the table to float at the right margin of the zone
No Text Wrapping	Centers the table in the zone and ensures that text is not wrapped around it
Properties	Displays the Table Properties dialog box so that you can set preferences for the table
Delete	Deletes the table at the cursor position

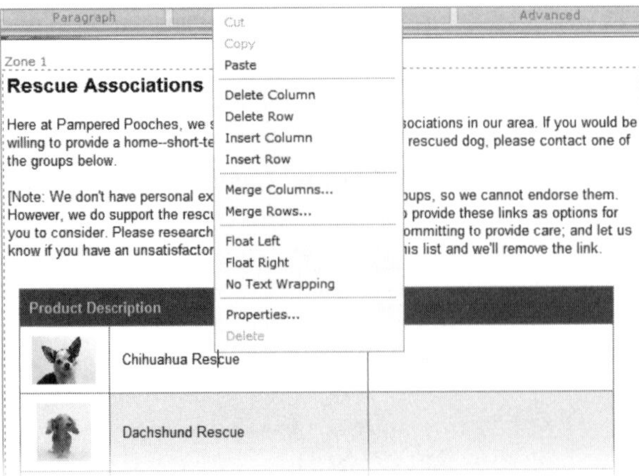

FIGURE 5-3 Right-click the table to display your choices for changing the table.

TIP

If you inadvertently add a column in a place you didn't intend, simply click the Close box of the page view. Office Live Small Business will ask you whether you want to save the changes to the page or cancel the changes. Click Cancel to abandon the changes and return to the Page Manager.

Adjusting Table Properties

You can customize the look of your table in several ways. You can choose a border color, control cell spacing and height, add a background color or picture, and customize the border width. To display the table properties, right-click the table and choose Properties. The Table Properties dialog box appears, as shown in Figure 5-4.

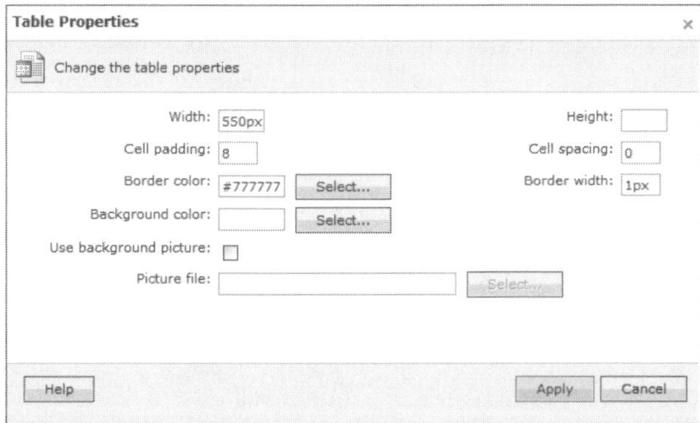

FIGURE 5-4 Use the Table Properties dialog box to customize the look of your table.

The Width setting refers to the entire table width, and Office Live Small Business adjusts the column widths according to the content of the table cells and the number of columns in the table. Experiment with your table to get a feel for the way in which the width setting affects the overall table. Similarly, the Height setting applies to the entire table.

Cell Padding and Cell Spacing control the amount of space surrounding each data item in the table. The Border Color and Border Width settings enable you to choose from a palette of 117 colors and set the width of the outer border. Note that the color you select for the border will also be applied to the interior cell divisions in the table; however, the Border Width setting will be applied only to the outside of the table.

You can set a color background for the entire table by clicking the Select button to the right of the Background Color box. Click a selection from the color palette, and the entire table background fills with the color you select.

NOTE You might need to adjust the color of the text in the table to make it easy to read after you fill the table with a background color.

For a special table effect, you can add a picture to the background of the table by clicking the Use Background Picture check box and clicking Select to the right of the Picture File box. After the Select Image dialog box appears, click the picture you want to use, and click OK. The picture is added to the table. Similar to adding a background color, however, use this feature sparingly and be prepared to change the text color and style so that the text can be seen easily against the background.

Enhancing Your Site Functionality with Web Modules

Web modules enable you to go beyond basic functionality on your site by adding special items that provide site visitors with additional features and options. Web modules are easy to add, move, and remove, so you can feel free to experiment with the ones that capture your interest. The process is simple: you click in the zone on the page where you want the module to appear (for example, click in Zone 1, Zone 2, or Zone 3, depending on the layout of your page), and choose the module you want from the Module list. Office Live Small Business includes the following Web modules you can add to your pages:

- Contact Us
- HTML
- Map & Directions
- Slide Show
- Live Spaces Blog
- Stock List
- Weather
- Form Designer
- List Publisher

The sections that follow introduce you to the basic steps involved in adding and working with Web modules on your site.

Adding a Web Module

To add a module to a selected page, follow these steps:

1. Click Web Site.
2. In the Page Manager, click the Edit link of the page you want to change.
3. Click to position the cursor at the point where you want to add the module.
4. Click the Module arrow in the Insert group. A gallery of modules appears (see Figure 5-5).
5. Click the module you want to add. The module is added to your page.

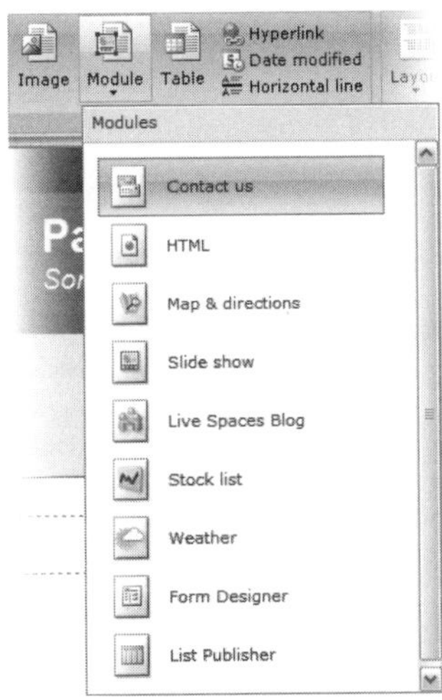

FIGURE 5-5 Select a Web module from the Modules list.

Moving a Module

Suppose that you just added a module to Zone 2 on the current Web page but you really meant to add it to Zone 3. How do you fix that? Simple. Click the module and drag it to the correct zone. The cursor position will show you where the module will appear when you release the mouse button. The module then appears in the new zone, resized to fit the available area.

Resizing a Module

If you want to resize the module you've added, it's not quite as simple as clicking and dragging (but it's not too much harder than that). Here are the steps:

1. Right-click the module.
2. Click Resize. The Resize dialog box appears (see Figure 5-6).
3. By default, Office Live Small Business sets the sizing of the module to fit the content added to the module. To change the default and resize the module to meet your exact specifications, you can enter specific sizes (in pixels) in the Width and Height boxes.
4. Click OK to save your settings and resize the module.

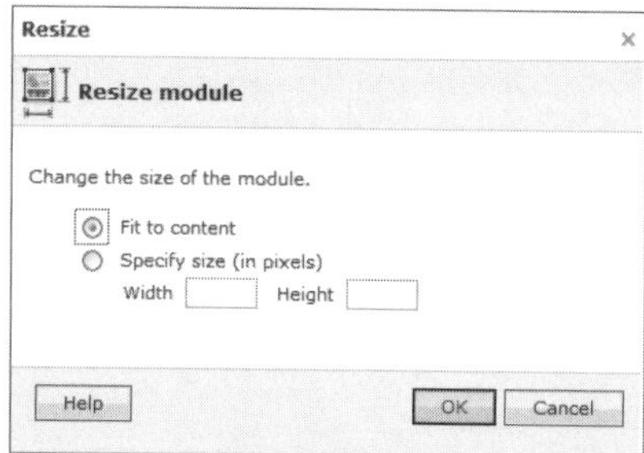

FIGURE 5-6 Change the settings in the Resize dialog box to change the module size on the page.

You might need to experiment with the sizing to get a feel for the width and height you want. When you click the Specify Size (In Pixels) button, the current sizes appear in the Width and Height boxes. Use those values as benchmarks and increase or decrease the values depending on whether you want to expand or reduce the size of the module.

Did you add the wrong module? Right-click the module and click Delete. Click OK. All things should be so easy.

Contact Us Module

The Contact Us module is a simple module that collects information from your site visitors. You might simply use it on your Contact Us page, or you can adapt it to be used to collect customer testimonials, questions, and more (see Figure 5-7).

To add the Contact Us module, click Module in the Insert group of the Page Editor and select Contact Us. The Contact Us dialog box appears, asking you to enter the e-mail address you want Office Live Small Business to use to send you an alert when a user fills in the Contact Us form (see Figure 5-8). Enter your address and click OK. If you want to enter more than one address, use a semicolon to separate the addresses.

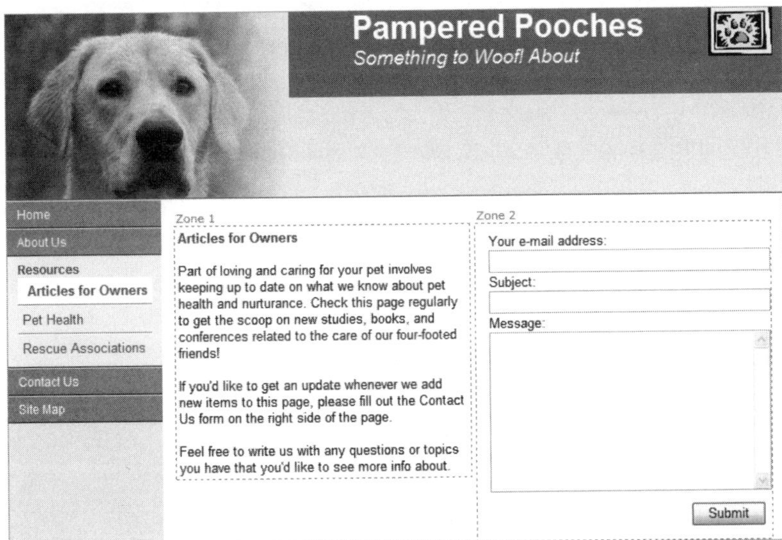

FIGURE 5-7 The Contact Us module enables site visitors to connect with you easily.

Contact Us

Change the Contact Us delivery settings

Type an e-mail address where you want an alert sent to when a customer fills out a Contact Us form. Separate multiple entries by a semicolon.

E-Mail address:

Help OK Cancel

FIGURE 5-8 Enter an e-mail address so that you'll be notified when a user fills out the Contact Us form on your site.

HTML Module

If you have some experience with HTML or you are familiar enough to copy and paste HTML from another site into your own, you might want to customize your page by adding an HTML module. Common HTML modules include clocks, site counters, local weather gadgets, and utilities. The example shown in Figure 5-9 shows a link to a book review that was created in HTML on another site and then copied and pasted into the HTML module in Office Live Small Business. By using content you've already added elsewhere (or using pieces of blog posts others have already published about your company—with their permission, of course), you can add testimonials, gadgets, and more to expand the functionality of your site and leverage content you already have.

To add the HTML module to your page, click Modules in the Insert group and choose HTML. In the Add And Edit HTML dialog box, paste the HTML content you've copied from elsewhere or type the HTML code you want to use in the module (see Figure 5-10). When you're finished entering information, click OK to save your changes and view the HTML module on the page.

FIGURE 5-9 The HTML module enables you to use HTML gadgets, modules, or content you are already using elsewhere or can create easily.

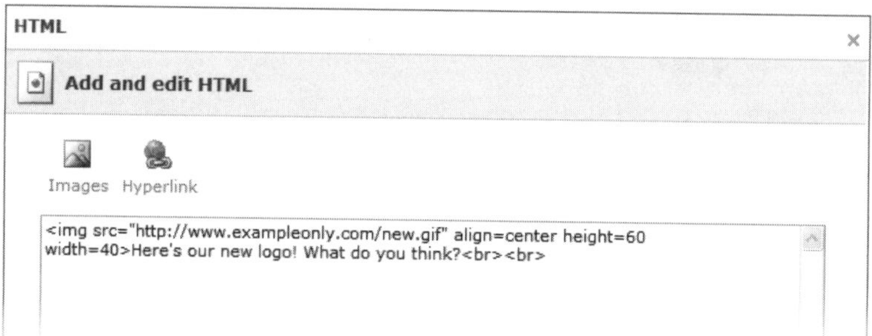

FIGURE 5-10 Enter or copy information into the Add And Edit HTML dialog box to add the item to the page.

If you want to make changes to the module content after you add it, simply right-click the module and click Properties. The Add And Edit HTML dialog box opens so that you can make the changes you need to make. Click OK when you're finished.

WANT TO GET SCHOOLED IN HTML?

If you love to know the whys and wherefores behind the way things work, you can find out more about HTML by starting with a few of these links (you might be surprised to discover how easy it is):

- HTML Tutorials: *www.w3schools.com/html/default.asp*
- HTML Basics: *www.ncsu.edu/cc/edu/html_trng/html_basics.html*
- HTML for Beginners: *www.htmlbasictutor.ca*

Of course, one of the beautiful things about Office Live Small Business is that busy small-business owners can create great-looking sites without ever having to learn HTML at all. So unless you have free time and really want to spend it learning to do something that's not mandatory for your site, you can save your exploration for a less-busy time (whenever that might be!).

Adding Video to Your Site

One of the most popular uses for the HTML module involves adding a video player to your site. Depending on the type of business you're in and the content your customers will expect (and want) to see, you might want to add video segments of product demonstrations, customer interviews, a word from the president, or simply something fun. When you add a video player in the HTML module of Office Live Small Business, you are including the code that links to the video on another site. This means that you might be embedding HTML from one of the sites listed on the following page:

- YouTube
- Google Video
- MSN Soapbox

When you are adding HTML from a third-party site of which you're a member, be sure to have your user ID and password information for that site handy. You will also need the identifying number of the specific video clip you want to include. On most sites, you can log in to your account, select the video you want to use, and then look for the Embed Video link or box, which will provide the HTML code you need in order to display the video on another site. When you find the Embed HTML code (see Figure 5-11), select it (be sure to include opening and closing brackets) and copy it into the HTML module dialog box. Click OK to save the video player and clip.

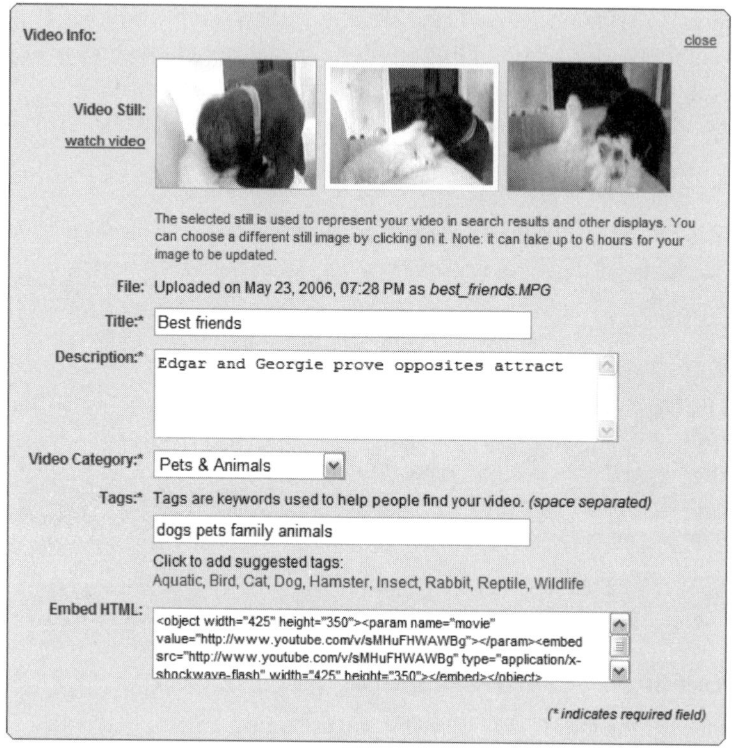

FIGURE 5-11 Look for the Embed HTML box on your video player's site and copy the code into your HTML module.

> **NOTE** Remember that copyright laws require that you include on your site only content that you have created (or that you have obtained the permission to publish).

Map & Directions Module

With the Map & Directions module, you can make it as easy as possible for potential customers to find and use your services. Similar to Windows Live Maps, this module asks you to enter your address and then choose the way in which the map and directions are displayed. Start by clicking in the zone on the page where you want to add the module; then click Module from the Insert group and choose Map & Directions. The Map & Directions dialog box appears (see Figure 5-12).

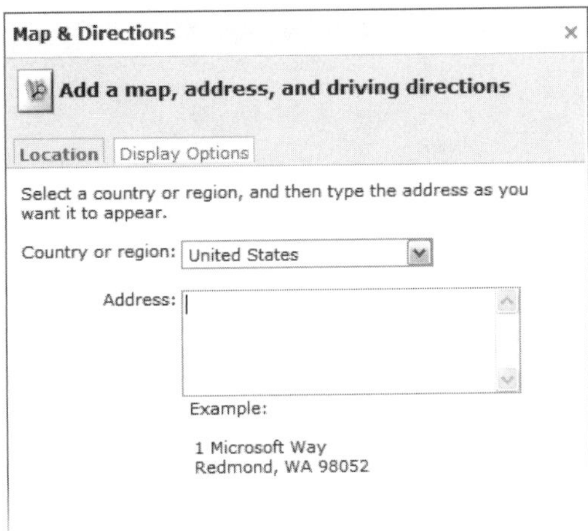

FIGURE 5-12 Type your business address in the Map & Directions dialog box and click Display Options.

After you enter your address in the Location screen of the Map & Directions dialog box, click the Display Options tab. On this page, you can choose whether you want to include an interactive map, what size you want the map to be, and how much interaction you want to provide (see Figure 5-13).

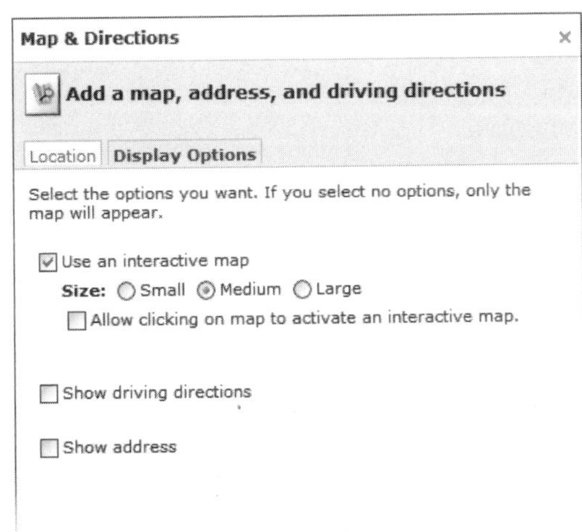

FIGURE 5-13 Choose your preferences for the map functionality and click OK.

TIP Think of the convenience items you like when you work with sites such as Windows Live Maps or MapQuest. Do you like features that enable you to zoom in on the map by clicking it, scroll right and left (or up and down) by dragging on the map area, or get specific driving directions? Use your experience as a guide when making similar decisions for your own site.

If you want driving directions and your business address to be visible to the user, click the Show Driving Directions and Show Address check boxes. Click OK to save your settings and add the module to the page.

Figure 5-14 shows a completed map with linked driving directions. Professional, isn't it? And you can add it to your Web site in less than two minutes (no kidding).

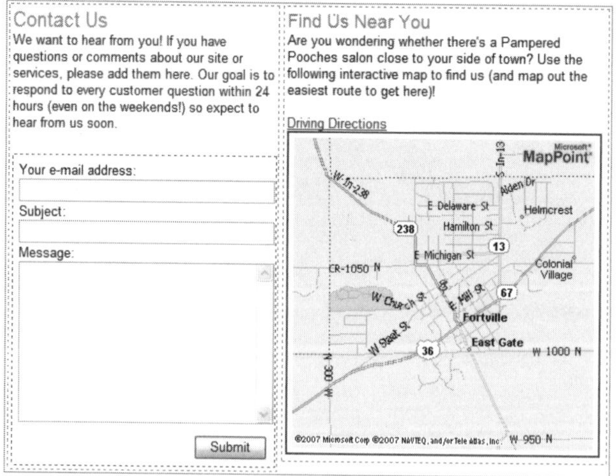

FIGURE 5-14 The Map & Directions module adds a sophisticated, convenient feature for your site visitors.

TIP

Want to provide multiple maps to multiple locations? Simple. Click in a different zone and add a new Map & Directions module in that area of the page. If you need to change the page layout to include more zones, click Layout in the Advanced group and select the new layout from the displayed list.

Slide Show Module

The Slide Show module gives you a great way to show off your products or services to the wider world. This module enables you to create a customized slide show that cycles through a series of photos—any photos—that showcase your stellar products or spotlight your happy customers. To add the Slide Show module to a zone on one of your pages, begin by clicking in the zone where you want to add the images. Then click Modules in the Insert group and choose Slide Show from the list. The Slide Show dialog box enables you to add photos using the Photo Upload tool if necessary, add an album title for the slide show, set the timing for the display of photos, and choose the pictures to be used. Here are the steps:

1. Display the page on which you want to add the slide show and click in the zone you want to use.
2. Click Modules in the Insert group of the Page Editor and choose Slide Show.
3. In the Slide Show dialog box, type a name for the slide show in the Album Name box (see Figure 5-15).
4. Click the Slide Interval arrow and choose the time you want to assign the display of each photo by clicking the value you want from the list.
5. If you want site visitors to be able to see and work with slide show controls (this enables them to page through the photos as they'd like), leave the Show Slide Show Controls check box selected.
6. Click the check box in the upper-left corner of each photo you'd like to include in the show.
7. Click Add. The photos are added to the Images In Slide Show area of the dialog box.
8. Reorder the images if you'd like by clicking an image in the Images In Slide Show area and clicking either the Move Left or Move Right buttons to change the position of the photo.

NOTE The photos will appear in the order you establish in the Images In Slide Show area, displaying from left to right.

9. Click Next.
10. Select a photo and add a caption (optional) by typing it in the Caption box (see Figure 5-16). Click Save Caption to save the text you enter for each photo. Repeat as desired for other photos in the slide show.

11. Click OK to save the module and add it to your page. Figure 5-17 shows how the Slide Show module looks after it is added to the page in the Page Editor.

FIGURE 5-15 Use the Slide Show module to add a continuously playing slide show to your site.

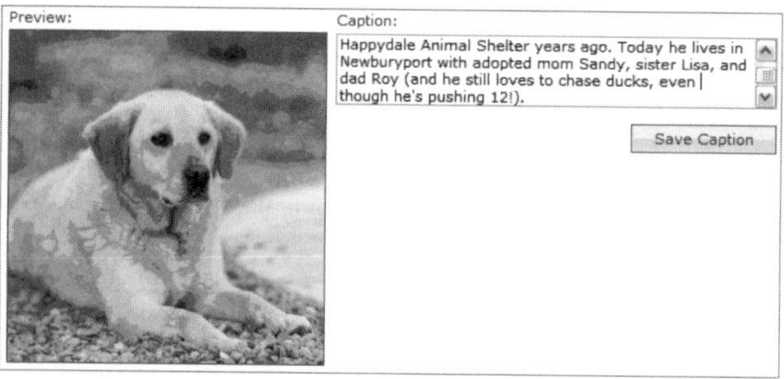

FIGURE 5-16 Add captions to individual photos to tell visitors more about your products, services, and success stories.

FIGURE 5-17 The Slide Show adds visual interest and helps visitors learn more about you and what you offer.

> **NOTE** The size of the slide show on the page will depend on the zone in which you add it. If your page is one large zone, the slide show will initially take up the entire width of the zone area. You can resize the Slide Show module by clicking it and dragging one of the handles in the corner or along the edges of the module to resize it. You can also limit the size of the module by creating it inside a smaller zone (such as Zone 2 or Zone 3 on a multizone page). To change the layout of your page to create additional zones, click Layout in the Advanced group and choose the layout with the zones you want to create. You can then cut and paste content into the different zones as needed.

Live Spaces Blog Module

Blogs are big, whether you are blogging to promote your business or simply to express your ideas and interests. Windows Live Spaces is a successful blogging, photo sharing, and personal networking site that enables you to post ideas, articles, links, photos, and more to your blog. If you want to add a blogging feature to your Office Live Small Business site, you can easily do that by adding the Live Spaces Blog module to your page. Simply fill in the name of your space in the box provided (see Figure 5-18) and, if you'd like to change the number of blog posts that are linked to your Office Live Small Business page, click the Number Of Posts To Show arrow and choose the number you want from the list. Click OK to add the module to your page.

TIP Windows Live Spaces is a free blogging service that packs a lot of punch. To find out more about what's available through Windows Live Spaces, go to *spaces.live.com*.

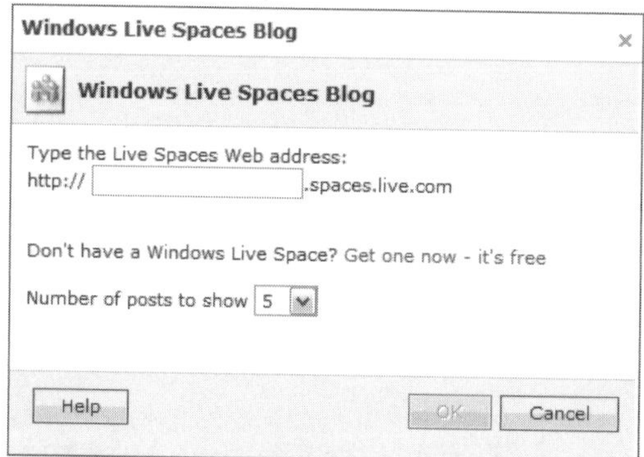

FIGURE 5-18 You can incorporate blog posts from Windows Live Spaces on your Office Live Small Business site.

Stock List Module

If your company serves customers who will be interested in knowing the latest stock prices for goods and services they care about, you can easily add a stock table to your site to display the latest trading information. If you don't know the codes for the companies you're interested in displaying, don't worry—the module provides a link for you to use to research the company information online.

Here's the process. Display the page you want to add the stock information to, and display the Page Editor. Click Module in the Insert group and click Stock List. In the Stocks dialog box (see Figure 5-19), enter the letters for the company name you want to add. If you are unsure about the letters, click the Find A Symbol link and locate the company by first selecting the industry area and then scrolling through the company list in the industry you select. When you've found the codes for the companies you want to use, enter each one in the Add A Symbol box, clicking Add after each addition.

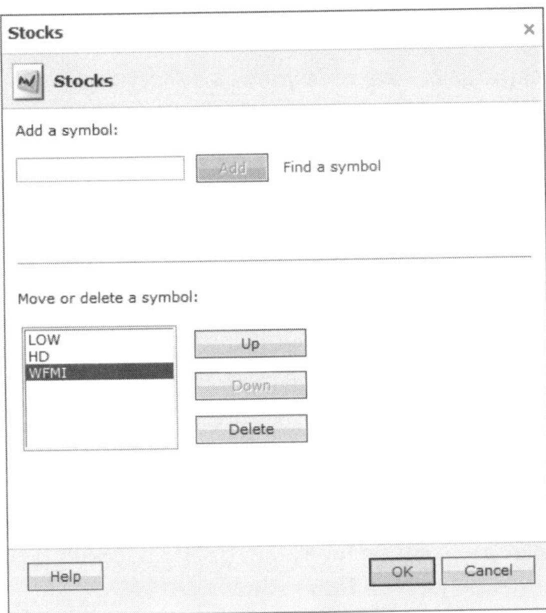

FIGURE 5-19 Add and order stock symbols for your stock list.

You can rearrange the items that appear on your list by clicking the stock you want to move and clicking Up or Down (or Delete, if you want to remove it altogether). When you're satisfied with the list, click OK to add it to your page (see Figure 5-20).

Zone 2

Barking Big

Here are a few of the builders and suppliers we've been keeping an eye on. If you're a do-it-yourselfer (most groomers are!), you might be interested:

Symbol	Price	Change	% Chg
LOW	22.19	0.40	1.84%
HD	26.28	0.03	0.11%
WFMI	35.08	-0.18	-0.51%

Quotes are by IDC Comstock and are delayed 20 minutes
Fund prices are from Morningstar.

FIGURE 5-20 You choose the stocks, and the module does the rest.

Weather Module

Especially if you serve a local audience, adding a Weather module to your site can be a great visitor service. (Plus, for some reason, most of us are simply interested in the weather.) You might want to post a Weather module on a page where you let site visitors know about upcoming events, for example—especially if those events will be held outdoors!

Here are the steps for adding the Weather module to your page:

1. Display the page you want to change. Select the zone you'd like to add the module to.
2. Click Module and click Weather.
3. In the Weather dialog box, type your ZIP code. Click Search. If the dialog box gives you a list of locations for that ZIP code, click the arrow and choose your city name from the list (see Figure 5-21).
4. If you want to display a four-day forecast, click the Show The 4-Day Forecast check box. Change the measurement unit if you live in an area where the temperature is tracked in Celsius.
5. Click OK.

The module is added to the zone in which you positioned the cursor. If you selected the four-day forecast, you will see a graphical representation for all four days, along with expected high and low temperatures for that period (see Figure 5-22).

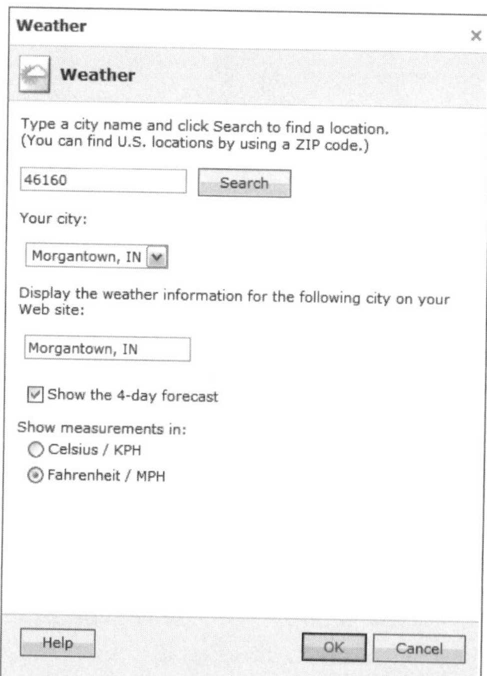

FIGURE 5-21 Enter the ZIP code for your area and select the name of your city.

FIGURE 5-22 The Weather module adds an attractive visual weather element to your page.

Form Designer Module

Office Live Small Business gives you a simple way to gather information from your site visitors when they come to find out more about your company. Using the Form Designer module, you can create a form that collects information and then sends the data to Contact Manager, Document Manager, or your Team Workspace, depending on the application you choose. Here's how it works:

1. Display the Web page on which you want to add the data form.
2. Click the zone on the page in which you want the form to appear.
3. Click Module and choose Form Designer.
4. Click the Application arrow and choose the application to which you want to send the data.
5. Click the List arrow and choose the data list to which you want the data added. The field area displays all the data items that will be included in the form by default (see Figure 5-23).

NOTE List options change depending on the application you select.

6. Click the check box of any fields you do not want to include on the form. If you want to remove the check marks in all fields at once, click the Display check box at the top of the list.

7. Click in the Display Name column and change the name of the field displayed on the form if desired.
8. In the Provide A Success Message area, type text you want visitors to see after they complete your form.
9. Click OK to save the form.

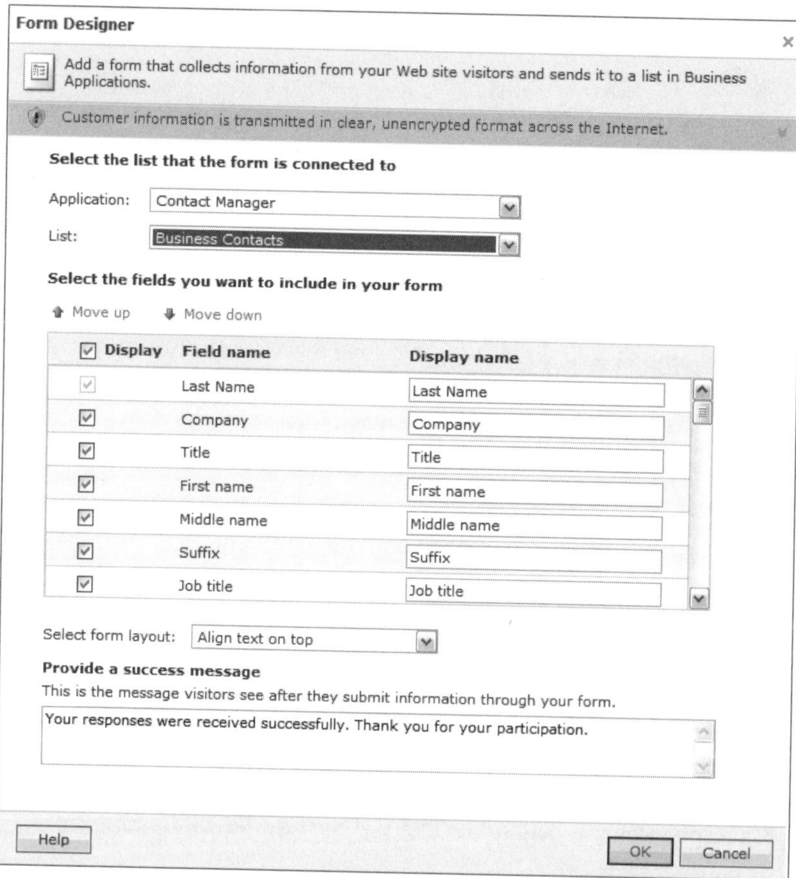

FIGURE 5-23 Choose the application to which you want the data to be sent.

Figure 5-24 shows an example of a simple form that collects the e-mail addresses of visitors who sign up for the site newsletter.

FIGURE 5-24 This is a simple example of a form published with Form Designer.

List Publisher Module

The List Publisher module enables you to publish data lists that you have created in Contact Manager, Document Manager, or Team Workspace to your Web page. This feature enables you, for example, to publish a class roster, an upcoming events list, or a list of available documents in a specific place on your page. To add a List Publisher module to one of your Web pages, follow these steps:

1. Click in the zone in which you want to add the module.
2. Click Module and click List Publisher.
3. In the List Publisher dialog box, click the Application arrow and choose the application from which you want to use the data.
4. Click the List arrow and choose the list you want to use. The field area displays all available fields that will be displayed in the module (see Figure 5-25).
5. Click the check box of any field you want to remove from the list. Change the display name for each field if desired.
6. Click OK.

FIGURE 5-25 List Publisher enables you to add data lists to your pages.

Figure 5-26 shows an example of data items displayed on the page by List Publisher.

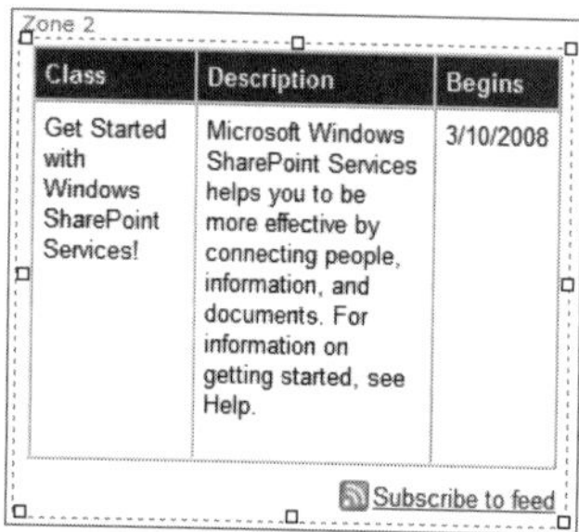

FIGURE 5-26 This is a simple list created with List Publisher.

Using Advanced Web Features

Just because Office Live Small Business is a simple way to create professional-looking Web sites, you don't have to be a beginning-level Web designer to use it. The latest version of Office Live Small Business includes an advanced mode that makes it possible for you to use the tools you're familiar with from other Web design applications to build, customize, and manage their Web pages. After you customize your pages, you can create new page templates based on those pages so that others can create pages for your Office Live Small Business site as well.

You can use the advanced Web features to do the following:

- Use cascading style sheet (CSS) styles in your site.
- Tailor your site header, footer, and navigation bar.
- Create pages that are used for forms and lists on your site.
- Include a site information module that displays information about your site anywhere on the page.
- Save a page as a template.

TIP Although the advanced features aren't rocket science, they also aren't for everyone. If you are comfortable with Web technologies and like to try new things (and have the time), the advanced features can add a level of customization to your site that can make updating, managing, and leveraging your work more efficient than ever.

Activating Advanced Features

Activating advanced Web features involves turning on options that are not automatically enabled when you begin working with your Office Live Small Business site. To activate the advanced features, follow these steps:

1. Click Web Site.
2. In the Page Manager, click the Site Actions arrow.
3. Click Activate Advanced Design Features (see Figure 5-27).
4. When prompted, click OK to activate advanced design features.

FIGURE 5-27 Choose Site Actions to find the option for activating advanced controls.

Working with a Style Sheet

One of the biggest features in the advanced design toolkit is the ability to apply and work with style sheets for your Office Live Small Business pages. After you activate the advanced tools, the Style Sheet tool becomes available in Advanced group of the Site Designer. Here's how to use it:

1. In the Page Manager, click the Edit link of the page you want to change.
2. Click the Site Designer tab. Notice the Style Sheet tool in the Advanced group (see Figure 5-28).
3. Click Style Sheet. The Style Sheet dialog box appears (see Figure 5-29).

> **TIP** If you aren't too familiar with CSS, it's a good idea to click the View Default CSS link in the Style Sheet dialog box so that you can see what the CSS style sheet used to format your Web pages look like. Reviewing the existing styles also helps you avoid overwriting any of the existing styles when you add your own.

4. Click the Apply Custom CSS Code To My Web Site check box.
5. You can type or paste CSS styles directly into the box in the Style Sheet dialog box. Any styles you add overwrite existing styles in the CSS being used behind the scenes to format your page.
6. Click OK to save the style sheet.

> **NOTE** If you are using CSS styles for the first time, make a copy of a page to practice with instead of modifying the styles on live pages.

FIGURE 5-28 The Style Sheet tool is added to the Advanced group when advanced design features are enabled.

FIGURE 5-29 You can type your own CSS styles directly into the custom CSS code area or copy and paste styles from another Web design program.

TIP

Want to learn more about CSS? There are a number of great resources available online if you want to do a little exploring. One creative and easy-to-use site designed early on to show CSS users and developers the dramatic way a page can be changed through the magic of style sheets is *csszengarden.com*. Other sites you might want to visit include the W3 School (*www.w3schools.com/css/default.asp*) and CSS Tutorial (*www.csstutorial.net/*).

WORKING WITH CSS

CSS, which stands for *cascading style sheet*, is a Web technology that enables you to organize and streamline the formatting of your site by using styles. A *style* is a format that you can easily apply to elements on your page. A *style sheet* is a collection of styles you can attach to a page so that the styles become available.

The beauty of CSS is that you can create one style sheet and attach it to as many Web pages as you like. This enables you to keep your formatting consistent across your entire site—or across multiple sites.

Even though Office Live is designed so that you don't have to work with style sheets or HTML to produce professional-looking Web sites, having the ability to work with CSS enables you to use styles to format your pages so that you can easily change the whole thing later by simply applying an updated style sheet. Suppose, for example, that you have a 15-page site that uses Arial as the font, a color scheme with purple and orange, and a certain kind of header style and table style. You can create CSS styles for each of those elements—and they are all saved in your CSS style sheet. A few months from now, you might want to redesign your site to showcase some great new features. Instead of going through each page one by one; selecting the text; and changing the font, color, and style, you can attach a revised style sheet to the page. The entire site will be changed to reflect the new styles.

Saving a Page as a Template

You will notice that as soon as you activate the advanced design features, a new feature is added to the options in the Page Manager. Now you can save a page you've created as a template for other pages. To save a page as a template, follow these steps:

1. In the Page Manager, click the Save As Template link for the page you want to use as a template for other new pages. The Save As Template dialog box appears (see Figure 5-30).
2. Change the template title and file name for the template, if you like.
3. Add an optional description to help those who might be creating a new page know which page elements or modules are included in the template.
4. Click OK to save the template.

After you save a page as a template, the page will be available in the Template Gallery on the Web Site page so that others can use the template for new pages on your site.

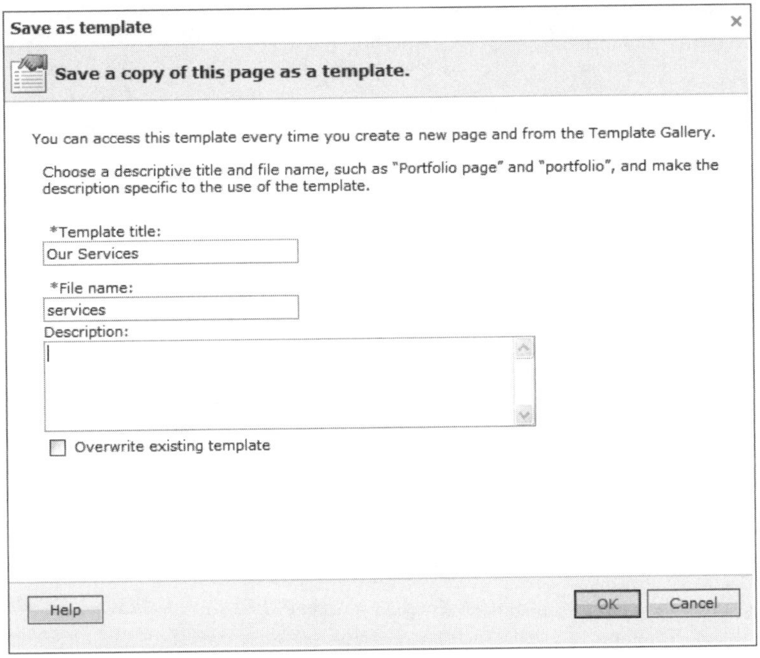

Save as template

Save a copy of this page as a template.

You can access this template every time you create a new page and from the Template Gallery.

Choose a descriptive title and file name, such as "Portfolio page" and "portfolio", and make the description specific to the use of the template.

*Template title:
Our Services

*File name:
services

Description:

Overwrite existing template

Help OK Cancel

FIGURE 5-30 Using the advanced design tools, you can save a page as a template and use it as the basis for new pages you create in the future.

THINK "PACKAGING"

If you find that you are really good at creating sites with Office Live Small Business, you might want to package what you've done and provide it to other users as they begin working with their own sites. Your clients can then use the site you created as the basis for their own work (which adds the extra benefit of consistency if you are all part of an association or franchise organization).

When the advanced design features are enabled on your Office Live Small Business site, a new option for Web packaging becomes available in the Design Site list in the Page Manager. Click Design Site and choose Package Solution, and the program will walk you through the steps for preparing your site to share with others.

Similarly, if you want to install a packaged site (also called a "solution") from another vendor or partner, you can click Design Site and select Install Solution.

YOUR BUSINESS ONLINE: Q&A INTERVIEW

Jay Harper, District Manager and VP of Operations (GMI)
The GMI Group: *www.thegmigroup.com*

Q *What are your favorite features in Office Live Small Business?*

A For typical business success, everyone must be prepared for change and feel comfortable with each and every course correction and deviation. Without Office Live, we lived with an 800-pound gorilla (Network Solutions) and had very little success with our stale Web site. Changing over to Office Live has given us a tremendous boost and helped us to relaunch ourselves far beyond our expectations. Why? Because we are not held down by a host who is inflexible, unresponsive, and difficult to work with. Office Live has been super to work with, and has given us smart changes that have improved our performance and look. We now embrace change and love seeing ourselves in real, living color, instead of the gray, near-colorless world we operated in before Office Live came into our lives.

Q *How does having a Web site help your business?*

A The response has been overwhelming from our client base and the industry. We have experienced "instant credibility" by having a site that gives greater insight to our commitments and services.

Q *How do you use the marketing and management features in Office Live Small Business?*

A adManager has improved our search engine responses with Google, Yahoo, Excite, and many others. Best of all was that it did not cost a whole lot. Just a simple ad account set at a certain amount per month, and it is that simple. Management of the site is extremely easy and adaptable.

Q *What do you want to do next with your site?*

A We are working on a video for the Home page, and we will start a section for e-work orders. I am eager to see the new changes coming from Office Live Small Business.

WHEN DO THE BELLS AND WHISTLES PAY OFF?

Adding special features and new functionality to your Web site is a bit like exploring a huge desert buffet. Sure, you can have all you want, but *should* you? Moderation might be the key word, depending on the needs and expectations of your audience. As you explore the tested-and-tried adages of the Web design pundits, you will find a common refrain—*less is more*. If you use that advice to temper your enthusiasm for easy-to-add Web gadgets (perhaps adding two and then waiting a month to get feedback and see whether users are actually trying them) and ease into Web gadgetry cautiously, you can be reasoned and practical about your site changes while keeping your audience firmly in mind.

The most important aspect of adding bells and whistles to your site is really the task of keeping your customer at the center of your thought. Do your customers need to see an animated logo? Sure, you want to put the photos of the great new building on your site, but will your customers really want to sit through a slide show of the building from all angles? (If the photos help show customers how reliable and successful you are, it might be a whistle you want to add.)

What you *don't* want to do is add so many gadgets and modules to your site that customers have a hard time finding what they need. For all the great design, terrific photos, and engaging copy on your pages, if users don't find what they are looking for, they will click away and look for a site that delivers what they want. You might have what users want, but if it's buried at the bottom of a page that showcases an unnecessary video at the top, they might not know it.

The moral? Before you add all the high-energy, attention-getting (and fun!) modules to your site, think carefully about what your site visitors really need and want to see. What will help them know what they need to know about you in order to purchase your product or service? Do everything you can to help them make that decision with a clear mind and heart—and give them an easy way to contact you with any questions that they have—and you're halfway home to creating an engaging and functional site that can really help you bring in the business.

What's Next

This chapter showed you the ways you can extend the basic functionality of your Office Live Small Business Web site. Whether you want to do something simple, such as adding tables or changing layout, or increase the fun and function with modules that deliver additional information and interactivity to your site visitors, the various tools are easy to learn, use, and manage. If you have Web design experience, you can activate the advanced design tools so that you can use CSS to control the look and feel of your site and save your pages as templates for future creations. The next chapter shows you how to keep an eye on all the Web traffic that will be flocking to your site.

Tracking Your Web Statistics

IN THIS CHAPTER, YOU WILL

- Learn why it is important to track your site.
- Get started with reports.
- Get the big picture with overview reports.
- Understand site visitors.
- Display site usage.
- Review referring sources.
- Track keywords.
- Check page usage views.
- Display system statistics.
- Review administration reports.

THE FIRST part of building a successful Web site involves creating and designing the pages. You need to get the site up so that people can learn about your company, see images of your prod-ucts and services, and learn a little bit about you. You might include links, forms, slide shows, and more to showcase your offerings and help users build the confidence they need to do business with you.

After you get the site up and running, you might want to add some special features (as you learned in the previous chapter), adding to your site's functionality to help it stand out. When you're feeling pretty good about your site having a presence on the Web, you will naturally begin to get curious about who's visiting you. Even before you begin marketing your site with keyword marketing and e-mail newsletters, you will see people somehow happen across your site.

Once you build it, they will come.

This chapter shows you how to use the Web statistics tools that are built into Microsoft Office Live Small Business. You learn why it's important to track your statistics, and you get some experience reading Web reports. When you add features that enable you to get your site into the top search engine rankings, you can expect to see your site visits climb.

Why Is It Important to Track Your Site?

The best thing about the Reports feature in Office Live Small Business is that it gives you food for thought—in other words, ways to see what's going on as people visit your site. You'll be able to educate yourself about who your visitors are, where they are coming from, what they're interested in, and whether their interest focuses on some products more than others.

By viewing reports in Office Live Small Business, you'll be able to tell

- How many people have visited your site from week to week.
- How site visitors are finding you.
- What kind of visitors they are (returning visitors, new visitors, or visitors who visit once).
- How a specific marketing event (newspaper ad, site design, newsletter, and so on) might be impacting your Web traffic.

Once you have the information you need, you can use it to make improvements to your site. Perhaps you'll decide to try search advertising. Maybe you'll send out an e-mail newsletter. Or perhaps you'll add some of what is drawing attention on your top-rated pages to some of the pages that visitors are skipping over. Whatever you decide to do, the reporting features in Office Live Small Business track the data and give you the means to make decisions that can impact your bottom line for the better.

SEE ALSO You can easily export the data from your Web site reports to be used in other analyses as well. See "Downloading Reports" in the "Reviewing Administration Reports" section later in this chapter for more information.

Getting Started with Reports

To get started in site reporting, click Reports in the navigation bar along the left side of the Office Live Small Business window. The Reports page displays a Getting Started area that provides links to two startup articles. In the left navigation panel, you see links to eight different types of reporting (the first reports appear on the Reports page):

- The Reports page displays the Web Site Usage Overview report and the Top Traffic Drivers report, giving you information about who is visiting your site and where they are coming from.

- The Visitors page gives you a breakdown of the number of visitors who come to your site daily. You can customize the length of the report and view different visitor groups.
- The Site Usage page shows the overall activity of your site and lets you know how many pages were viewed during each site visit.
- The Referring Sources page shows you how visitors found your site, which sites were most often the referring sources, and the type of source each referrer was.
- The Keywords page displays the most effective sources by which people used the keywords you specified; you can also see which keywords worked best by using the reports on this page.
- The Page Usage report shows you which pages on your site got the greatest number of visits during the time frame you specify.
- The System Statistics page gives you valuable information about the types of browsers your site visitors are using, as well as the screen resolutions and color capabilities of their systems and the operating systems they are using.
- The Administration area enables you to view conversion points (pages that display when a visitor completes a task, such as filling out a form) and download reports.

Each of the sections that follow gives you details on creating each of the reports available in Office Live Small Business.

NOTE The reporting features in Office Live Small Business will be beneficial to you whether you are using the basic free services or you have purchased the add-on services that enable you to extend the reach of your business. If you sign up for Store Manager, E-Mail Marketing, or adManager, you will also be able to track the information gathered through online sales, marketing campaigns, and keyword search results.

The Big Picture: Overview Reports

In the center of the Reports page, you can see a chart that gives you an overall picture of your Web traffic (see Figure 6-1). In just a glance, you can see

- Which visitors were new to your site.
- Which visitors visited only once.

- Which visitors were returning visitors.
- How many visitors came to your site from week to week.
- How many site visits related to marketing events you added to the site.

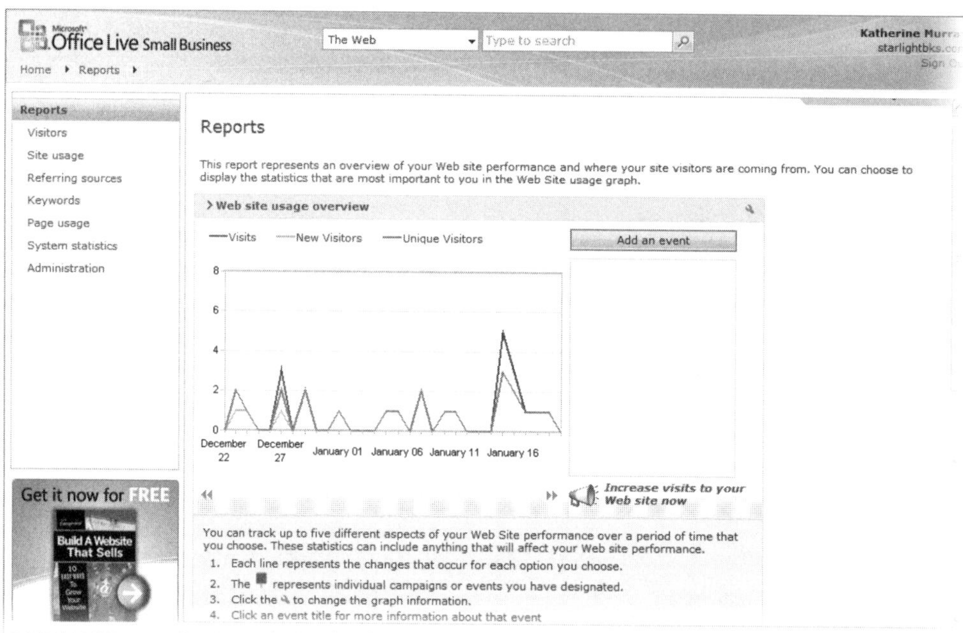

FIGURE 6-1 The Reports page displays a Web Site Usage Overview report.

Adding a Marketing Event

Your Web reports will be even more effective if you use the tracking capability in Office Live Small Business to add triggering events. The Reports page gives you the option of entering key marketing events that may (and hopefully will) result in a boost in your online traffic. To add a marketing event so that it will be included in Web reports, follow these steps:

1. In the Reports page, click Add An Event.
2. In the New Event dialog box (see Figure 6-2), enter a title and description for the event.

3. Click the Type arrow and choose the event from the list. You can choose from the following types of events:
   - Newspaper ad
   - Phone book ad
   - Seminar
   - Site map submission
   - Coupon
   - Web site change
   - Press release
   - Others
4. Enter the financial investment the marketing event requires.
5. Select the start and end dates of the event (if your newspaper ad ran for a week, for example, make sure that the start and end dates reflect the entire time the ad was running).
6. Click OK.

FIGURE 6-2 Create an event so that Office Live Small Business can track the results in relation to your Web traffic.

Top Traffic Drivers

If you scroll down to the lower half of the Reports page, you will see another overview chart that shows you the top five referring sites. A referring site is the last site a user visited before coming to your site. The Web tracks the path from that site to this one. And paying attention to your referring sites gives you a clue about what users are finding that is triggering their attention to your site.

The top traffic drivers are most likely the most heavily visited sites around—Google, Yahoo, and others—but you might also see what's known as a *direct link* (which means that a user actually clicked in the address bar of his or her browser and typed your URL directly) as well as other sources (see Figure 6-3).

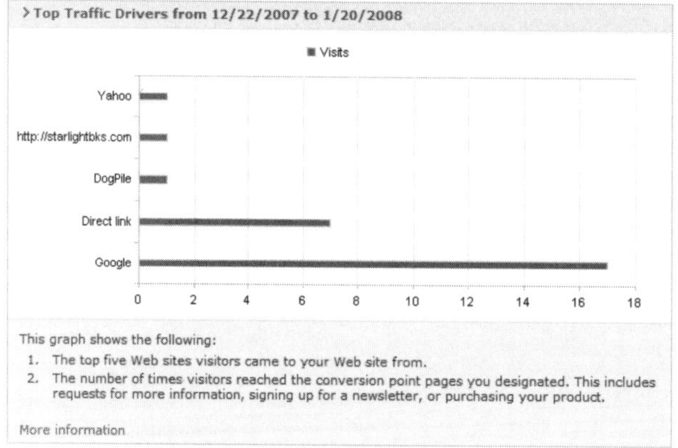

FIGURE 6-3 The Top Traffic Drivers chart shows you the sites your visitors were viewing before coming to your site.

NOTE The Top Traffic Drivers chart shows both site visitors and the number of conversion points reached in a site visit. A *conversion point* is an action a site visitor completes. This might include signing up for more information, ordering a copy of your annual report, or scheduling an appointment.

Understanding Your Visitors

Click Visitors to display a page of reports showing information about the specific visitors who come to your site. The Visitors Report page, shown in Figure 6-4, gives you quick information about the following items:

- The number of new visitors during a specific period of time

- The number of unique visitors during a period you select
- The number of visits per day, broken down by new, unique, and repeat visits

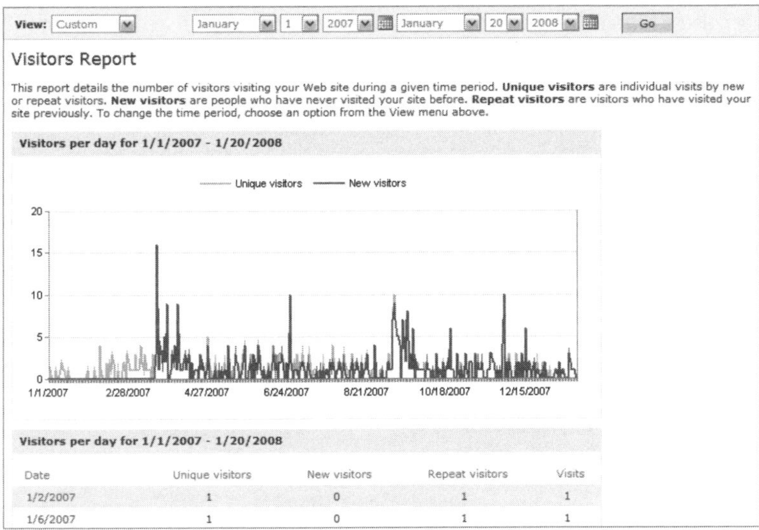

FIGURE 6-4 The Visitors report shows new and unique visitors as well as daily visits.

Setting Report Dates

Stretching across the top of the window in several of the report views is the View bar, which enables you to choose the type of report you want to display, as well as the start date and end date for the gathered data. To select the report type and start and end dates, follow these steps:

1. Click the View arrow to display the list of options. You can choose from the following:
   - Past 12 months
   - This month
   - This day
   - Custom
2. Select Custom. Set the beginning date by clicking the Month, Day, and Year arrows. Alternatively, you can click the Calendar control to select the date from the Calendar tool.

3. Choose the end date for the report by clicking the Month, Day, and Year arrows and choosing the date you want from the lists. Again, you can use the Calendar tool instead if you choose.

4. Click Go to enter the date and have the reports and charts redrawn accordingly.

Displaying Site Usage

The Site Usage report enables you to get a sense of the number of site visits and the page views your visitors displayed while they were on your site. A visit is counted as one visitor arriving at your site; views relate to the number of pages the visitor displayed during the site visit. In the report shown in Figure 6-5, the greatest number of page views was displayed in March.

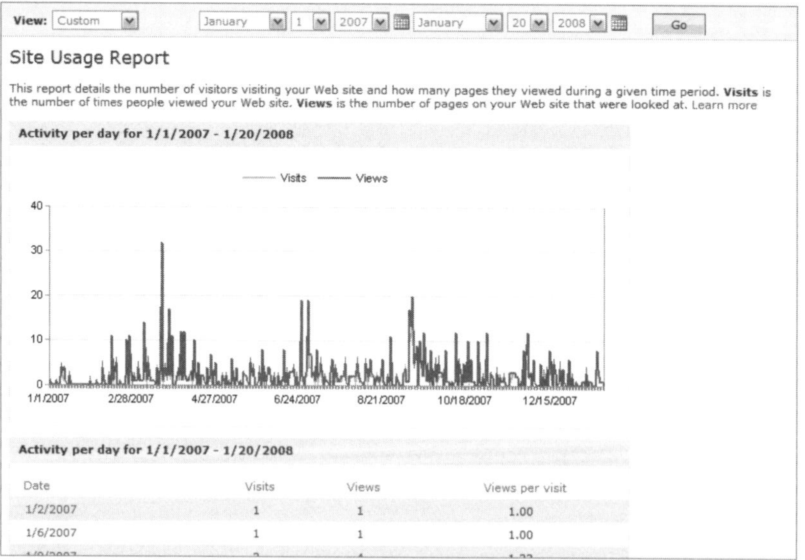

FIGURE 6-5 The Site Usage report shows the daily activity on your site.

In the lower half of the Site Usage report, a daily report of visits and views, as well as an average of views per visit, is displayed. You can scroll through the list and see the result for each page in the report range you specified at the top of the report page.

Reviewing Referring Sources

The Referring Sources report shows you the sites your visitors were viewing before arriving at your site (see Figure 6-6).

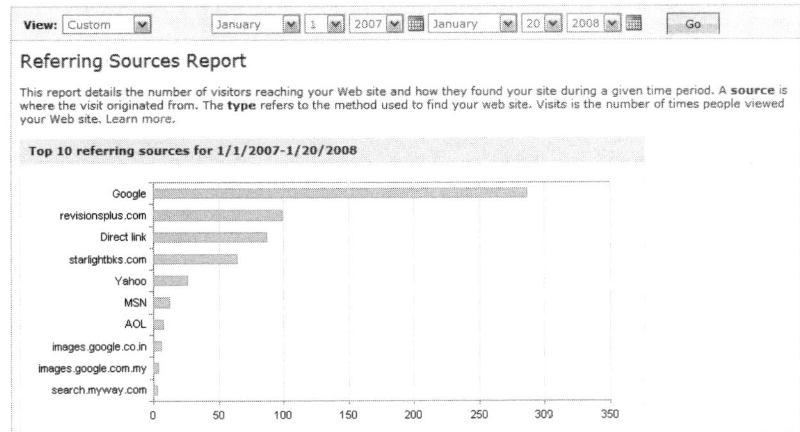

FIGURE 6-6 The Referring Sources chart shows you which sites refer the greatest number of visitors to your site.

Scrolling down the report page, you'll see a listing of the top 200 referring sources, listed in order of the number of referrals they provided (see Figure 6-7). This list can help you see where your visitors are coming from and perhaps give you a few ideas about where you might want to place search ads or where you think your keywords are bringing some benefit.

Top 200 referring sources for 1/1/2007-1/20/2008

Source	Type	Visits
Google	Organic search	287
revisionsplus.com	Web Site referral	99
Direct link	Direct link	87
starlightbks.com	Web Site referral	64
Yahoo	Organic search	26
MSN	Organic search	12
AOL	Organic search	8
images.google.co.in	Web Site referral	6
images.google.com.my	Web Site referral	4
search.myway.com	Web Site referral	3
sg3.msntv.msn.com	Web Site referral	3
us.f564.mail.yahoo.com	Web Site referral	3
blockedreferrer	Web Site referral	2
pma-online.org	Web Site referral	2
DogPile	Organic search	1

FIGURE 6-7 The Referring Sources list lets you know the type of referrals you receive.

The Type column provides you with important information about the type of referral each site provided. An *organic search* is simply a regular search in which a user enters a search word or phrase in the search box; your page was displayed as a result. A *Web site referral* occurs when a user clicks a link that is displayed on another Web site. A *direct link* occurs when a user clicks in the address bar in the browser window and types your URL.

Tracking Keywords

Keywords give search engines the information they need to locate your Web site when a user searches online. Every Web page has the capacity to record keywords—in fact, you should make it a natural part of your Web page-creation process to add keywords for every page you design. Office Live Small Business makes it possible for you to get even more benefit from your keywords by purchasing keyword search advertising with adManager. This enables your site to do more than just show up in search results when a user enters a word that happens to be one of your keywords; instead, your site is placed at the top of the search results in a sponsored ad section, giving it even more visibility and increasing your chances that the link to your page will be clicked.

Office Live Small Business enables you to create Web reports that show how well your keywords are working. If you are using adManager and are purchasing and managing search advertising, additional report data will be available in the keyword area. Figure 6-8 shows the page available with the basic Keywords report.

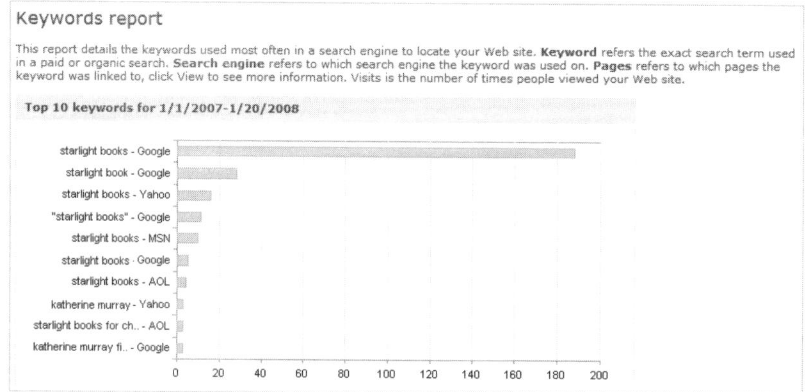

FIGURE 6-8 The Keywords report shows the top 10 keywords for the period you specify.

The listing at the bottom of the Keywords Report page shows each keyword, along with the corresponding search engine and the number of times the keyword was used.

Checking Page Usage Views

The Page Usage report shows you which pages in your site have been visited most often. Similar to the other reports available in Office Live Small Business, you can specify the start date and end date to change the content of the report to reflect the period you want to review (see Figure 6-9).

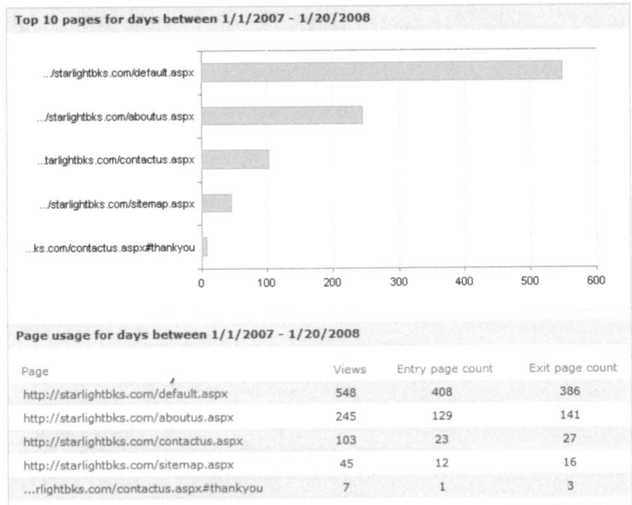

Page usage for days between 1/1/2007 - 1/20/2008

Page	Views	Entry page count	Exit page count
http://starlightbks.com/default.aspx	548	408	386
http://starlightbks.com/aboutus.aspx	245	129	141
http://starlightbks.com/contactus.aspx	103	23	27
http://starlightbks.com/sitemap.aspx	45	12	16
...rlightbks.com/contactus.aspx#thankyou	7	1	3

FIGURE 6-9 The Page Usage report shows you the most popular pages on your site as well as the number of views each has received.

The Page Usage listing at the bottom of the report shows you the top-visited pages and includes the number of views during the time frame you specified. The listing also shows the number of times that page served as the entry point for your site (meaning that visitors landed on that page) and the exit point (the last page viewed before visitors left your site).

TIP

The Page Usage listing can give you a clear picture of which pages visitors are most interested in viewing in your site. Is there one page that leaves people cold? Is there another that's off the charts? Consider what makes each of those pages unique and see whether you can use that information to ramp up interest in other pages on your site.

Displaying System Statistics

The System Statistics report provides you with interesting information about the technology being used by the people who visit your site (see Figure 6-10). You probably know about the variety of Web browsers, screen resolutions, and operating systems in use today. Knowing what percentage of your visitors are using older technologies, limited color displays, or browsers that might be blocking graphics can be helpful as you think through what content you want to include to reach the broadest possible audience.

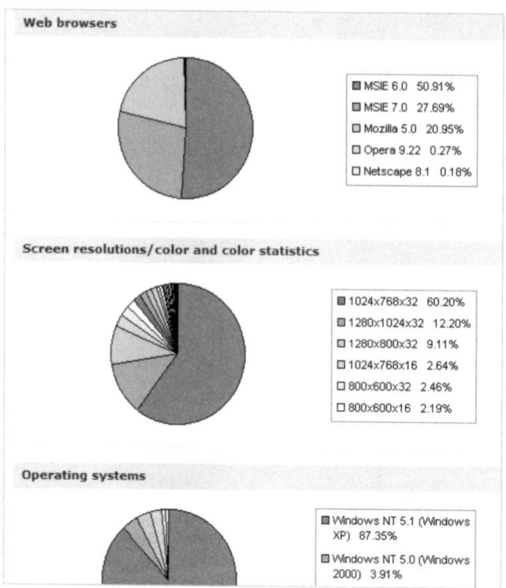

FIGURE 6-10 System Statistics shows you which browsers, screen resolutions, and operating systems your site visitors use.

Reviewing Administration Reports

Office Live Small Business includes three different types of activities in the Administration section. You can set, modify, and manage conversion points; get code for tracking statistics on other sites; and download reports in a form usable in other business applications.

Working with Conversion Points

You can create conversion points that let site visitors know they have completed a task on your site. For example, a conversion point might say "Thanks for filling out this form" after a user enters e-mail information in an online subscription form.

To create a new conversion point, follow these steps:

1. Click Reports in the navigation bar.
2. Click Administration.
3. Select Conversion Manager.
4. In the Conversion Manager page, click New. The Add A Conversion Point page is displayed.
5. Click in the Point Name box and type a name for the conversion point that describes the task that the user has completed (for example, "subscription complete" or "product ordered").
6. Click in the Page URL box and type the address of the page that appears after the task is completed. For example, if you have a standard "thank you" page in your site, enter the Web address for that page.
7. Click OK to save the conversion point.

Getting Code for Other Sites

The Get Code command enables you to copy the code your Office Live Small Business site uses to track Web statistics throughout the site. You can then paste this code on any Web page you create—even if you've used other Web design software. If you place the code you copy from the Get Code page at the bottom of the Web page you create, the statistics for that page will be tracked and displayed alongside your Office Live pages.

To get the tracking code, click Reports in the navigation bar and then click Administration. Click Get Code. The Get Tracking Code window appears (see Figure 6-11). Click the Highlight Code button to select the tracking code; then press Ctrl+C to copy the code to the Clipboard. Open the Web page you want to track, and paste the copied code at the bottom of the page. Save the page and publish as usual. The page will begin tracking visitor information that will be available through Office Live Small Business reporting.

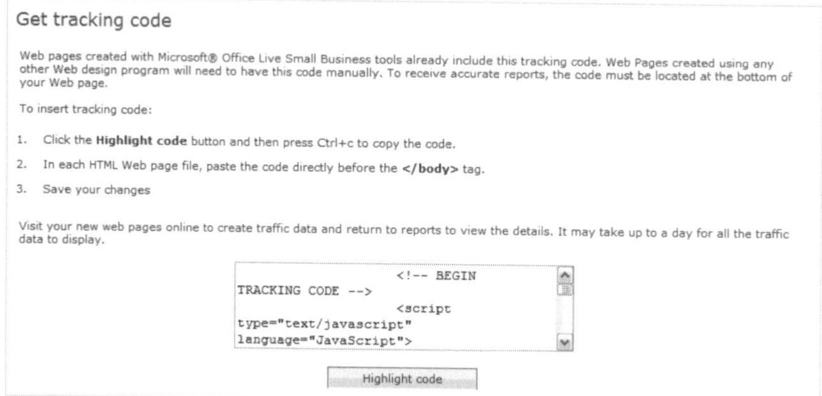

FIGURE 6-11 Copy and paste tracking code from your Office Live Small Business site to other pages you create in other applications.

Downloading Reports

Web reports aren't just for the Web enthusiasts in your business—they are for everyone. Financial people will want to see them. Content people will want to see them. Your mother will want to see them (really, she will). You can download your reports into a form that is easy to use in other common applications, such as Microsoft Office Excel. Here's how to do that:

1. Click Reports in the navigation bar and select Administration.
2. Click Download Reports.
3. In the Download Reports window (see Figure 6-12), select a start date and an end date.
4. Click the check boxes of data you want to include in the report.
5. Click Run Report.

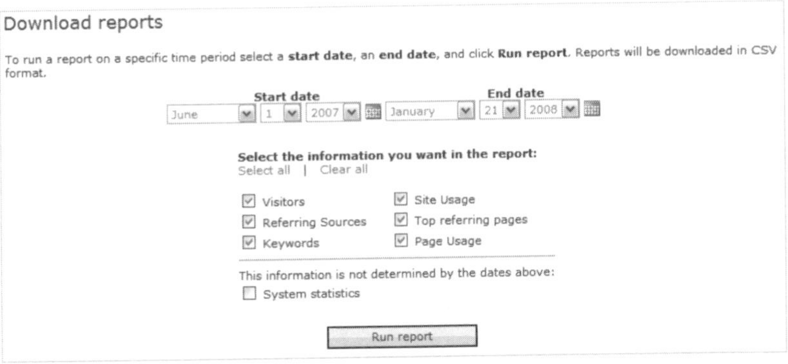

Download reports

To run a report on a specific time period select a **start date**, an **end date**, and click **Run report**. Reports will be downloaded in CSV format.

Start date: June 1 2007 End date: January 21 2008

Select the information you want in the report:
Select all | Clear all

- [x] Visitors
- [x] Referring Sources
- [x] Keywords
- [x] Site Usage
- [x] Top referring pages
- [x] Page Usage

This information is not determined by the dates above:

- [ ] System statistics

Run report

FIGURE 6-12 Download site report data so that you can use it in other applications.

Office Live Small Business prepares the report and displays the File Download dialog box, asking whether you want to open or save the file. Click Save to save a copy of the file to your computer. In the Save As dialog box, navigate to the folder where you want to store the file, and click Save. The report is saved in Comma Separated Values (CSV) format, and you will be able to open the file and view it using Excel.

WEB STATS: WHAT'S REALISTIC?

Web statistics are a little like exit polls: They are great if you want to notice possible trends, but not the most solid foundation for decision making. Use the Web stats you gather through Office Live Small Business to learn about your site and the people who view it. When you let your curiosity guide you—*I wonder why most people come from Yahoo and not Google, and why do they skip the video page but spend time reading the newsletter?*—you have a good chance of learning how to best meet your customers' expectations.

Your Web stats might surprise you. One week they might appear flat and lifeless, but the next week they are heading up to the top of the charts. It's hard to say which blog might have given you a stray mention or where you could have been picked up on a Best-of-the-Web list. But Office Live Small Business can help you find those referring sources and make better choices about keywords so that you improve the likelihood that you'll be in the right spot on the Web again in the future.

What's Next

This chapter rounds out our discussion of all things Web. Now you know how to create the basic site in Office Live Small Business; add special features, Web modules, and more; and now, track the masses as they follow the links to your door. The next chapter helps you move a few steps closer to your customers by showing you how to use Office Live Mail, IM, and Microsoft Office Outlook Connector to stay in touch with clients, vendors, teammates, and more—all smoothly integrated with Office Live Small Business.

Staying in Sync with Microsoft Office Live Small Business Mail

IN THIS CHAPTER, YOU WILL

- Get on the e-mail fast track.
- Get back to Microsoft Office Live Small Business.
- Check, create, and send e-mail.
- Work with contacts.
- Use instant messaging with peers, vendors, clients, and more.
- Update your calendar.

CONSIDER THIS: You've been preparing an important presentation for several weeks that could lead to a huge opportunity for your business. You've been asked to speak to a gathering of potential investors who are looking for new projects to fund. And it's possible that someone in the group will choose yours! Part of the challenge of grasping new opportunities is that when you're a one-person shop, everything falls on your shoulders. You need to keep the orders processed and respond to customer e-mail. You need to stay on top of vendors and follow up with manufacturing concerns. How will you do this while you're on the road? Who else knows your business better than (or even half as well as) you?

Microsoft Office Live Small Business recognizes that as the owner of a small business, you often are trying to be all things to all people *and* be in multiple places at once. To help you stay in touch with all the important people who keep your business moving, the e-mail features in Office Live Small Business enable you to read and respond to e-mail; set up messages; work with groups; and even use instant messaging with clients, vendors, and staff—all from any Web access point.

That means that if your laptop dies during the trip (heaven forbid!), you can still access your data and your relationships by using the Web browser on the hotel's computer. There's no need to be out of touch or out of sync if you are using Office Live Small Business.

Getting Started with Office Live Mail

The first thing you will notice about Office Live Small Business Mail is that the newest mail you receive is always visible on your Home page. This means you can see at a glance whether an important message has arrived while you've been away (see Figure 7-1).

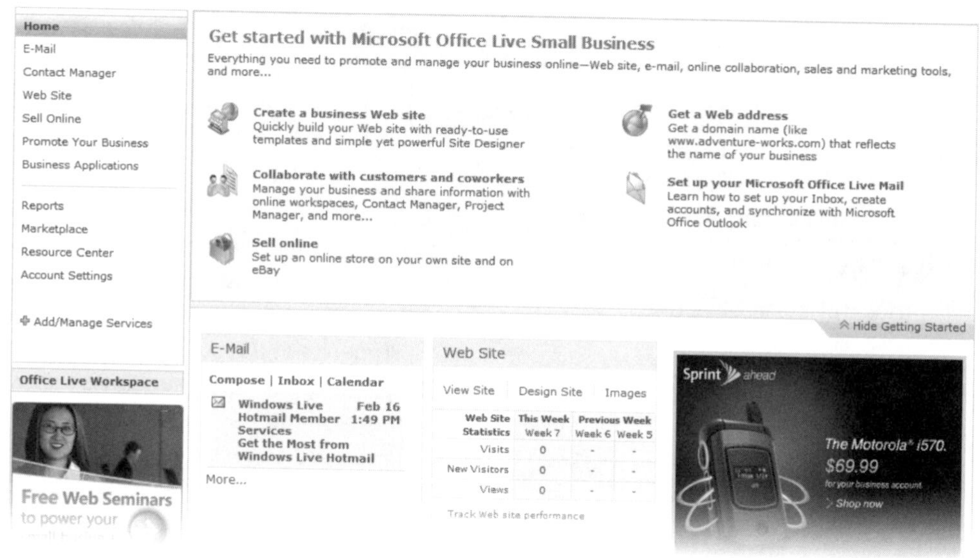

FIGURE 7-1 Your e-mail is always visible on the Home page of Office Live Small Business.

The E-Mail Fast Track

You can check your e-mail, create a new message, or update your calendar directly from your Office Live Small Business Home page. In the E-Mail area of the Home page, the most recent messages are displayed, along with three options.

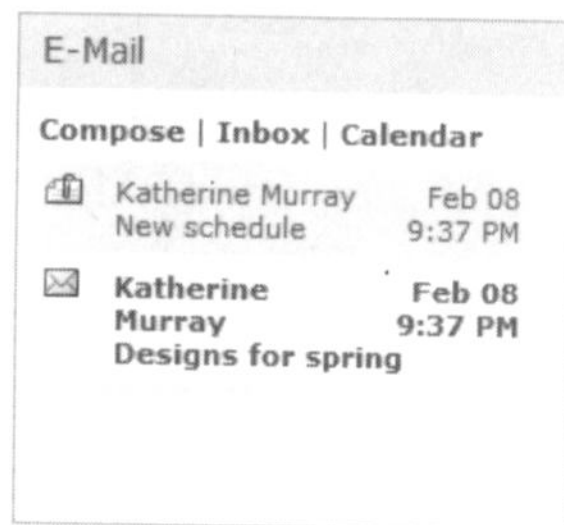

You can view the most recent e-mail messages you've received by clicking the message you want to view directly in the E-Mail box on the Home page. You can also click the following options in the E-Mail box to perform specific e-mail tasks quickly:

- Click Compose to display a new e-mail message window.
- Click Inbox to view the message in your inbox.
- Click Calendar to view your schedule for the day.

In the sections that follow, you learn how to use each of these items—and more—to communicate with and manage contacts and appointments in Office Live Small Business.

TIP

In Chapter 3, "Getting Started with Microsoft Office Live Small Business," you learned how to set up your e-mail accounts. If you need to add users to your account or change your earlier settings, you can do so by clicking Account Settings in the navigation bar and choosing E-Mail Accounts.

Getting Back to Office Live Small Business

Because Office Live Small Business is integrated with Windows Live services, you'll notice that you are moving among the different services as you use the e-mail and calendar features in Office Live Small Business. Suppose, for example, that you click Compose in the E-Mail box on the Home page. Instantly a new message window is displayed. You can create and address your e-mail message and send it by clicking Send.

Now that you've sent the message, though, how do you get back to Office Live Small Business? Here are the steps:

1. Click the Windows Live logo in the upper-left area of the window.
2. Point to Other Live Services.
3. Click Office Live (see Figure 7-2).

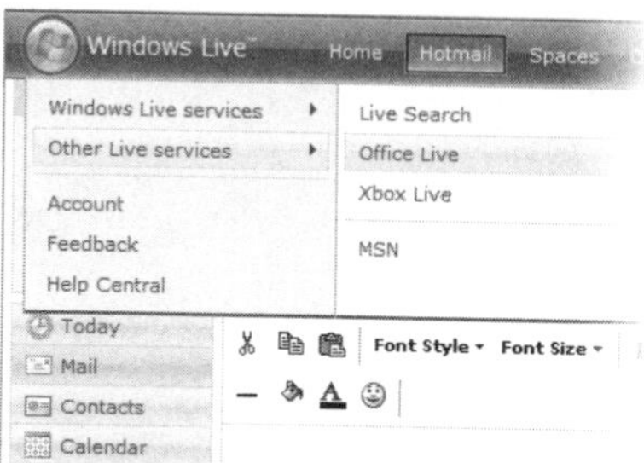

FIGURE 7-2 Return to your Office Live Small Business account by choosing Other Live Services and clicking Office Live.

Checking, Creating, and Sending E-Mail

If you've used Web-based e-mail before, you'll have no trouble finding your way around the e-mail portion of Office Live Small Business. The beauty of e-mail in Office Live Small Business is that it is seamlessly integrated with the other features on your site and available from any place you have Web access, 24/7. You can create up to 100 e-mail accounts in Office Live Small Business and track any number of contacts, with a huge range of information.

What's more, Office Live Small Business enables you to track more than simple name, address, and e-mail information. You can use the Contact Manager to collect, organize, and work with an extensive amount of customer information, including accounts, contacts, opportunities, marketing campaigns, and more.

Click E-Mail in the navigation bar on the left side of the Office Live Small Business Home page. The E-Mail window appears, looking similar to the screen you see in Figure 7-3.

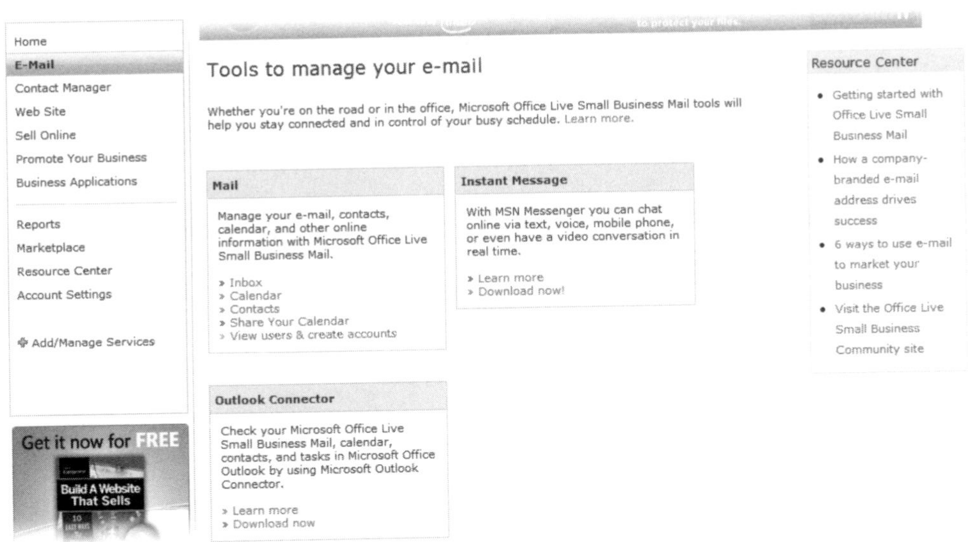

FIGURE 7-3 The E-Mail window gives you everything you need to stay in touch with customers, vendors, and staff.

The three different areas in the E-Mail window give you access to three separate methods of connecting with customers, vendors, and staff. The Mail area includes connections to your e-mail and enables you to do the following:

- Check, create, send, and manage e-mail.
- Add and manage contact information.
- Add, update, and manage appointments on your calendar.
- Create, assign, and update tasks for groups and individuals (and, of course, yourself).
- Share your calendar and tasks with others in your contact list.
- Create and manage e-mail accounts for site users.

The Instant Message area gives you the option of downloading Windows Live Messenger so that you can trade messages, images, files, and more in real time with customers, vendors, staff, and friends. If you don't have Windows Live Messenger, you can download the utility directly from your Office Live Small Business page.

The Outlook Connector area gives you the option of downloading a utility that enables you to view your Office Live Small Business mail, contacts, calendar entries, and tasks in Microsoft Office Outlook. Again, a link is included on the page so that you can download the utility without leaving your Office Live Small Business account.

E-Mail Basics in Office Live Small Business

To get started with your e-mail, click Inbox in the E-Mail area. The Windows Live Hotmail window opens, displaying the e-mail messages currently in your inbox and giving you the tools you need to view, respond to, and organize your messages (see Figure 7-4).

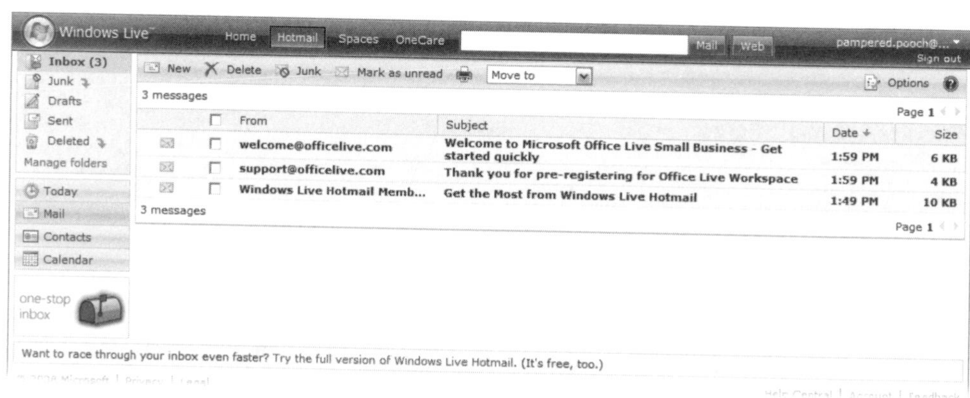

FIGURE 7-4 The Inbox lists the messages that need your attention.

Reading Your Messages

Unread messages in your inbox are displayed in bold type so that you can easily spot the ones you haven't read yet. To open one of the messages in your inbox, simply click either the From or Subject link for the message you want to see. The message opens, as you see in Figure 7-5.

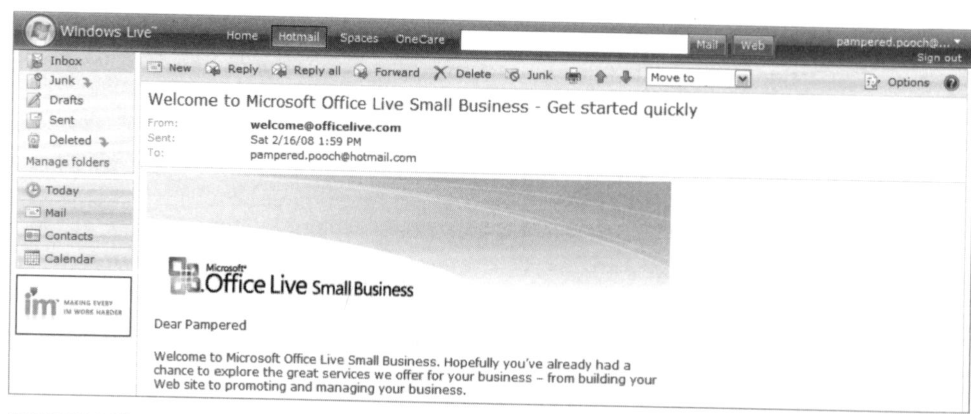

FIGURE 7-5 The message you select opens in the E-Mail window.

You can read through the message, using the vertical scroll bar as needed to view the rest of the message. After you read the content, you can use one of the tools in the toolbar to respond to the message, delete it, or file it away for future use. Table 7-1 introduces you to the tools in the Mail window.

TABLE 7-1 Mail Tools in Office Live Small Business

TOOL	NAME	DESCRIPTION
New	New	Displays a new mail message window
Reply	Reply	Opens a new message window in response to the sender of the current message
Reply all	Reply All	Opens a new message window and copies all recipients of the current message
Forward	Forward	Creates a new message window that includes the current message
Delete	Delete	Deletes the current message
Junk	Junk	Marks the existing message as junk mail and moves it to the Junk Mail folder
	Print	Prints the current message
	Previous Message	Displays the previous messages in the Inbox list
	Next Message	Displays the next message in the Inbox list
Move to	Move To	Shows a list so that you can move the current message to a new folder

Replying to a Message

When you want to reply to the current message, click Reply or Reply All. The contact who sent you the message will now appear in the To line. If multiple contacts were included on the message and you click Reply All, all contacts will appear in the header of the message.

By default, the header area of the message displays only the To line and the Subject line. You can add Cc (copied to) and Bcc (blind copied to) lines to the header area by clicking the Show Cc & Bcc link. To add contacts to the To, Cc, and Bcc lines easily, click in the line you want to add the contact to, and then click the contact name in the Contacts list along the right side of the message window.

TIP

You can use Office Live Small Business Mail to send messages from up to five other accounts as well. This lets you coordinate your accounts so that you can easily send messages from one point. To enable this feature, click the From arrow and choose Add An E-Mail Address; then follow the prompts to add other e-mail addresses to your Office Live Small Business account.

The tools available in the Reply window are different from the tools you saw in the message window. As Figure 7-6 shows, these tools enable you to prepare, check, and send your message. For example, to

- Attach a file or photo your message: Click the Attach arrow and click your choice.
- Check the spelling of your message: Click Spell Check.
- Save a draft of the message: Click Save Draft.
- Set the importance of the message: Click the Set Priority To arrow.
- Close the message without saving it: Click Cancel.
- Send the message to the recipients you selected: Click Send.

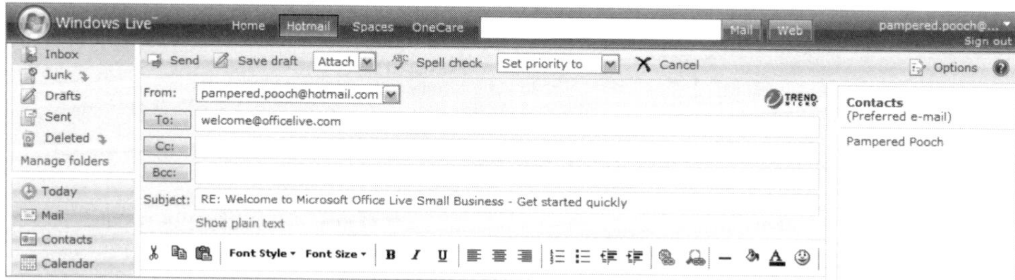

FIGURE 7-6 The tools across the top of the message window enable you to prepare, check, and send the message.

Composing a New Message

You can create a new message by clicking Compose on your Office Live Small Business Home page or by clicking New in the Inbox window. The new message window includes the tools and fields you saw in the Reply window (refer to Figure 7-6).

When you are replying to a message, the Subject line includes the subject of the previous message, preceded by "RE:." When you are creating a new message, you will create your own Subject line. To help keep your message out of other peoples' junk filters, enter clear subject lines and avoid using punctuation characters if possible.

In addition to the tools at the top of the window, you can use the formatting tools across the top of the message area to set the font size, style, alignment, color, and format for your message. If you want to add a little lightheartedness, you can insert emoticons in your notes as well (see Figure 7-7).

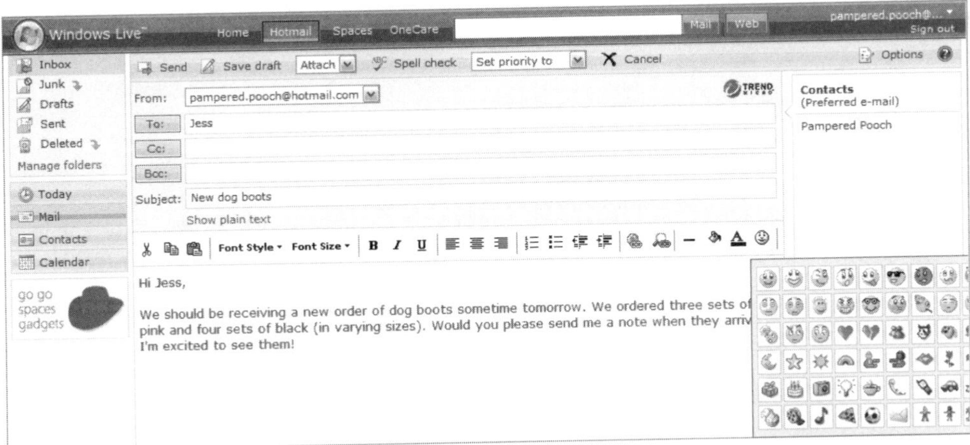

FIGURE 7-7 Use the formatting tools to control the appearance of text and add emoticons.

You can easily attach files to messages you send from Office Live Small Business by clicking the Attach arrow, choosing File or Photo, and choosing the file you want to attach. The mail utility will automatically scan any files you attach and alert you if there is any risk associated with the files you attach. Similarly, when you receive messages from others that include file attachments, the mail utility scans those attachments for viruses and potential problems.

Organizing Your Mail by Using Mail Folders

You can use the Move To list in both the inbox and message window toolbars to organize your messages in folders so that you can easily find and open them later. The navigation bar along the left side of the window shows you the different folders created automatically to organize your mail. In classic view, the Manage Folders list appears at the bottom of the folders list. You can add to those folders (or remove ones you don't want) by clicking Manage Folders.

When you click Manage Folders, the folders window appears, listing the different folders already created and showing you the number of messages in each and the amount of storage space they use (see Figure 7-8).

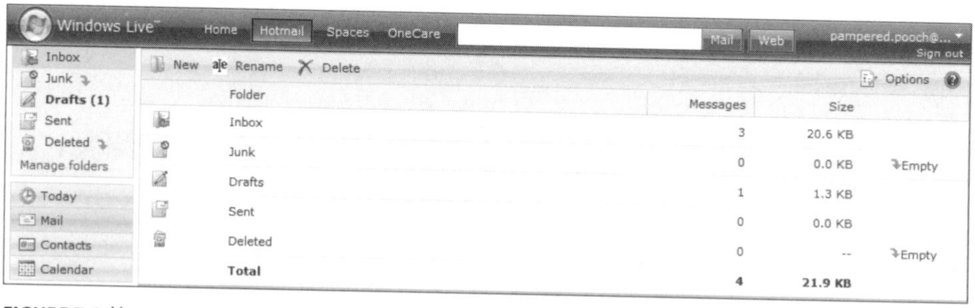

FIGURE 7-8 You can create your own mail folders to organize the messages you receive.

To add a new folder, click New. The New Folder window appears. Type a name for the new folder and click Save.

To rename a folder you've added, click the check box of the folder in the folders list and click Rename in the tools row.

You can also delete a folder you no longer need by clicking its check box and then clicking Delete.

> **NOTE** You cannot rename or delete the folders that are created by default in Office Live Small Business.

You can move messages to the new folders you've added when you're working in either the inbox or the message window. To move multiple messages from the inbox, follow these steps:

1. Click the check boxes of messages you want to move to a specific folder.
2. Click the Move To arrow.
3. Choose the folder name from the list.

Office Live Small Business moves the messages you selected to the folder you specified.

To move a message you're viewing in the message window to a selected folder, click the Move To arrow and select the folder from the list.

Streamlining Message Filing with Filters

You can automate the process of filing messages by creating filters for your e-mail. This enables you to create a filter that sends all messages from a particular vendor, for example, into a folder for the product the vendor represents. Here are the steps for creating a filter for incoming messages:

1. Display your e-mail inbox.
2. Click Options in the right side of the toolbar.
3. Click More Options and choose Automatically Sort E-Mail Into Folders from the Customize Your Mail group.
4. Click New Filter. The Edit Filter window appears, as Figure 7-9 shows.
5. In Step 1, click the arrow of the first field and choose the first filter option. Repeat for the second and third field selections. This step tells Office Live Small Business how to filter the mail you receive. Table 7-2 lists a few examples:

TABLE 7-2 Creating Mail Filters

FIELD 1	FIELD 2	FIELD 3
From address	Contains	Xbox
From name	Equals	Microsoft
Subject	Contains word	Order

6. Choose where you want the filtered messages to be sent (Inbox, Junk, New Folder, or Delete These Messages). If you click New Folder, click in the blank following the option and type the name for the new folder.
7. Click Save. The Automatically Sort E-Mail Into Folders window shows you the newly created filter.

TIP You can easily modify any filter you create by returning to this window and clicking the Edit link. You can change the filter fields or destination at any time.

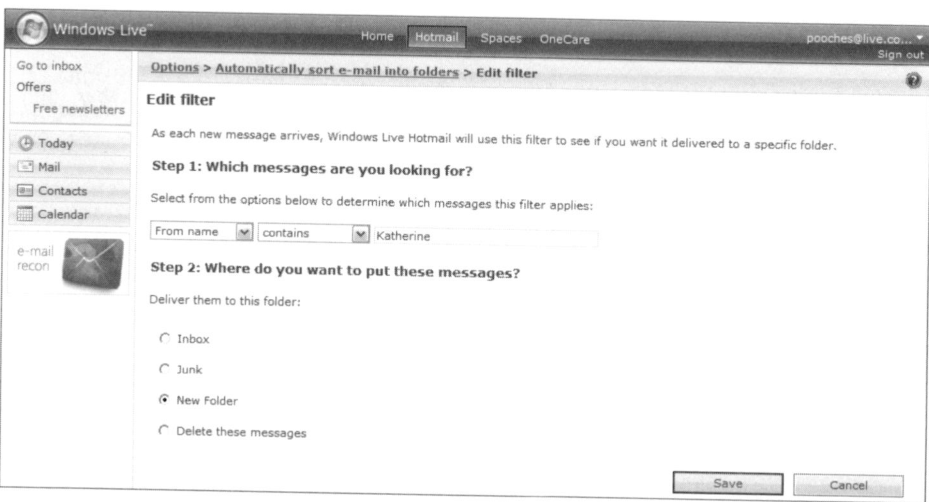

FIGURE 7-9 Add a filter to file your messages automatically.

CREATE AUTOMATIC E-MAIL REPLIES

You don't have to be at a big company to send automatically generated messages that let customers, vendors, and peers know you're out of the office and will contact them when you return. To create automatic e-mail replies, click E-Mail in the Office Live Small Business navigation panel and click Inbox. In the Mail window, click Options on the right side of the toolbar. Click More Options and then click Send Automated Vacation Replies in the Manage Your Account area.

In the Vacation Reply window, click the Send Vacation Replies To People Who E-Mail You button, and type the text you want to send in the message window. You can format the note as desired, using the formatting tools in the top of the message area.

If you want the automatic replies to go only to those users who are already in your contacts list, click the Only Reply To Your Contacts check box. By default, this check box is selected; to avoid receiving junk e-mail (which can increase when companies realize your account is "live" because the message was responded to), leave this option selected.

Click Save to save the new message and enable the automatic feature. Remember to return to this window and choose Don't Send Any Vacation Replies to discontinue the automatic sending.

Getting the Spam Out

Most of us are getting pretty good at spotting spam—we certainly get a lot of practice! When you use e-mail as part of Office Live Small Business, you get the added benefit of having the latest antivirus utilities working to weed out the bad stuff and let the good stuff through. Office Live Small Business Mail includes the following anti-spam features:

- A simple link on each e-mail message enables you to mark the e-mail as safe or unsafe.
- A color-coding system shows you at a glance which messages the system believes are suspicious. A white bar at the top of the message means the message is from one of your contacts, yellow means the message is from someone not on your contacts list, and red lets you know the message is suspicious.
- A Junk Mail tool is built into the e-mail toolbar so that you can easily identify (and weed out) unwanted messages.
- A Not Junk tool enables you to retrieve messages inadvertently caught in your junk mail filter.
- A Report Phishing Scam command enables you to instantly report a dangerous or suspicious solicitation.

MAIL DEFINITIONS

- **Junk mail** is any unsolicited mail you receive from companies or individuals advertising services, Web sites, or products.
- **Spoofing** is sending e-mail messages with fraudulent or stolen account information.
- **Phishing** is sending e-mail messages that masquerade as legitimate companies in an effort to trick you out of sensitive information (such as credit card numbers, expiration dates, and more).

Marking as Junk or Not Junk

When you receive a message that is definitely junk mail, you can mark the message as junk with a simple click of the button. If the message is part of a phishing scam, you can report the sender to Microsoft so that other users can be alerted (and this sender can be checked out). To mark a message as junk mail, follow these steps:

1. In the Office Live Small Business Home page, click E-Mail and select Inbox.
2. In the Inbox list, click the message you want to mark as junk mail.
3. Click Junk in the toolbar. A drop-down list appears, as you see in Figure 7-10. Click Junk to mark the selected message, and then click OK. If you want to send a message report to Microsoft, click Report Phishing Scam and click OK.

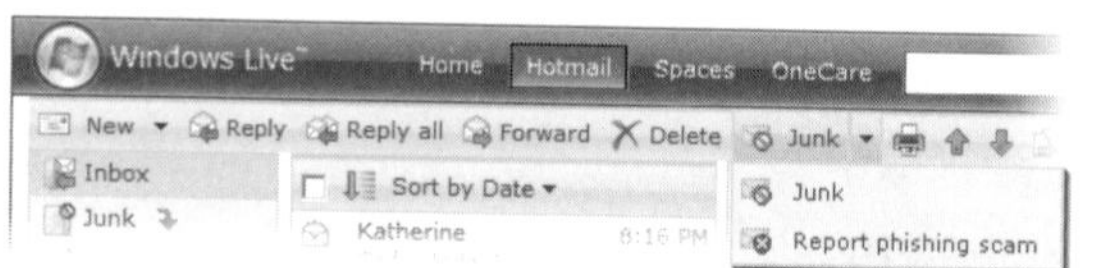

FIGURE 7-10 Click Junk to mark a message as junk mail, or report it as a phishing scam.

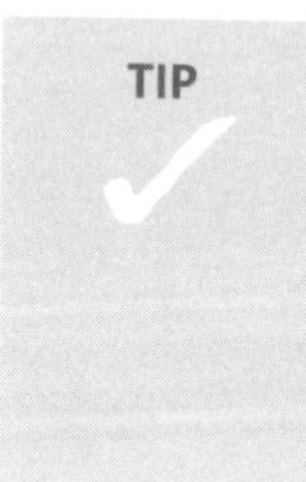

TIP Savvy spammers know just where to gather the e-mail addresses of unsuspecting users. Common gathering points include discussion boards, e-mail newsletter lists, and mailing lists. If you join a new list or discussion board and then begin getting an increased volume of spam, unsubscribe from the newly added list as soon as possible. You can also look for RSS feeds to gather the information you want to have without subscribing to lists.

Marking Senders as Safe or Unsafe

Although Office Live Small Business Mail helps you see quickly which messages are trustworthy and which are not, you can teach the system to recognize the reputable users you want to receive e-mail from as well as the users you want to block.

To mark a sender as safe or unsafe, follow these steps:

1. Click the message in your E-Mail box on the Office Live Small Business Home page, or click Inbox and choose the message in the Inbox list.

2. In the message header, click Mark As Safe for senders you know to be reputable, or click Mark As Unsafe for senders you want to save to the Blocked Senders list (see Figure 7-11).

3. If you click Mark As Safe, the Add Contact option appears in the message header. To add the sender to your contact list, simply click Add Contact.

4. If you click Mark As Unsafe, Office Live Small Business displays a message box telling you that Microsoft may share the address with other users to cut down on spam. Click OK to continue.

FIGURE 7-11 Click Mark As Safe or Mark As Unsafe to tell Office Live Small Business Mail how to recognize the sender.

Using Junk Mail Filtering

You can use filters to tell Office Live Small Business Mail how to handle the junk mail you receive. By setting the filtering level, you can control the level of screening the mail utility uses when reviewing the incoming messages. Here's how to check and change the junk mail filter on your account:

1. On the Office Live Small Business Home page, click E-Mail.

2. Click Inbox.

3. Click Options in the right side of the toolbar, and then click More Options.

4. Select Filters And Reporting in the Junk e-mail group. The Filters And Reporting window appears (see Figure 7-12).

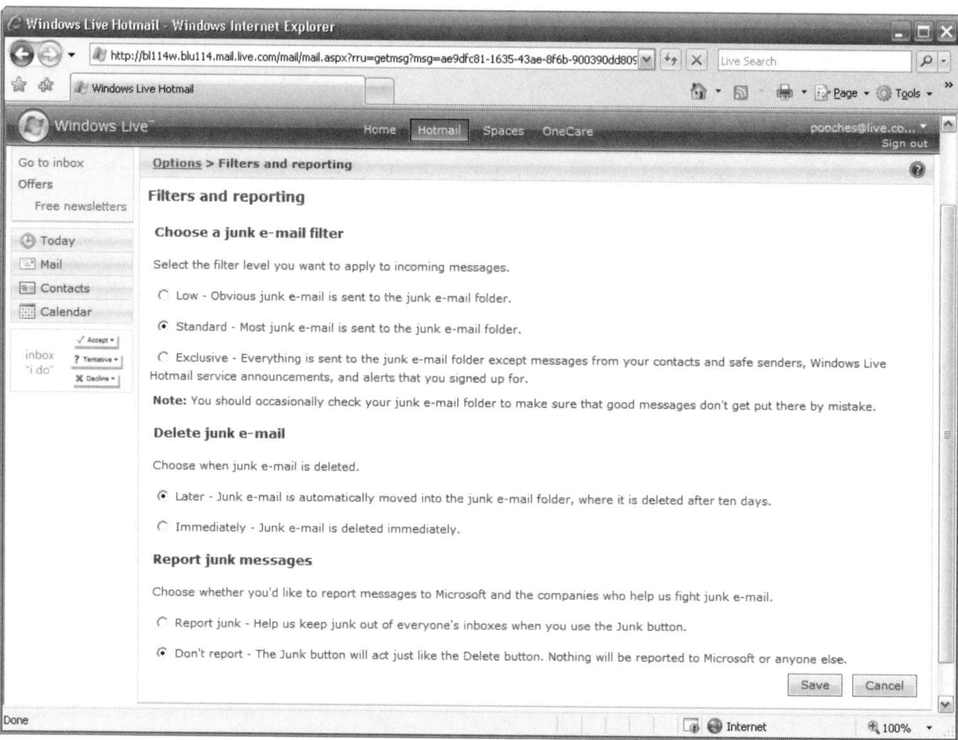

FIGURE 7-12 Change junk mail filtering to increase or reduce mail screening.

By default, Office Live Small Business Mail sets the junk mail filter to Standard, which sends most messages identified as junk mail to the Junk mail folder. If you want to allow more of those messages to come through so that you can review them and make the choice yourself, click Low in the Choose A Junk E-Mail Filter list. To raise the level of protection so that only messages from your contacts arrive in your inbox (everything else is sent to the Junk mail folder), click Exclusive.

The Filters And Reporting window also enables you to indicate how you want Office Live Small Business Mail to handle the junk mail you receive. By default, the messages stored in the Junk mail folder are not deleted right away—this gives you time to review the messages and make sure wanted messages aren't being sent there by mistake. If you want junk mail messages to be deleted as soon as they are sent to the Junk mail folder, you can click Immediately. But for best results, until you get used to the mail service and the types of mail Office Live Small Business Mail classifies as junk, it's a good idea to leave Later selected.

The last set of options in the Filter And Reporting window controls your choices about reporting phishing messages to Microsoft. The default setting is Don't Report, but you can change it to Report Junk so that clicking Report Phishing Scam will send the message to Microsoft for follow-up.

INSTALLING AND USING THE OUTLOOK CONNECTOR

If you're a Microsoft Office Outlook 2003 or 2007 user, you will be pleased to know that you can download and use a simple utility called the Outlook Connector that enables you to synchronize your mail, contacts, tasks, and appointments with those features in Office Live Small Business. Download the Outlook Connector by clicking E-Mail in the Office Live Small Business navigation bar and clicking Download Now in the Outlook Connector box. Follow the prompts on the screen to download the utility and save it to your desktop; then double-click the file and follow the Microsoft Office Outlook Connector Setup Wizard to install the file.

When the installation is complete, Outlook will restart and display the Microsoft Office Outlook Connector box so that you can enter your Office Live Small Business e-mail address and password. Enter the information and click OK.

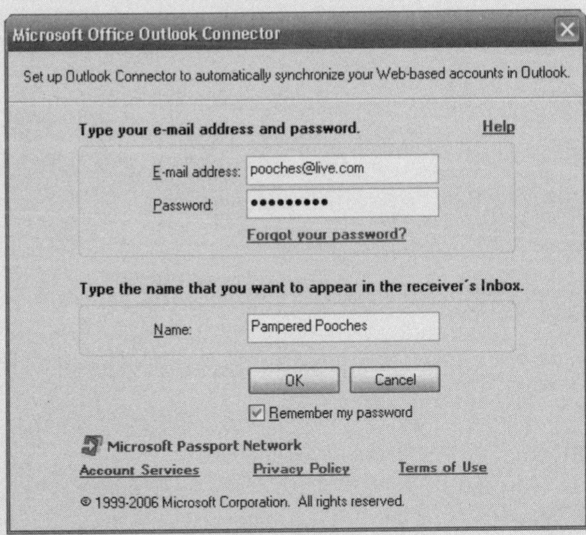

You will be prompted to restart Outlook, and when you do, the new account will be added automatically to your All Mail Folders List.

To find out more about the Outlook Connector, see Office Live Small Business help at *office.microsoft.com/en-us/officelive/FX101984871033.aspx*.

Working with Contacts

If you've used Web-based e-mail in the past, you are probably familiar with the way in which contacts are stored online so that you can connect with them easily. Office Live Small Business Mail automatically displays any contacts you have available through Windows Live services. So if you have a Windows Live Spaces account, for example, any contacts you've added as friends in that account will appear in your Contacts list.

To display Office Live Small Business Mail contacts, click E-Mail on the Home page and click Contacts in the Mail box.

Adding a New Contact

To add a new contact, click New in the toolbar to display the Edit Contact Details window in Office Live Small Business Mail. In order to create a new contact, you need only a name and the person's e-mail address. But the following fields are offered by default:

- First name
- Last name
- Nickname
- Personal e-mail
- Windows Live ID
- Mobile phone

If you know the contact's Windows Live ID and plan to use Windows Live Messenger, go ahead and enter the ID at this point and click the Use This Address check box.

Office Live Small Business Mail gives you a wide range of other information items you can include for each contact if you choose. To see the additional fields, click Show All Fields and enter the information you want to capture.

After you add the data for your contact, click Save.

Importing Contacts

Office Live Small Business includes a utility called the Contacts Importer that can import your existing contacts from Microsoft Office Outlook and Microsoft Outlook Express.

If you have additional contacts you want to import from other services, you can import contacts from the following e-mail services:

- Windows Contacts
- Windows Live Hotmail
- Yahoo! Mail
- Gmail

The e-mail contact information needs to be saved in Comma Separated Values (CSV) format before it is imported into Office Live Small Business Mail.

To use the Contacts Importer, begin by creating a new group in which to store the imported contacts. Here are the steps:

1. In the mail window, click Contacts, click Add To Groups, and choose New Group.
2. The new group appears highlighted in the left column. Type a new name for the group and press Enter.
3. Click the new group. The Import Contacts link appears in the center column.
4. Click Import Contacts.
5. Click Download And Run Contacts Importer.
6. Click Run when prompted to run or save the utility; enter your Office Live Small Business user ID and password.
7. The Contacts Importer displays the address books that will be imported; if you see address books listed that you do not want to import, click the check box of that address book to deselect it.
8. Click Next. A listing of contacts appears, giving you the option to deselect contacts you choose not to import right now. Make any necessary changes, and click Next.
9. After the utility finishes importing the contacts, click Close.

CONTACT MANAGER IN OFFICE LIVE SMALL BUSINESS

In addition to the Contacts area available in Office Live Small Business Mail, the program offers a powerful business application called Contact Manager (available in the left navigation panel on the Office Live Small Business Home page). Contact Manager enables you to take contact management to a whole new level. Using Contact Manager (which is covered in detail in Chapter 10 , "Working with Business Applications"), you can create accounts, customers, events, transactions, and more. You can keep track of every communication, task, and meeting relating to specific clients, and produce reports that help you evaluate which of your efforts are bringing the biggest benefit.

Instant Messaging Peers, Vendors, and Clients

The world of communication has grown smaller and faster over the last several years. Today, being able to contact others via e-mail is the norm, not the exception. But if e-mail isn't fast enough for you (you do have to wait for the other person to get around to a reply, after all), you can use an instant message to pop up over their other applications and ask or answer a question in a more immediate way.

Instant messaging (IMing) is really a predecessor to texting—it's been around awhile in a number of different forms. Early on, IMing wasn't accepted in the professional realm; it was something friends and family used to stay in touch during the day. But as new versions of IM software were developed, they offered a full range of features and a more secure experience, and businesses started jumping on the bandwagon.

Office Live Small Business includes Windows Live Messenger as its instant messaging client. This program enables you to send and receive communications that include not only text but also photos, data files, and even video. What's more, by using Windows Live Messenger you can reach your contact via computer, mobile phone, PDA, or even by voice.

Downloading Windows Live Messenger

To add Windows Live Messenger, click E-Mail on the Office Live Small Business Home page and click Download Now in the Instant Message box. On the Windows Live page, click the orange Get It Free button to begin the download. Review the settings on the Set Up page. (By default, Messenger will select the Windows Live Search as your default search engine, set your Home page to MSN, sign you up to participate in Microsoft's information collection program, and add the search toolbar to your browser.) Then click to remove the check mark for any item you don't want. Click Install to download the software.

The installation process displays a status box as it performs an initial check on your system and prepares to download the utility (see Figure 7-13). Because Windows Live Messenger is part of the Windows Live family of services, a number of utilities are available to you in addition to instant messaging. Click any of the items in the displayed list that you also want to add to the basic instant messaging capabilities, and click Add To Installation. Any items you select will automatically be included in the installation process as the instant messenger program installs. When the process is complete, click Close.

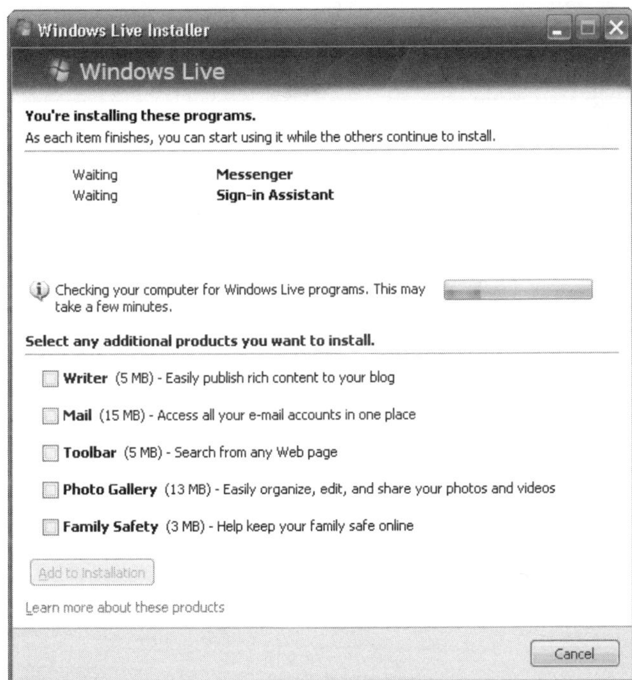

FIGURE 7-13 You can choose to add other Windows Live services as you download Windows Live Messenger.

Using Windows Live Messenger

After Windows Live Messenger is installed, the sign-in window will appear on your screen (see Figure 7-14). Enter your Office Live Small Business e-mail address and password, and click Sign Me In Automatically if you want to log in to Windows Live Messenger each time you sign on. Additionally, you can have the instant messaging utility remember your e-mail address and password by selecting the Remember Me and Remember My Password check boxes. Click Sign In to start Windows Live Messenger.

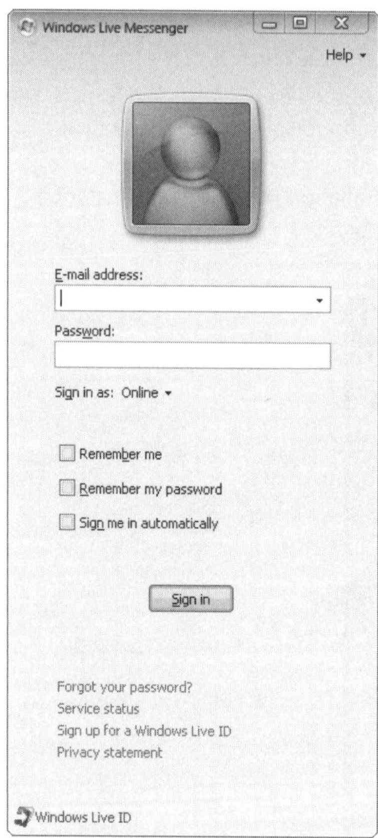

FIGURE 7-14 Use your Office Live Small Business e-mail address and password to sign in to Windows Live Messenger.

Setting Up Windows Live Messenger

Any contacts you already have in your Office Live Small Business account will show up automatically in the Windows Live Messenger window. You can actually begin sending instant messages right away. Before you do, however, you may want to customize the look and feel—and tailor the information displayed in the Messenger window—so it fits the way you want your business to appear online.

For example, you might want to do the following:

- Change the display name to show your business name.
- Add your business logo to the display photo (this will be visible to contacts with whom you trade messages).
- Add your business brand statement or slogan to the <Enter A Personal Message> line.
- Change the color scheme so it reflects the color you use in your branding.

Change Your Display Name

If you logged in using an account that pulls up your personal name as the display name, you can easily change that to reflect your business name. (That way, each time someone sees your name in the Windows Live Contacts list, you are marketing your business!) When you click the arrow to the right of your login name, a menu appears (see Figure 7-15).

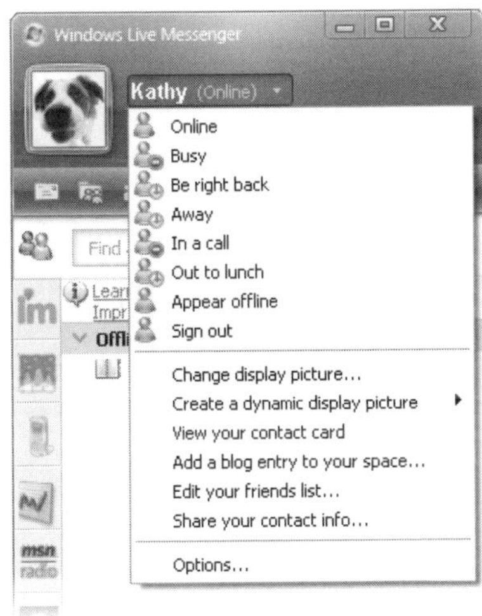

FIGURE 7-15 Click the arrow to the right of your login name to display a variety of options for customizing Windows Live Messenger.

Click Options at the bottom of the list to display a window of choices for customizing your Windows Live Messenger account. Type your business name in the first box in the Display Name area. Click OK to save the change.

Add a Photo

To change the photo used in your Windows Live Messenger window, you can click Change Picture in the Options dialog box or choose Change Display Picture from the drop-down menu available when you click the arrow to the right of your display name.

In the Display Pictures dialog box, scroll through the displayed list and choose a different photo. You can also upload your own photo (you'll want to do this if you have a logo you want to use): Click Browse, navigate to the folder containing the file you want to use, select it, and click Open. Click OK to add the picture to your Windows Live Messenger window.

You can also create a dynamic picture—an image that displays movement (blinking eyes, moving hands, changing expression) in the photo display area. To view the types of dynamic pictures that are available, choose Create A Dynamic Display Picture from the menu and choose the service you want to view.

Add a Brand Statement

You can use the status line immediately below your display name to show the tag line of your business. Display the Options window and click in the second box in the Display Name area. Type your brand statement, and then click OK.

Be sure to keep your tag line short and memorable so that others can see it clearly in their Windows Live Messenger windows.

I'M SPREADING THE WORD

The worldwide popularity of Windows Live Messenger gives it a wide reach and the possibility of significant impact in many of the important issues facing the world today. To use some of that potential in service of the greater good, Windows Live has developed the I'M Spreading the Word program, which enables all Windows Live Messenger users to contribute to causes they care about simply by including a special code beside their names in Windows Live Messenger.

Here's how it works. Choose a cause you want to support and type the code for the cause to the right of your name at the top of the Windows Live Messenger window. Here are the codes and their organizations:

*9mil	ninemillion.org
*bgca	Boys & Girls Clubs of America
*help	StopGlobalWarming.org
*hsus	The Humane Society of the United States
*komen	Susan G. Komen for the Cure
*mssoc	National Multiple Sclerosis Society
*naf	National AIDS Fund
*red+u	American Red Cross
*sierra	Sierra Club
*unicef	UNICEF

Type the code after your name (for example, "Pampered Pooches *unicef"). Each time you use Windows Live Messenger to start a conversation, Microsoft donates a portion of the advertising revenues to the organization you selected. At the time of this writing, the I'M initiative has been in place for 11 months, and more than three quarters of a million dollars has been raised, simply through instant messaging.

For more about the I'M initiative, go to *im.live.com/Messenger/IM/Home/Default.aspx*

Sending and Receiving Instant Messages

The process of sending and receiving instant messages is very simple. To send an instant message to someone on your contact list, simply double-click the contact's name, type your message, and click Send.

When you receive an instant message from one of your contacts, a small message box appears on your screen. You can open the Windows Live Messenger window by clicking the message box; then you can respond by typing your message and clicking Send.

In addition to trading simple lines of text, you can share photos, files, videos, presentations, and more. You can also include others in the conversation so that multiple people in your group can participate.

SEE ALSO Although going into further detail on Windows Live Messenger is beyond the scope of this book, you can find all kinds of great Messenger ideas in *Microsoft Windows XP: Do Amazing Things* by Joli Ballew (Microsoft Press, 2003).

Updating Your Calendar

In addition to the tools for checking and working with your e-mail, the Mail box on your Office Live Small Business E-Mail page offers a variety of tools that can help you stay organized, reach clients, and stay up to date on important tasks. The Calendar and Share Your Calendar links make it easy for you to add appointments, create events, assign tasks, and more, all from your Office Live Small Business account.

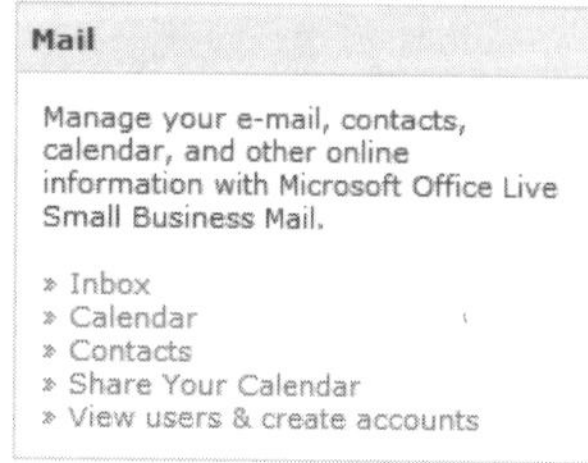

Adding an Appointment

Start the process by clicking Calendar in the Mail box on the E-Mail page. In the Calendar window, click New (in the far left side of the toolbar), and click Appointment (see Figure 7-16). The new appointment window appears, giving you options for entering the subject, place, time, and category of the appointment, as Figure 7-17 shows. You can also set a reminder for yourself about the appointment, select the way in which you want the item to appear on your calendar, and invite others to attend as well. After you enter your information, click Save.

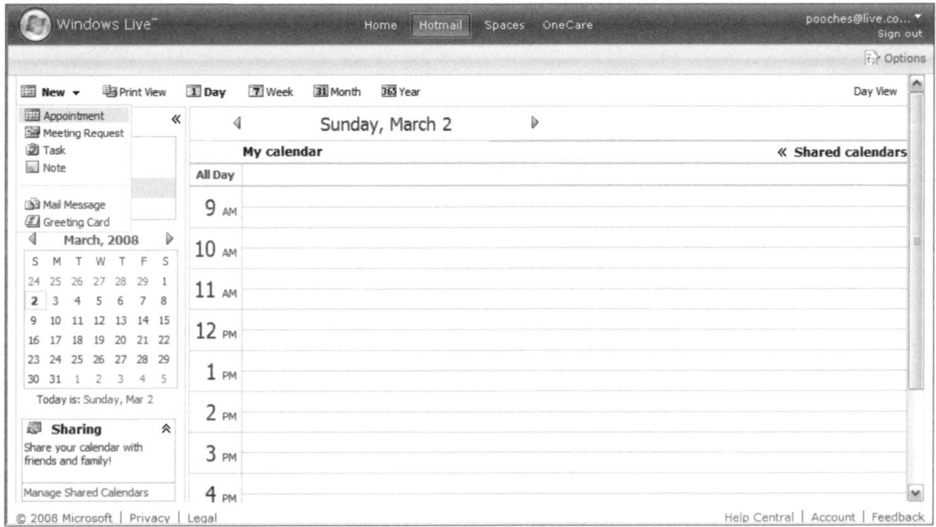

FIGURE 7-16 Add to your schedule by clicking a time slot and typing your information or by clicking New and choosing Appointment.

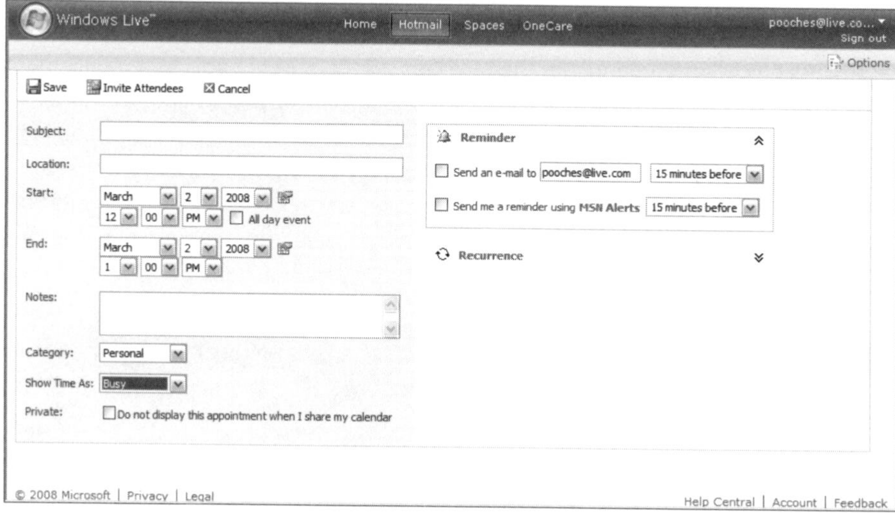

FIGURE 7-17 Add the subject, place, time, and category for your appointment.

NOTE If you want to hide this meeting from others who may view your shared calendar, click the Do Not Display This Appointment When I Share My Calendar check box at the bottom of the meeting information area.

After you save the appointment, it appears automatically on your calendar on the day and at the time you specified. If you invited others to the meeting, a small group icon will appear to the left of the appointment name. You can edit the appointment at any time by clicking the link.

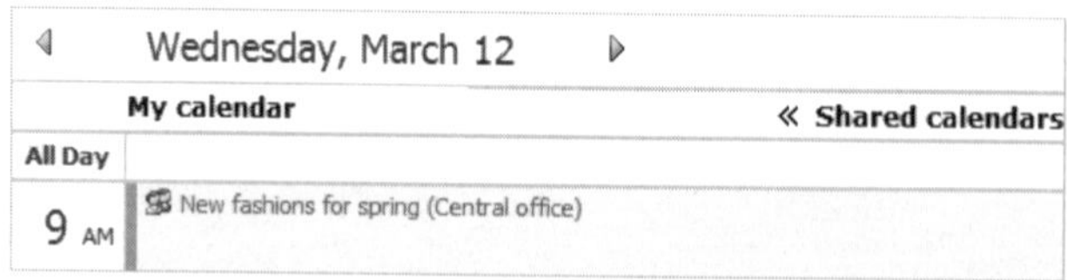

CHANGING CALENDAR VIEWS

Your Office Live Small Business calendar provides multiple views you can use to zoom out or zoom in on appointments coming in your future. You can choose from any of the following views:

- Day view
- Week view
- Month view
- Year view

By default, the calendar displays Day view, which lists each day in half-hour increments on the right side of your window. You can scroll down through the list to move from morning to night. Additionally, you can move from day to day by clicking the arrows to the left and right of the date, as shown in the preceding illustration.

Week view lists an entire week at a time, displaying only scheduled appointments in the appropriate slots. Scroll through the week by scrolling down the list; display any appointment by clicking its link. You can move from week to week by clicking the arrows to the left and right of the week, or by clicking another day or week in the monthly calendar view in the left column.

Month view displays a traditional monthly calendar, providing the scheduled appointment as a link on a particular day. You can move from month to month by clicking the arrows to the left and right of the month name or by clicking another month in the navigation grid on the left.

Year view displays the "big picture" of the full calendar year, enabling you to move easily from month to month or leap ahead into the future to plan a weekend away or the new conference you're talking about hosting. You won't see any scheduled appointments at the Year level; this view simply gives you the scope of the year so that you can use Month, Week, or Day views to display and modify appointments.

Sharing Your Calendar

When you are working with others closely—in an office or outside of one—being able to schedule time together is important. You can save yourself a lot of time and energy by simply sharing your calendars instead of trading e-mail and phone calls trying to find a time to meet.

A shared calendar enables others who have the necessary permissions to see whether you're available at a specific time on a certain day. You can control the amount of information others see and determine how the information looks to others.

To begin sharing your calendar, follow these steps:

1. Display the Calendar window by clicking Calendar in the Mail box on the Office Live Small Business E-Mail page.
2. In the Sharing box on the left side of the Calendar page, click Manage Shared Calendars.
3. Click Share Your Calendar.
4. Click the name of a person you want to share your calendar with from the contacts list, and click Next.
5. Choose whether you want this person to be able to see all your appointment details, or only that you are free or busy. Click Next.
6. Add a note inviting the person to share your calendar, and then click Finish.

An invitation with a link is sent to the contact you added to your shared calendar, and the person will be able to view only the appointment information you elected for them to see.

You can change the permission level or stop sharing your calendar at any time by clicking Manage Shared Calendars and modifying your settings as desired.

Adding Tasks and Notes

The process of adding tasks and notes to your Calendar in Office Live Small Business is one of those simple but elegant procedures that can add a lot to how organized—or disorganized!—you feel as you grow your business. If you are working with a virtual team, you can use tasks and notes to help keep team members up to speed on the latest stages and developments in a project. Each team member will be able to see the tasks and notes that apply to his or her part in the job.

To create a task using Office Live Small Business, follow these steps:

1. Click Calendar in the Mail box on the Office Live Small Business E-Mail page.
2. In the Task box on the left side of the Calendar window, click New.
3. In the Task window, enter the subject, date, status, and any notes about the task. Set a reminder if you want to receive an alert or e-mail message prompting you to complete the task.
4. Click Save to save the task.

The new task appears as a link in the Task box; you can view, update, or delete it at any time by clicking the link and changing the task information as needed.

To add a note using Office Live Small Business, follow these steps:

1. Click Calendar in the Mail box on the Office Live Small Business E-Mail page.
2. Click to expand the Notes box in the left side of the Calendar page.
3. Click New.
4. Type the subject and note in the Note window (see Figure 7-18).
5. Choose a category for the note.
6. Click Save.

Save Cancel

Subject: Too many sweaters

Category: Business

Content: I'd like for us to think about what else we can add to the fall line in addition to the great sweaters we already have. Hats? Boots? Matching collars and leashes? Let's be creative with our dollars this year.

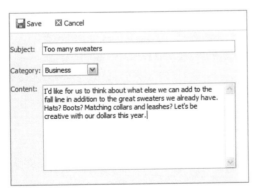

FIGURE 7-18 You can add notes to your Calendar view that provide information for future events and tasks.

BUSINESS COMMUNICATIONS—DOS AND DON'TS

Communicating is about connection—two people understanding an idea, two groups working together on a project, a vendor inspiring a customer, a customer sharing a successful purchasing experience with your company. Thinking through the impact your business communications will have on your customers is an important first step in making sure your messages are saying what you want them to say.

- **Do** have a communications strategy. When you're first starting out, it may not seem necessary to include a far-reaching communications strategy in your startup plans. But if you envision your business growing, knowing *what* you want to say to clients and prospective customers, *how* you'll say it (and how often), *which* means of communications you'll use, and *who* receives it are all important pieces of information. Sit down over coffee with your partners one morning and talk through the ways in which communicating with customers figures into your business. You may be surprised by the number of the ideas you have.
- **Do** have a mission statement. Right off the bat, know your reason for existing as a business. Be able to state it in as few words as possible. (Some people call this the "elevator pitch," the ability to explain your business purpose and focus in the time it might take to ride up a floor or two on an elevator.) Being clear about your purpose makes the rest of your communicating easier because you are aware of the overarching reason you're in business.
- **Don't** mix messages. Especially at first, it's tempting to try to be all things to all people. But if you have a mission statement of "making the dog world a happier place, one bath at a time," somebody is going to get confused if you add "and iguanas, too" at the end of that statement. If you find that your messaging is spilling out beyond the confines of your brand, it may be time for a little strategic planning, but don't start the change in e-mail messages and business documents.

- **Do** be aware of key opportunities for contact. What does the sales process look like for your customer? Think through each stage of contact a customer has with your company. At which points would *you* want to receive communication from a company you're considering purchasing from? Do you want a reminder about a product you recently viewed? You definitely want a thank-you and order confirmation note. How about a follow-up survey or a newsletter offer? Make a list of natural opportunities for contact with your customer during your own sales process, and use that as the basis for communications you send as you build relationships with people who visit your site.
- **Don't** confuse customers by replying from different e-mail addresses. If you are using Outlook Connector and answering e-mail offline, be sure to choose your business branded e-mail account when replying to messages. That way, each time your business e-mail appears in someone's inbox, it is reinforcing your business brand. Sending a message from a different account seems disorganized and loses that opportunity for reinforcement.
- **Do** use Contact Manager so you can track all communications with a specific customer. Use Office Live Small Business Contact Manager to store, view, and create reports on all the messages, events, tasks, and appointments you create with all the contacts in your contacts list. This powerful tool enables you to take communications to a higher level by tracking and following up on all the potential communication activities your business brings.
- **Don't** wait for customers to follow up with you. After a sale is completed on your site, you may be thinking, "No news is good news." In other words, if you don't hear anything from a customer, you can assume that the sales experience was successful. Although that mindset may work if you're mainly interested in putting out fires as they occur, it can cost you a big opportunity. Sending a follow-up note to customers who have recently purchased something from your site can leave an important and lasting impression that your business cares about the customer's experience and wants to receive feedback on how to improve the process.

What's Next

In this chapter, you learned about the primary communications features included with Office Live Small Business: e-mail, instant messaging, and calendar features. The next chapter introduces you to the new online sales features in Office Live Small Business. Soon you'll be creating product pages, posting items, and selling online like a pro.

Selling Products Online

IN THIS CHAPTER, YOU WILL

- Learn about Store Manager in Microsoft Office Live Small Business.
- Activate Store Manager.
- Set up shipping methods.
- Prepare for payments.
- Add products and photos.
- List your products.
- Turn on your shopping cart.
- Activate your store.

AS YOU'VE seen throughout this book, Microsoft Office Live Small Business is a powerful suite of Web applications bringing everything that you, as the owner of a small business, need to promote, market, and manage your business. This chapter focuses on a key new feature that Office Live Small Business offers: the ability to sell your products online.

With Office Live Small Business, you now can create a customized e-commerce experience that presents your products in a professional, polished way on your site. You can offer an effective and easy-to-use shopping cart experience that makes purchasing from your site—or from your product listings on eBay—as safe and as simple as possible for your customers.

This chapter shows you how to activate Store Manager, set up shipping and payment options, create your product pages, add a shopping cart, and take the whole thing live, all in less than a single afternoon. What used to take a huge amount of resources—time, money, and staff—you can now do on your desktop (or laptop) using Office Live Small Business.

What Is Store Manager?

Store Manager is a new e-commerce utility that is an add-on service available through Office Live Small Business. Unlike some of the core services in the suite of applications, Store Manager is a subscription-based feature that enables you to dramatically extend the reach of your products and expand the capabilities of your site.

Store Manager is included in the latest version of Office Live Small Business that became available in February 2008. Users who sign up for Store Manager can do the following:

- Use professionally designed e-commerce templates to design a professional storefront for their sites.
- Create product pages with text, images, and even video.
- Easily modify and manage their product catalogs.
- Create product pages and listings for their own sites as well as for eBay.
- Track and create reports of sales data to keep an eye on what's working and what's not.
- Add on an easy-to-use checkout experience that will keep customers coming back.

Activating Store Manager

By default, Store Manager is deactivated when you begin working with Office Live Small Business, so your first step is to sign up for the service. Start by clicking Sell Online in the Office Live Small Business Home page. The Store Manager page appears (see Figure 8-1).

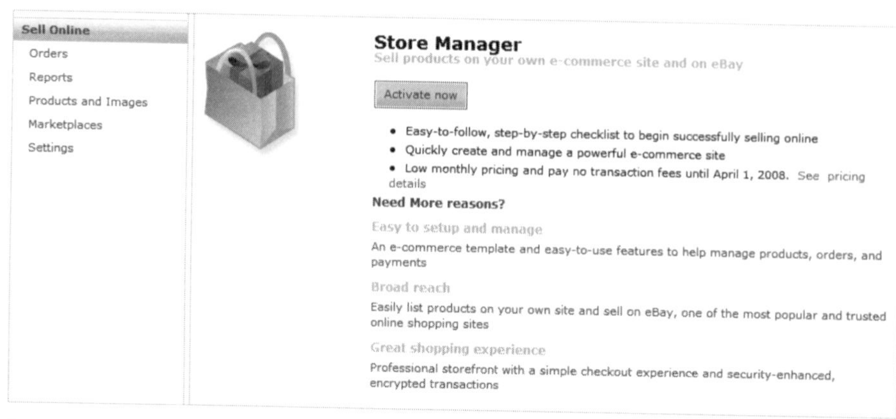

FIGURE 8-1 You activate Store Manager on the page that appears when you click Sell Online.

Click the Activate Now button. The Add Services page appears. In the Your Selection area, you see the service you have elected to add to Office Live Small Business (in this case, Store Manager). In the Your Plan area, you see the plan you're signing up for and the price. Store Manager costs $39.95 per month, which enables you to add e-commerce features to your site and to sell your wares on eBay. An initial discount is available for new users: You can use Store Manager free of charge for one month and then pay $29.95 a month for six months following signup.

Enter your contact and credit card information, read the authorization information, and then click Complete My Order. A confirmation message will appear, thanking you for your order. Click the Return To Office Live button to go back to the Office Live Small Business Home page.

Getting Started with Store Manager

Now when you click Sell Online in the navigation bar on the left side of the Office Live Small Business window, a different screen appears (see Figure 8-2). The Getting Started area lists six tasks you can complete as you set up your site for online sales:

- Set up shipping.
- Set up payment processing.
- Add products and images to create a product catalog.
- List your products for your online store or for your eBay account.
- Turn on your shopping cart.
- Go live with your new store.

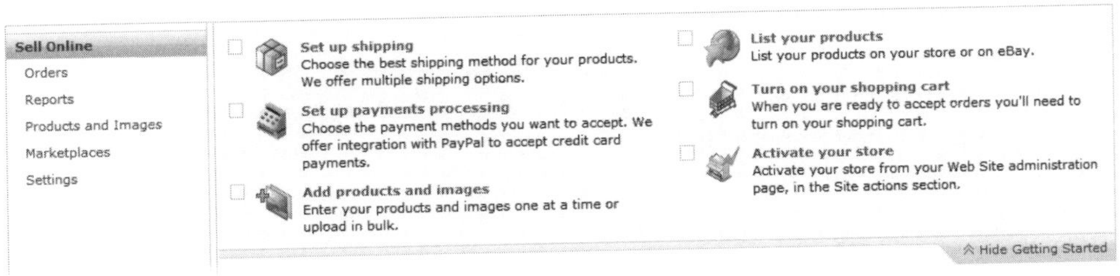

FIGURE 8-2 After you activate Store Manager, the Sell Online page displays your next steps.

In addition to the tasks highlighted in the Getting Started area, the Sell Online page gives you a quick look at the status of your online sales. The Orders In Process area on the bottom left of the screen shows you at a glance whether new orders have been added since the last time you visited the site. The Sales area will eventually display ongoing reports of sales from your site.

TIP

If you're just getting started with e-commerce, you may not have done the research needed to gather the shipping, sales tax, and payment information you are required to enter before taking your online store live. Office Live Small Business requires you to set up at least one shipping method and one payment method before you can go live with your site. If you want to follow along with the examples here, you can create placeholder accounts that you then fill in with correct data after you've gathered the information you need.

Setting Up Shipping

Knowing how you'll get your products to the customers who order them is an important piece of your sales puzzle. Many entrepreneurs know the headaches involved in finding cost-effective, reliable shipping vendors.

Office Live Small Business helps you add your own shipping vendors to your online sales and choose the type of shipping method you need for your business. Here's how to do it:

1. In the Getting Started area, click Set Up Shipping.
2. The Shipping Overview page appears. Click New Shipping Method (see Figure 8-3).
3. First you will choose a shipping method. Click the Shipping Type arrow and choose one of the following from the displayed list:
   - **By Item** When you choose to calculate the shipping costs by item, you have the option of choosing different shipping charges for each item. You indicate the shipping charge on the product details page, and that cost is applied during the sale.
   - **By Order Weight** When you choose to calculate the shipping costs by the weight of the order, all items ordered are totaled, and the shipping charges are applied at the point of sale.
   - **By Cost** When you select this option, the shipping charges are applied according to the subtotal of the completed order.

TIP Of the three shipping types, only By Item is a fixed price; both By Order Weight and By Cost enable you to calculate and modify shipping charges based on the destination of the order.

4. After you click your choice, the Create Shipping Method window appears so that you can enter additional information (see Figure 8-4). Here's a quick list of what each of these items means:

   - **Shipping Method Name** This name will be visible to your customers when they use the shopping cart, so it's a good idea to use something recognizable, such as UPS or FedEx Ground.
   - **Minimum Weight (lbs)** This refers to the smallest order that you are willing to send by this shipping method. For example, if it's not cost-effective for you to use FedEx with orders weighing less than 10 pounds, enter 10 in the Minimum Weight (lbs) box.
   - **Weight Increment (lbs)** This is the cost you add to the order when it exceeds the base weight amount.
   - **Maximum Weight (lbs)** This is the largest order you are willing to send by this shipping method.
   - **Free Shipping If Order Over** Click this check box if you want to offer free shipping as a sales incentive on large orders. If you click this item, be sure to enter the dollar amount of the order in the box as well.
   - **Domestic** In this area, click the arrow to choose whether you want to set one domestic rate for all states, set shipping rates individually for different states, or choose not to ship domestically.
   - **International** In this area, click the arrow to specify a flat rate outside the United States, set international rates, or leave the default value set to Do Not Ship Internationally.

5. After you fill in all the shipping information, click Save.

After you save your shipping method, it will appear on the Shipping Overview page, as shown in Figure 8-5. On this page you can add new shipping methods; you can also edit, delete, or disable the ones you've already created.

Shipping Overview

Create one or more shipping methods (for example: UPS Ground). There are three types of shipping methods you can create: by item, by order weight, or by order cost. The shipping methods you create will appear in the shopping cart at checkout.

Shipping Methods

+ New shipping method

There are no shipping methods available. To create a shipping method click New shipping method

FIGURE 8-3 When you click Set Up Shipping, the Shipping Overview page enables you to add a new shipping method.

Create Shipping Method

Enter details about your shipping method below.

Shipping type: By order weight
* Shipping method name:
* Minimum weight (lbs):
* Weight increment (lbs):
* Maximum weight (lbs):
Free shipping if order over: $

Domestic

For domestic shipping, you can either specify a flat rate, or specify a rate for each U.S. state. Select an option from the drop-down list.

Specify a flat rate for shipping within the U.S.
Base shipping amount: $
* Incremental shipping amount: $

International

You can choose whether or not to enable international shipping. Select an option from the drop-down list.

Do not ship internationally

Save Cancel

FIGURE 8-4 Fill in your choices for shipping domestically and internationally.

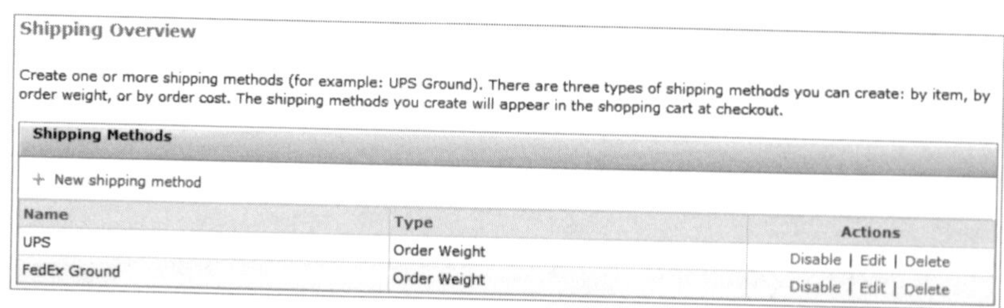
Shipping Overview
Create one or more shipping methods (for example: UPS Ground). There are three types of shipping methods you can create: by item, by order weight, or by order cost. The shipping methods you create will appear in the shopping cart at checkout.
Shipping Methods
+ New shipping method
Name
Type
Actions
UPS
Order Weight
Disable | Edit | Delete
FedEx Ground
Order Weight
Disable | Edit | Delete

FIGURE 8-5 You can add to or modify shipping methods at any time.

■ REMEMBER **Check your shipping charges periodically to make sure that fluctuating gas prices are not taking a bite out of any profits you make through online sales.**

Getting Ready to Process Payments

The next step in setting up your site for online sales is choosing the types of payments to accept. Click Sell Online in the navigation bar, and then click Set Up Payment Processing in the Getting Started area. Office Live Small Business displays the Payments page (see Figure 8-6).

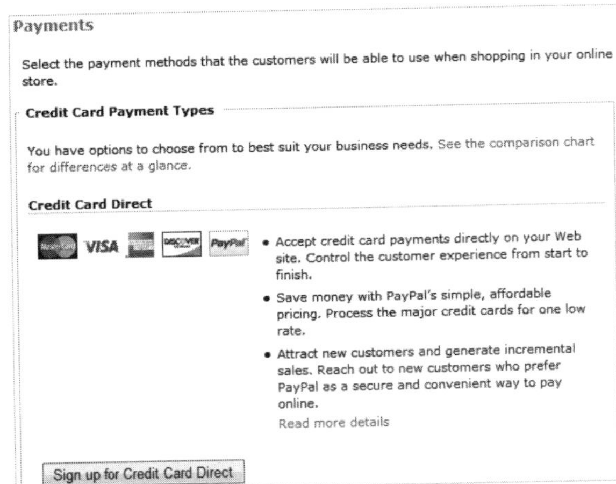

FIGURE 8-6 Choose a payment method to enable payments on your site.

The Payments page offers several options for collecting payment from your online customers:

- **Credit Card Direct** You can accept payments through the four major credit cards (American Express, Discover, MasterCard, and Visa) as well as PayPal. This option is offered through a partnership with PayPal's WebSite Payments Pro program, which gives you an option of two methods of payment for the service: 2.9 percent and $0.30 per sale, or a flat fee of $30 per month for unlimited transactions. The main benefit of this option is that customers don't have to leave your shopping cart experience to use major credit cards to pay for their purchases.
- **PayPal Express** You can let PayPal handle all the credit card information, and you pay fees only when you accept a payment from a customer. The methods of payment are similar: 2.9 percent and $0.30 for sales up to $3,000 in a month's time; then a reducing percentage as sales increase during the month. There is no monthly fee with this option. The downside of this option is that customers are taken from your site to PayPal when they choose to pay for their purchase using a major credit card.
- **Traditional Payment Methods** You can arrange to accept checks, money orders or cashier's checks, or cash.

NOTE If you choose either Credit Card Direct or PayPal Express, you will be taken through the process of signing up for PayPal. If you already have an existing PayPal account, you can use that information, although you should be careful to keep your business and personal accounts separate.

After you make your choice and enter any necessary information, click Save to save the payment method you've selected.

Creating Your Product Pages

Now the fun begins. You get to create the product catalog pages for your site. This is where having some creative energy—or some talented people who specialize in creative arts—will really come in handy. As you design your product pages, you will have the opportunity to add information in each of the following areas, so they are worth thinking about before you begin creating your pages:

- Product name
- Product numbering or ID
- Product price
- A short description of your product
- A longer description, if desired
- The category of the product
- Keywords that describe your product
- Photos of the product
- Dimensions
- Weight

TIP You may want to create an Excel spreadsheet that includes a column for each product with each of these items represented. That way you can be sure to be consistent in the way you number, name, categorize, and describe the various products in your catalog.

To get started, click Sell Online in the Office Live Small Business Home page, and then click Add Products And Images in the Getting Started area. The Product List page appears, as you see in Figure 8-7.

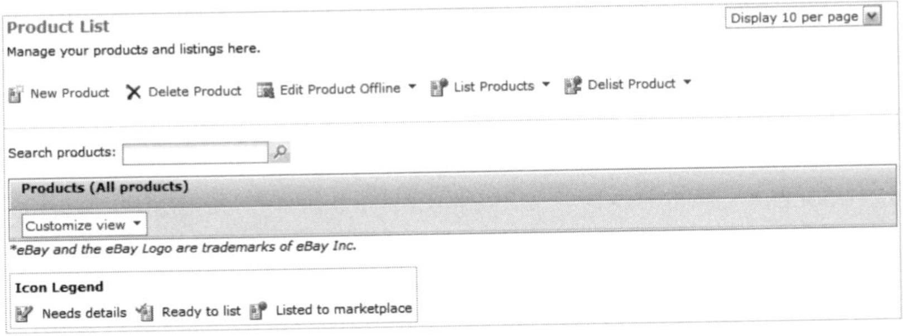

FIGURE 8-7 Begin by creating a new product listing for your catalog.

Click New Product, and the fun begins. In the Add/Edit Product page (see Figure 8-8), you will enter the information that describes and categorizes your first product. Notice that the Add/Edit Product page is set up with two tabs. At the top of the page you see Core Product Details and eBay Details. For now, leave Core Product Details selected, and you can add the basic information for your product following the description in the following sections.

FIGURE 8-8 Add product information on the Add/Edit Product page.

Adding Product Information and Price

Your first task requires entering the product name and ID you have given to your product. If you currently use a numbering or classifying system to help keep you sane during inventory time, use that system for your Office Live Small Business online store. If you are just starting out and can name and/or number products any way you want, think carefully about the names you choose and the numbering you design.

Here are a few questions to consider:

- If this is a product you have created yourself, is there a brand name attached to the product (for example, Flex-i-bend Leashes, Wags Natural Dog Bones, or TruePoint Clippers)?
- Do you carry more than one type and size of a particular product? Will you create separate product listings for each?
- Do you need a way to distinguish online sales items from in-person sales?
- Does your product ID include important information such as product type, model number, and stock order date? (For example, a product ID for a case of carrot-flavored natural dog bones might be NDB0308C—Natural Dog Bones; arrived in March 2008; carrot-flavored.)

Setting the price of your product requires a lot of thought and testing, so if you are just considering this for the first time, discuss your proposed price with others before posting it online. Most retailers charge at least 100 percent markup on their original wholesale prices, and others use a 150 percent or even a 200 percent markup to break even with operating expenses, salaries, and promotion and distribution expenses.

To add the Product name, Product ID, and Price, click in each of those fields and type the information you want to provide.

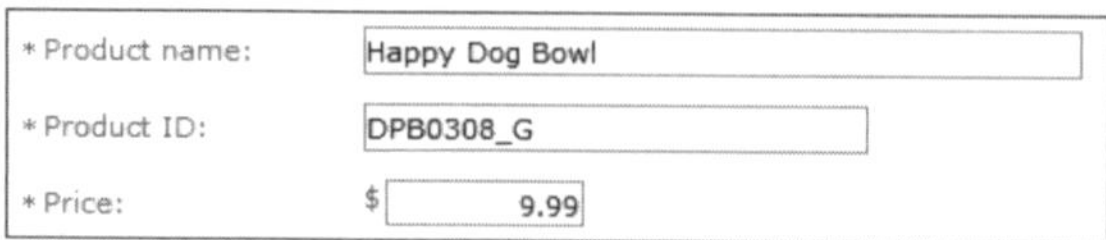

Writing Product Descriptions

When was the last time you sat down after dinner and read a catalog cover to cover? Most of us are looking for specific information when we browse a catalog. We want to see a simple description that lets us know whether the item sounds like something we need or want. We're curious about dimensions, materials, and durability. In other words, will we get our money's worth? Do your best to answer those key customer questions in your descriptions instead of dancing around them with fluffy or overblown text.

The short description is required for your product listing; the information you add here will appear beneath the product name in your store and in the customer's shopping cart. Keep this description brief—you have only 1,075 characters to use.

The Description area offers you the chance to provide more detail about the product. Here's where you have more room to discuss your product's value proposition. You have a 10,000-character maximum for the description—but try to stick with the facts consumers need to make a good purchase decision.

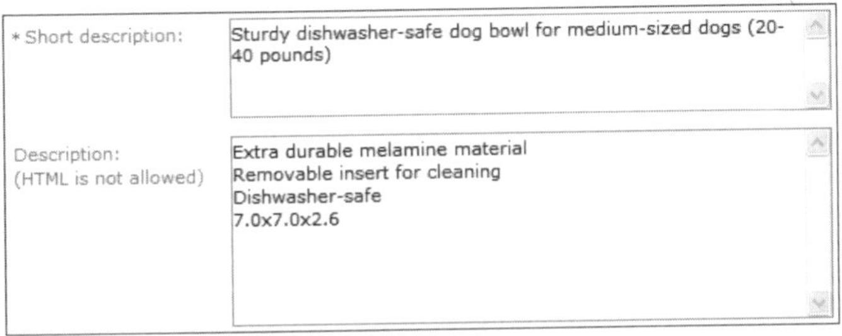

Creating and Using Categories

The product categories you create on your site help you keep things organized and give your visitors a way to find specific items when there are many different types of products for sale on your site. On the Pampered Pooches site, for example, categories might include these:

- Dog Beds
- Dog Boots
- Dog Coats
- Collars and Leashes
- Grooming Supplies
- Owner Wear (where you'll find that "I Heart Newfoundlands" t-shirt you've been looking for)

To add a new category to your product listing, follow these steps:

1. Click the Category arrow, and choose Add New Category. The New Category dialog box appears (see Figure 8-9).
2. Click in the Enter Category Name box and type the new name for the category.
3. Click OK.

This creates a new category at the top level. To add a subcategory to the level you just added, click the Category arrow again and choose Add New Category. In the New Category dialog box, click the Select Parent Category arrow and choose the category within which you want to create the new category. For example, the Dog Bowls subcategory could be created inside the Feeding Supplies category.

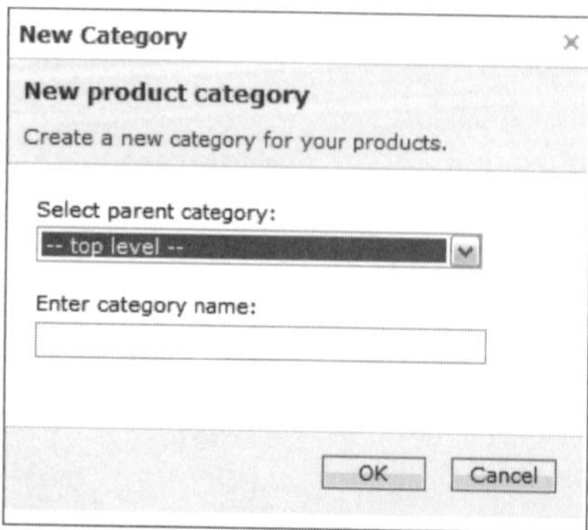

FIGURE 8-9 Add a new category or subcategory in the New Category dialog box.

Assigning Keywords to Your Products

Earlier in this book, you learned about keywords and what they can mean to the placement of your site in search results. A well-placed, targeted keyword can bring lots of paying customers to your virtual door. To get the greatest possible use of the keywords that work for you, add those same keywords to your product pages to help extend the reach of your site.

In the Pampered Pooches site, keywords in use include *dog grooming, pet grooming, dogs, dog training, dog bathing, dog supplies, grooming services, show dogs,* and *animal rescue.* You can use additional keywords in the Keywords field on the Add/Edit Product page, but there is a 512-character maximum. Be sure to separate keywords with commas so search engines know where one keyword stops and another begins.

Choosing Product Photos

A good product photo is a great salesperson, letting prospective customers know what they'll be getting for their money and reassuring them that the goods will be worth the cost. For that reason, make it a policy to upload only high-quality photos of your products.

What makes a photo good?

- The image is sharp and in focus.
- Lighting is adequate and consistent across the photo.
- The color is bright and realistic.
- The object is centered and clear, without other unnecessary elements in the shot.
- The setting for the object is professional.
- The object is photographed so that customers can envision using it themselves.

You can upload up to six photos for each product listing in Store Manager. To get the best use out of the multiple photos, capture photos from different angles and perspectives, or show the product in different settings and uses.

To upload photos for your product, follow these steps:

1. In the Add/Edit Product page, click the Add icon in the Pictures row.
2. In the Add Images To Product dialog box, click the Select Images From arrow and choose My Computer. The page changes to allow you to upload your product photos to the Online Image Folder (see Figure 8-10).

Add Images to Product

Select images

Use the drop-down list to locate image files to add to your product, from either your image folders or other folders on your computer. Each product can have up to six images. Once you have located the images that you want to add, select the check box next to the images, and click **Done**.

Select images from: My computer

Upload Image

Image to add: Browse...

Add image to: Online Image Folder

Image caption:

Notes:

Done Cancel

FIGURE 8-10 Add your product image and caption in the Add Images To Product dialog box.

NOTE Until you've added images specifically to your Office Live Small Business site, no images will be available through the Online Image Folder selection.

3. Click the Browse button and navigate to the folder storing the first product photo you want to add.
4. Leave the Add Image To setting at Online Image Folder, and then type a short caption for the photo in the Image Caption box.
5. Add notes about the photo if you want, or click Done to save the photo and add it to the Add Images To Product page.
6. Continue adding other photos if you like, or click Done when you are finished.

The image is added to the Add/Edit Product page listing. You can continue to add more photos or move on to the Shipping charges.

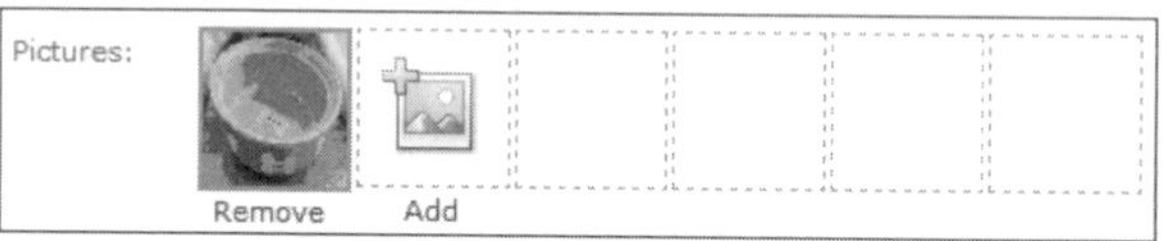

Finishing the Product Page

Now you get down to product specifics that come into play at the end of the sale. If you selected a Per Item shipping method in the Shipping section earlier, you can enter the amount you want to charge per item shipped in this box. If you want to add an overall shipping and handling fee, enter it in the Shipping Surcharge field.

Enter the weight and packaging dimensions in the next four fields (Weight, Packaging Height, Packaging Width, and Packaging Length) and then change the tax exempt status if it applies to the sales of your particular product. In the Private Notes box, you can enter notes that will not be visible to your customers (for example, "Drop price of this item in August to move inventory before the supply show in September").

Click Save to save your product page and return to the Product List page. The new product appears in the Products box, as you see in Figure 8-11.

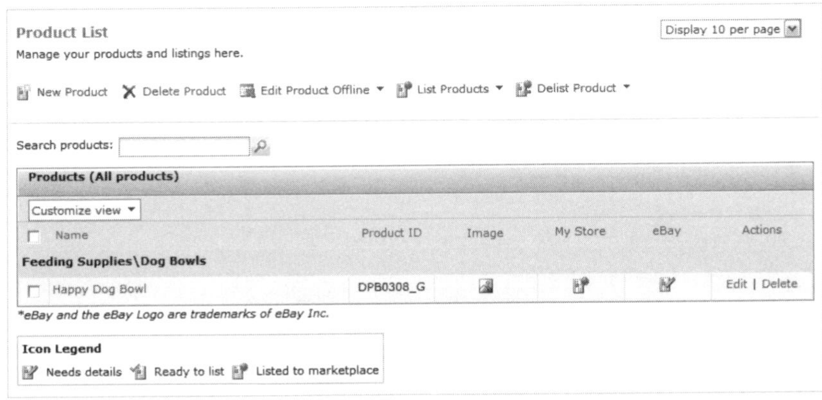

FIGURE 8-11 The product now appears on the Product List page.

Preparing to List with eBay

The icon legend on the Product List page shows that the eBay information for this product listing still needs more information. To reopen the product page, click Edit in the Actions column. In the product page, click the eBay Details tab.

If you already have an eBay account and it has been activated for Store Manager, you will see a variety of options that enable you to choose the type of sale to make (Auction, Fixed Price, or eBay Stores). You can also provide product information, starting and reserve pricing, payment methods, and shipping information (see Figure 8-12). Complete the information as you want it to appear on your eBay listing, and then click Save.

If you haven't yet set up an account with eBay, you will be prompted to do that. Click the prompt that says Click Here To Get Started With eBay! and then, on the second page, click Get Started With eBay! If you are not yet an eBay member, a window appears that gives you an opportunity to create an eBay account. Follow the prompts on the screen or enter your existing eBay information. Be sure that your eBay account is set up as a Seller's account. (You will need to provide your contact info and a credit card, but the process doesn't cost anything.) After the process is complete, you will receive an e-mail message asking you to activate your eBay account. Click the button; you can now return to the Add/Edit Product page in Office Live Small Business and click the eBay Details tab to continue adding your eBay listing information.

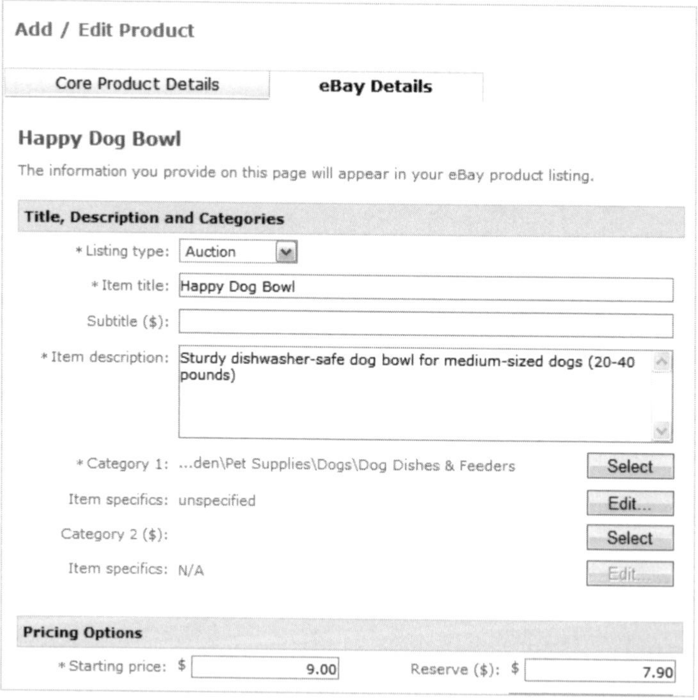

FIGURE 8-12 Fill in the eBay Details page before you save your listing.

Listing Your Products

The process of actually listing your products on your own Office Live Small Business store or your eBay account is so simple you might miss it.

Ready? In the Product List page, click the check box to the left of the item(s) you want to list. Then, in the toolbar at the top of the Product List page, click the List Products arrow. Two options appear, as shown in Figure 8-13.

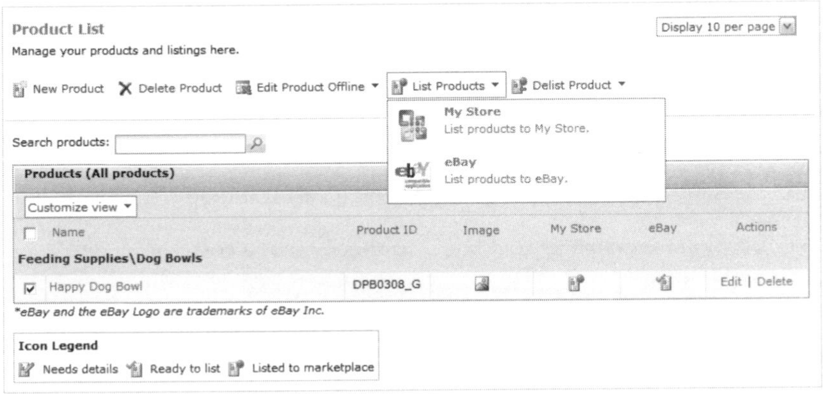

FIGURE 8-13 To list your products for sale, choose List Products.

Choose My Store to list the selected products to your own e-commerce site on Office Live Small Business. Click eBay to post the items for sale as an eBay listing.

Office Live Small Business displays a List Products dialog box (see Figure 8-14), in which you are asked to confirm the listing of products you selected. If you want to make further changes before listing, click Cancel and return to the Product List page to make the modifications you want to make. To complete the listing, click OK.

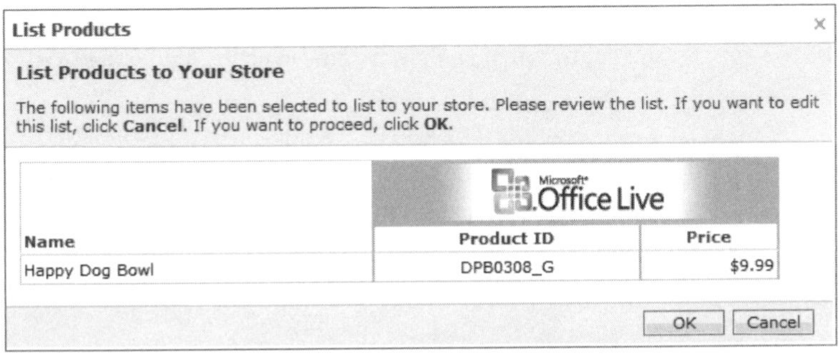

FIGURE 8-14 Office Live Small Business asks you to review the listing before it is completed.

Turning on Your Shopping Cart

Once you've added a product listing to the store on your site, you can turn on your shopping cart to make it possible for customers to purchase your product. The shopping cart experience in Office Live Small Business is simple and smooth; depending on the payment methods you selected earlier in the process, customers will be able to view and purchase your products in an easy-to-use, streamlined process.

To turn your shopping cart on, click Sell Online and then click Turn On Your Shopping Cart in the Getting Started area. Alternatively, you can click that option in the list of Quick Links that appears on the Sell Online page. In the Shopping Cart Options page (see Figure 8-15), you can do three things:

- Turn on your shopping cart.
- Change the message displayed when your shopping cart is turned off.
- Display a gift option that enables customers to specify that a cost not be displayed because the order is a gift.

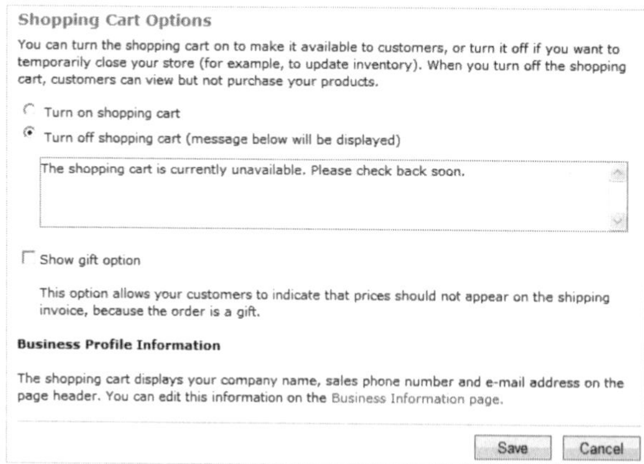

FIGURE 8-15 Change your shopping cart settings by turning on the cart, changing the display message, or activating gift options.

To turn on the shopping cart, follow these steps:

1. Click Turn On Shopping Cart and, if desired, select the Show Gift Option check box.
2. Click Save to save your changes.

Activating Your Store

The last step of adding e-commerce to your Office Live Small Business site involves going live with your store. It's a big moment! And the process is simple.

To activate your store, follow these steps:

1. Click Sell Online and choose Activate Your Store in the Getting Started area.
2. The Activate My Store page appears, warning you that any unsaved changed in your Product List or detail pages will be lost. If you're unsure whether you saved your latest changes, click Cancel, return to the Product List page, and click Save.
3. When you're ready to activate the store, click Activate Now.

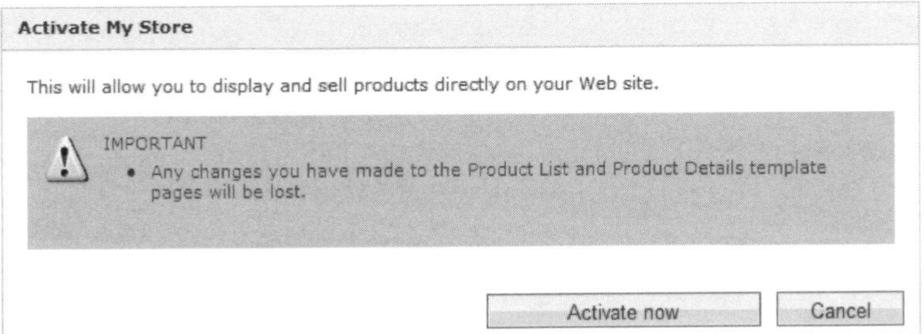

You are taken to the Web Site page of your Office Live Small Business account so that you can view the new Product List page and the items you have listed for sale. Test out the new products, click all links, and click Add To Cart to go through the sales experience your customers will have. Congratulations! You are now the proud owner of an e-commerce Web site!

TEN TIPS TO INCREASE ONLINE SALES

1. **Know your audience.** At the heart of every transaction is good communication—something was offered (you posted your products in your Office Live Small Business store), and something was accepted (when your customer bought your product). In order to make that transaction happen, customers need to know clearly what you're offering and why it should appeal to them. In order to sell effectively to those customers, you have to know who they are, what they want, what they expect to see, and what kind of information they want to find in a product listing. If you do your homework and know what types of product listings resonate with your target audience, you can tailor your own product listings in a similar way and increase your chances of big-time sales success.
2. **Write great copy.** Along with what your customers want to see goes the question of how they want to see it. Depending on the type of products you sell, your customers might like an irreverent sense of humor (or not). They might be "touchy-feely" (or not); they might want to hear solid, reliable, secure undertones in your copy (if you give "touchy-feely" text to a banking crowd, they might be concerned about the accuracy or security of your product).
3. **Include quality photos.** Don't post a photo about any product that presents it in anything less than the best possible light. Why? Because that subpar photo may be the one your customer uses to make a purchasing decision. When a customer is looking at the products on your site (Congratulations! That's half the battle), make sure you're displaying the best possible quality for that small moment of attention you're getting. Remember, the average consumer looks at a page for only a few seconds before deciding whether to look closer or click away. A good photo appearing in those few seconds may persuade your customer to stick around for a better look.
4. **Answer users' questions.** Consumers are much more comfortable purchasing online today than they were a few years ago, but people still want their questions answered. Include a FAQ page on your site so customers can see you're anticipating their questions and care about answering them.
5. **Show that you're trustworthy.** Everything on your site tells a customer whether you're a good purchasing risk or not. If your pages are professionally done, your links work, your text reads well, and your photos are strong, all those almost subliminal pieces of information reinforce the idea that you're a reputable seller. Uneven page design, oddly worded copy, missing or broken links, and mom-and-pop looking photo selections can detract from the overall trustworthiness of your site. And that can translate directly into dollars spent on online purchases.

6. **Help provide a safe user experience.** Office Live Small Business helps safeguard your users' data by partnering with PayPal to enhance the security of financial transactions. Adding similar security protection can be an expensive undertaking if you're creating a site with an independent ISP.
7. **Make the process intuitive.** Office Live Small Business helps you create an easy-to-use shopping cart and purchasing experience. Be sure to regularly review the sales experience from the customer's point of view so that you can be confident things are working as they should and the process is as simple to follow as possible. Ask others you know—friends, peers, relatives—to test your shopping experience as well and give you feedback about areas that are difficult to understand or navigate.
8. **Let users contact you.** Customers want to know there's a real person behind the site and that they can get their questions answered in a timely way. Be sure to display contact links prominently on your site—especially on your Product List page.
9. **Promote, promote, promote.** After working on your Product List page and pulling together great photos and copy for your catalog, you may be so excited about opening your online store that you forget about another important piece: online marketing. Although there is that common saying, "If you build it, they will come," that doesn't necessarily hold true in online sales. In order to build and increase the sales you make online, you need to market your site and products to the masses, using search ads, e-mail marketing, and more. (Luckily, the next chapter takes you right into this very topic.)
10. **Ask "How did we do?"** Be careful not to assume that you're doing a great job in online sales just because you're not hearing any complaints from customers. Take the initiative to ask people who've purchased something from your site to rate their sales experience. Be prepared for honest—and not all positive—feedback, and make changes to improve your process.

What's Next

In this chapter, you walked through the process of adding e-commerce capabilities to your Office Live Small Business site. You also learned how to prepare and list products on eBay from within your Office Live Small Business account. The next chapter continues building the momentum by using Web ads, e-mail marketing, and more to shine a spotlight on your site.

Promoting Your Business

IN THIS CHAPTER, YOU WILL

- Advertise on the Web.
- Get started with online promotions.
- Set up adManager.
- Create an ad.
- Create e-mail marketing campaigns.

WE'VE ALL heard the hopeful saying, "If you build it, they will come." To one degree or another, all Web sites are built on that premise. You post a site, enhance it, and maintain it because your customers *will* come to see your products, find out about your company, and look for your smiling face. But here's the catch: Thousands of business owners like you are thinking the same thing, depending on curiosity and happenstance to lead potential customers to their sites. Luckily, there's something you can do to tip the odds in your favor. That something is called *promoting your site.*

When you think of the phrase *Web promotions*, you may get a mental image of those cheesy flashing banner ads that promise you the moon if only you'll come take their quick survey. For now, put that image out of your head. That's a gimmick, not the kind of professional promotion you need to shine a light on your site so that people will notice. Microsoft Office Live Small Business offers two simple-but-sophisticated tools you can use to help you help others find your site easily. First, we'll begin with the standard—search advertising with adManager—and we'll follow with E-Mail Marketing.

Advertising on the Web

Online advertising has been enjoying steady, healthy growth since 2002 (the year the dot-com bubble burst). According to eMarketer, an online marketing research group, 2006 spending on Web ads topped $16 million, and the 2007 data is shaping up to show more than $21 million in Web advertising alone.[1]

If you've looked into Web advertising, you may have been overwhelmed by the number of choices and range of options from which you had to select. Banner ads, leaderboards, pop-ups, CPCs—how do you find your way through the maze of terminology and know what's worth investing in and what's not?

Office Live Small Business makes it simple for you by offering two straightforward and effective Web advertising methods:

- adManager enables you to set the keywords for your site, write an ad, set a budget, and control the appearance of your site in Web search results.
- E-Mail Marketing makes it easy for you to create newsletters and e-mail marketing pieces and track the results you receive (so you can improve future marketing efforts).

WEB AD RESOURCES

If you want to know all the ins and outs of Web advertising, here are a few good sites that provide you with the basics of online marketing as well as give you access to the latest in marketing trends:

- The basics of Web advertising: *www.theindependentpublisher.com/run/making_money/advertising.shtml*
- Clickz: *www.clickz.com*
- Marketing Sherpa: *www.marketingsherpa.com*

---

1 eMarketer. 2008. *e-Marketer's Ten Key Predictions for 2008*. Available online at *www.emarketer.com/Article.aspx?id=1005790&src=article_head_sitesearch*

Getting Started with Online Promotions

You will find what you need to get started with online promotions in the Promote Your Business option in the left navigation bar on the Office Live Small Business Home page. When you click the link in the navigation bar or in the Getting Started area, the page shown in Figure 9-1 appears.

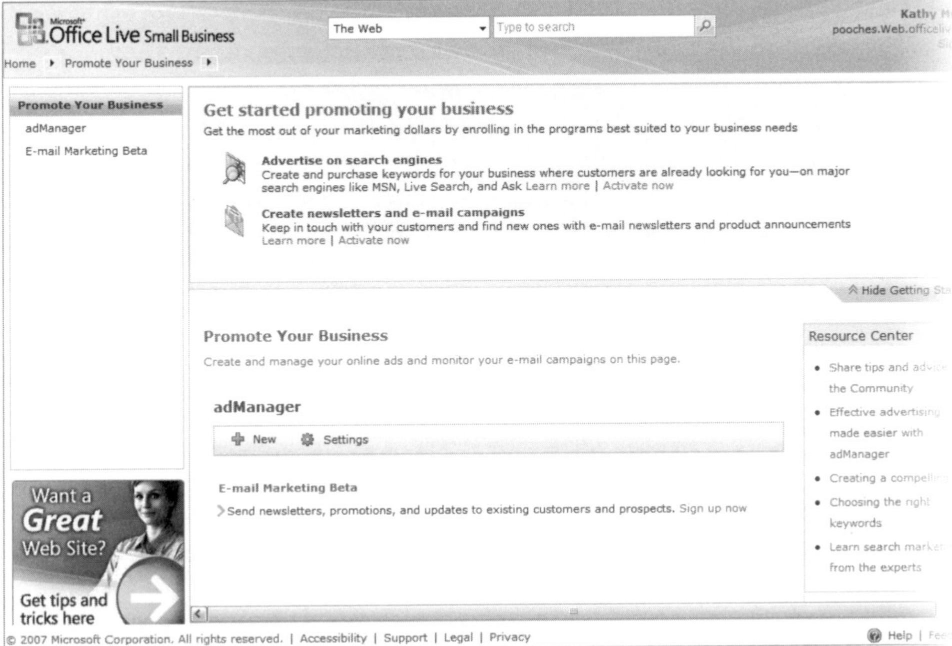

FIGURE 9-1 Choose Promote Your Business in the navigation bar or the Getting Started area to display your marketing options.

TIP

The Resource Center provides articles with tips and suggestions for using adManager and E-Mail Marketing to promote your business.

WHAT KIND OF PROMOTIONS DO YOU NEED?

Depending on the type of service or product you offer, you may want to try different types of online promotions. These questions can help you think through what might work best for your site:

- **Are you selling a product to a specific group of people?** If so, choosing your keywords carefully and using adManager to ensure good placement in search results will be important. That way, you can improve the placement your site ads get in search results—a key way to reach a specialized audience.
- **How do people find the products that are similar to yours?** Think through the ways you would find a competitor's product. What phrases would you use online to search for the product? Would you notice links or banner ads on other sites? Would you sign up for a newsletter if you thought it had something relevant to your needs?
- **Will your customers be likely to purchase from you repeatedly?** If your product or service is something that customers will want to buy regularly (for example, pet treats), consider adding a monthly e-mail newsletter or regular messages to keep that relationship going. Search placement is still important for those customers who are finding you for the first time, but e-mail marketing can help build relationships over a longer period of time.

Setting Up adManager

Both adManager and the E-Mail Marketing are add-on services in Office Live Small Business, which means that you pay an additional fee to use the services. With adManager, you set a budget for the amount you want to spend each month in search engine advertising. The cost is reasonable, and the process is simple.

To get started with adManager, follow these steps:

1. Click the Activate Now link in the Getting Started item for the service you want to add.
2. In the Ad Settings page (see Figure 9-2), click the Language arrow and choose the language in which you want your ad to appear.
3. Click the Location arrow and select whether you want the ad to appear worldwide, in specific countries or regions, or only in selected cities.

> **NOTE** Consider carefully where you want your ad to display because this can ensure that you get the most for your marketing dollar. If you have a grooming salon for pets, the best use of your advertising budget will be in displaying your ad to a local audience searching for dog grooming services. If you sell your product to a worldwide audience, Display Worldwide would be the better choice.

4. If you selected Select Countries Or Regions or Select Cities, additional lists will appear so that you can choose the countries, regions, or cities where you want the ad to appear. Click the country or city you want; then click Add to add it to the Selected list.

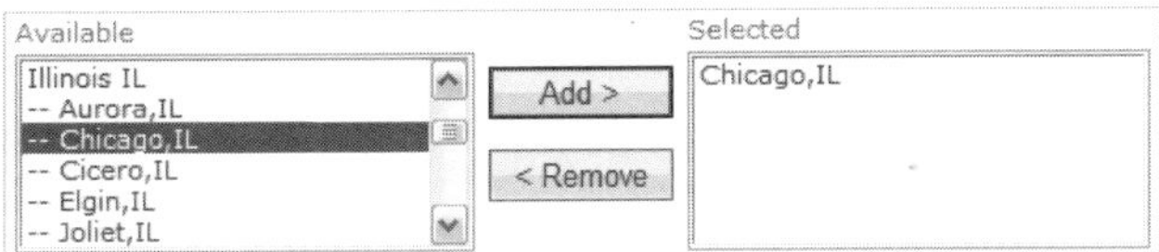

5. Click OK to save your settings.
6. In the Search Engine Accounts And Budget area, two search engines are displayed: Live Search and Ask Sponsored Listings Network. Click Set Up Account for the Live Search item.
7. Verify or enter your contact information and click OK.
8. Enter a user name, enter a password, and choose and answer a secret question, as shown in Figure 9-3. Click OK.
9. Enter your payment information, including your name, credit card type, credit card number, expiration, and verification number. Note that adManager will charge a one-time $5.00 activation fee. Click OK.
10. Enter a monthly budget amount. You can enter anything from $2.00 to $10,000.00. As your site is displayed in search results, your credit card will be charged only up to the amount you specify here. Click OK.

11. Review the Microsoft Terms And Conditions, click the check box, and click Finish.

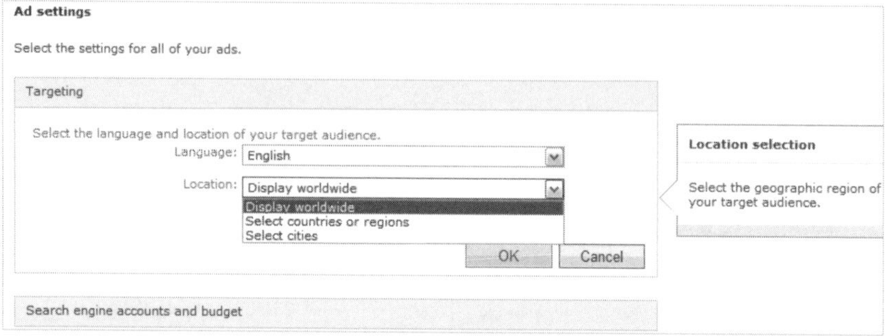

FIGURE 9-2 As you set up adManager, choose the language and location in which you want your ads to appear.

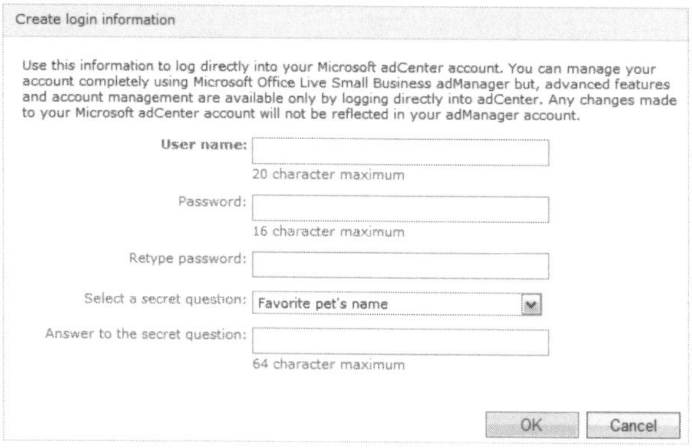

FIGURE 9-3 Create your account for the search engine on which you want to advertise.

Congratulations! You've just activated adManager, and now you're ready to create your first ad.

Creating an Ad

Before you jump right in and create your first ad, it is a good idea to do a little homework and see what others are including in their ads. What seems to work well and what doesn't?

If you're using Windows Internet Explorer 7 or 8, click New Tab or press Ctrl+T. If you're using an earlier browser, leave Office Live Small Business open in the current window and open another browser instance. In the new window, go to *www.live.com* and enter a search word or phrase that is similar to the keywords you plan to use on your own site. Click Search. A page similar to the one shown in Figure 9-4 appears.

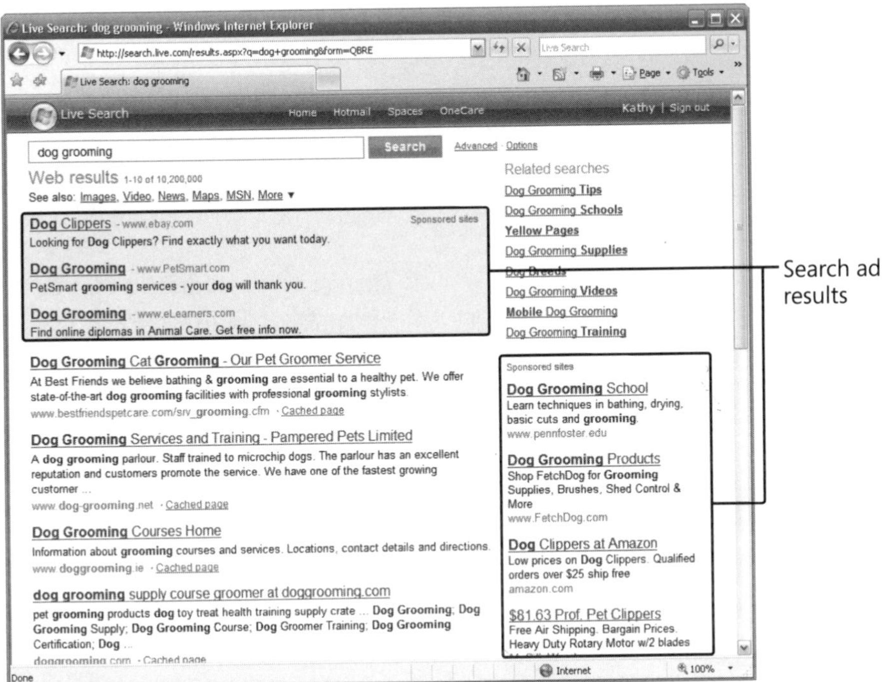

FIGURE 9-4 Notice how your competitors use search ads.

Review the ads and notice the following items:

- The number of words used in the heading
- How often the search phrase appears in the ad
- The number of words in the text description
- Whether the price of the item appears in the link
- What audience the ad seems to be targeted for
- Which ads sound reputable and which do not
- How much detail each description includes

After you finish reviewing the ad results, return to Office Live Small Business and prepare to create your ad. Here are the steps:

1. In the Ad page, click in the Headline box. Type a headline for the ad that displays what you want your potential customers to notice first about your ad (see Figure 9-5). The headline you enter can be up to 25 characters in length.

2. Click in the Line 1 Text box. Enter a description of your product or service (up to 34 characters).
3. Click in the Line 2 Text box. Type a second line of text, if desired—this line can be up to 35 characters in length.
4. Check the URL that appears in the Display URL box. (Your Office Live Small Business Web address will appear automatically here.)
5. Click in the Destination URL box if you want to change it. This address is the page potential customers will see when they click the link in your ad. The Preview box shows how your ad will look.
6. Click OK to save your ad.

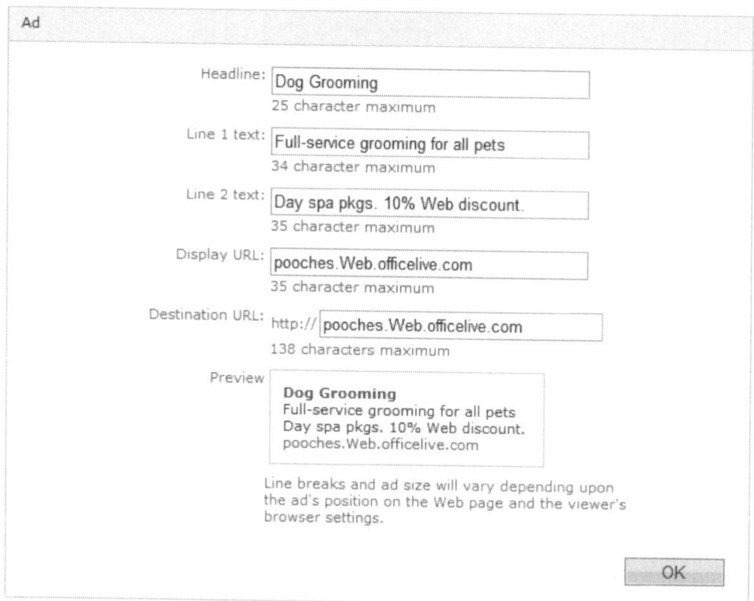

FIGURE 9-5 Enter the description for your ad and notice how it appears in the Preview box.

DOS AND DON'TS FOR AD COPY

There are some rules that govern the type of content you can put in your ads. Keep these items in mind as you draft the text for your search ad:

- Avoid using inappropriate or illegal content or references in your ads.
- Be sure to follow through with your promises. For example, if you advertise a discount for Web purchases, feature that discount prominently on your site so that customers see the offer when they arrive.
- Leave out unnecessary punctuation (especially exclamation points).
- Be truthful in your advertising and make sure your product descriptions accurately reflect what you offer.
- Make sure the ad is unique; adManager does not allow duplicate listings.

Selecting Keywords for Your Ad

Your next step is to choose the keywords, the words your customers and potential clients will enter in the Search box when they are looking for what you have to offer. Choosing the right keywords has a direct impact on the success of your ad—if you choose keywords that match the words and phrases customers will enter in the Search box, your ad will appear in the search results they see.

TIP

Before selecting or adding keywords for your ad, talk with others in your business, or ask friends and relatives how they would be likely to search online if they were looking for a product or service like yours. Be sure to include those words as well as possible alternate phrasing (for example, a customer might search for "dog grooming" or "pet grooming" or "flea baths").

The Select Keywords page (see Figure 9-6) appears after you click OK in the Ad page. On the left side of the page, adManager lists some words and phrases that are already part of your site. Scroll through the list and click any of the words you want to use as keywords. You can also click in the Type Your Own Keyword box and enter a keyword not reflected in the list. Click Add to add the keyword to the My Keywords list on the right side of the page. Continue adding keywords until you've included all words and phrases that accurately reflect your site.

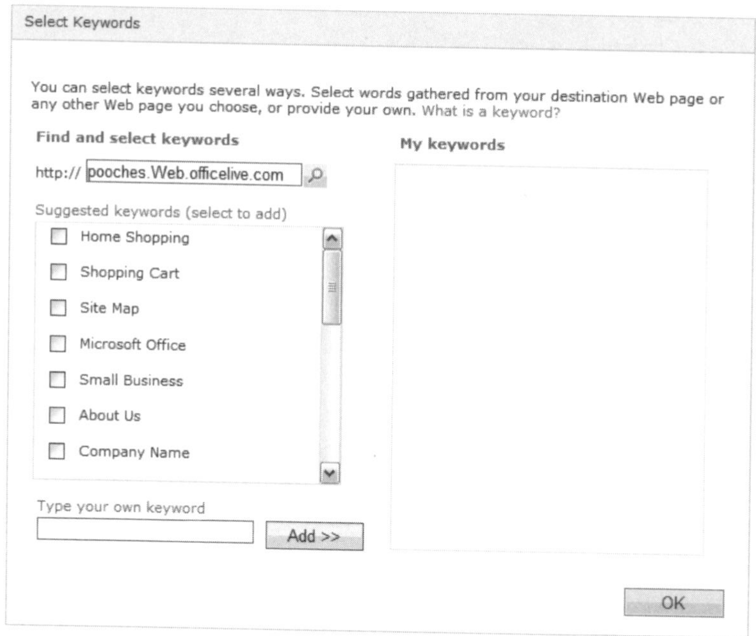

FIGURE 9-6 Choose keywords from the list or type your own on the Select Keywords page.

The Set Your Keyword Pricing page (see Figure 9-7) enables you to enter a specific bid amount for each keyword you've entered. You can control the amount you spend for each keyword in your list. (You can also click Delete if you decide you don't want to use a specific keyword after all.) adManager will enter recommendations for you if you click the Recommend Prices button. The recommendations are not bottom-dollar prices; they are prices that will be competitive with other ad services, meaning that you will get a higher ad placement in a results list if you enter an amount close to the recommended price.

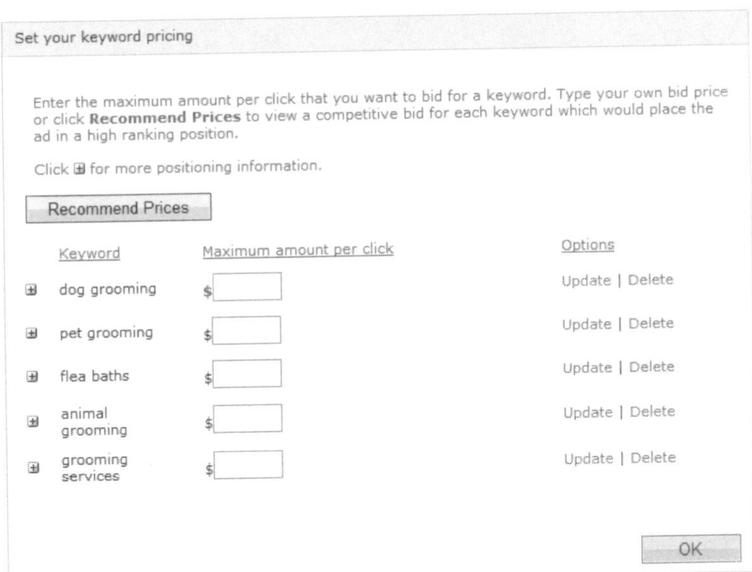

FIGURE 9-7 Office Live Small Business can recommend competitive pricing for you to ensure higher placement in search results.

> **NOTE** Office Live Small Business will alert you if the prices you entered (either by typing the amounts in the blanks or clicking Recommend Prices) exceed the budget you have established for your adManager account. You can then either change the per-click amounts or increase your budget.

When you are happy with the amounts you've set for your keyword pricing, click OK. The next page displays an overview of all your choices up to this point in the process. Review all the information displayed for you and click Finish to complete the process.

Displaying Ad Summaries

After you create and choose keywords for your search ad, it appears on the Ad Summary Page (see Figure 9-8). This listing shows all the ads you are currently using and lets you know how many times the ad has been viewed, how many times it's been clicked, and how much you've spent on the ad.

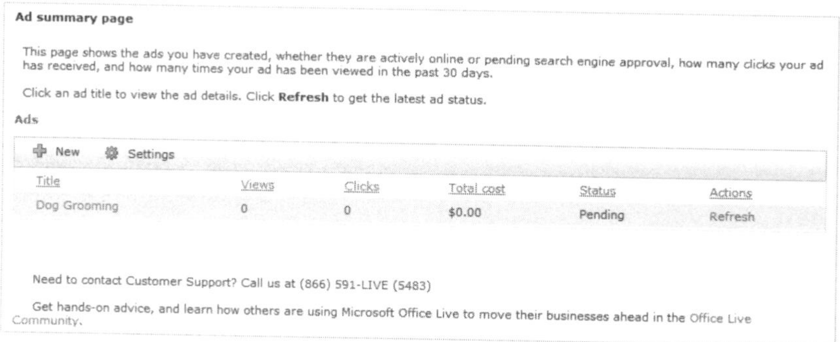

FIGURE 9-8 Get quick information about the status and effectiveness of your ads on the Ad Summary page.

Reporting Ad Results

A big part of making your adManager program successful involves keeping an eye on the kinds of results you get and adjusting your keywords, advertising budget, or search engines as needed. By creating reports based on your search result data, you can find out the following information:

- Which keywords users are responding to
- How many of the people seeing your ads are actually clicking them
- What percentage of visitors are purchasing your products
- Which search engines give you the best results

To create adManager reports, follow these steps:

1. From the Office Live Small Business Home page, click Promote Your Business.
2. Click adManager.
3. Click Reports. adManager gives you two options at this point:
   - Keyword Detail displays information about the keywords that are working effectively for your site.
   - Keyword By Engine enables you to see how many of your ads translated to clicks that brought users to your site.

4. Click the report you want to run and click the arrow to display the list of possible views (see Figure 9-9).

5. Click the view you want and click Go.

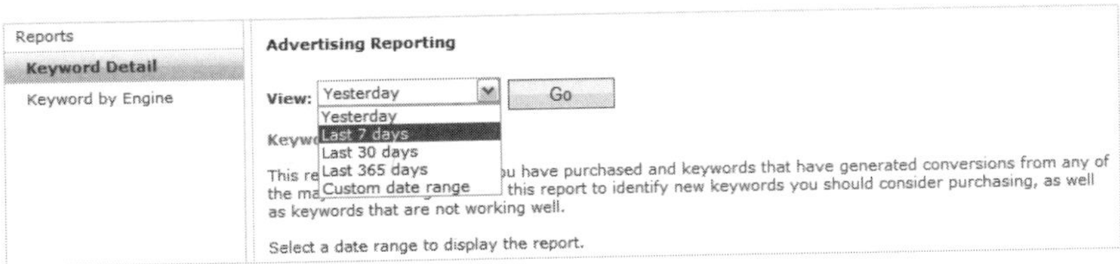

FIGURE 9-9 Choose options on the Advertising Reporting page and create a report that shows the results of your Web advertising.

NOTE Some views may not be available, depending on the length of time adManager has been available on your site.

Creating E-Mail Marketing Campaigns

The E-Mail Marketing feature enables you to create e-mail newsletters and targeted e-mail messages that spread the word about your business to up to 200 contacts per month. You can send up to 200 messages per month at no cost, with a $.05 cost per message for messages over 200.

Activating E-Mail Marketing

Your first step in adding E-Mail Marketing to your promotion services involves clicking Promote Your Business from the Office Live Small Business Home page and clicking E-Mail Marketing. The page displays an overview of the feature and offers you an Activate Now button. Click it to get started, and then follow these steps:

1. If necessary, log in using your Windows Live ID and password.

2. Your account information appears as you've entered it for Office Live Small Business. Review your information, and enter payment information as needed. Click Save And Continue.

NOTE You will be asked to enter credit card information even though the service is currently free of charge.

3. After reviewing your information, click Complete My Order.
4. Click the Return To Office Live button.

The Office Live Small Business Home page appears.

Creating a Campaign

Now, when you click Promote Your Business from the Office Live Small Business Home page, E-Mail Marketing is available to you. The process of creating a new campaign in E-Mail Marketing involves choosing the people you want to receive the communication, adding the content, and choosing when you want the message to be delivered. To create an E-Mail Marketing campaign, follow these steps:

1. Click Create Campaign to get started. The Create Campaign page (see Figure 9-10) appears.

TIP After you click Create Campaign, E-Mail Marketing enables you to click an Add button to select the groups of contacts you want to include as recipients. You might have already entered these contacts in Contact Manager; if not, you can import them from other data files. For more about working with your business contacts in Office Live Small Business, see Chapter 10, "Working with Business Applications."

2. Click Add. The Add Subscribers By Group dialog box (see Figure 9-11) appears.
3. Select the check box to the left of the group you want to send the campaign to. Click OK.
4. In the Campaign Details dialog box (see Figure 9-12), enter the information you want to appear in the From and Subject lines. Also be sure to enter an e-mail address for replies.

5. If you want to track the effectiveness of your e-mail campaign, leave click tracking set to Yes. This tracks the number of times recipients click links in the e-mail message they receive.
6. Click the Design Your Campaign link. The Campaign Editor opens.
7. In the Campaign Editor, follow the text prompts to add a title, a tag line, and content for your e-mail newsletter.
8. Similar to the tools available in the Web Design utility, the tools in the Campaign Editor enable you to choose the format of text, add images and tables, and insert links and lines. Customize the content to reflect the message you want to send. Click Save to save your changes.
9. Click View to see how the newsletter will look to the message recipients.
10. When you are happy with the way the newsletter looks, click the Close box.
11. Back in the Campaign Details area, click OK.
12. The Test Campaign And Schedule Delivery area appears. Enter an e-mail address you want to use to test the newsletter. Click Send Test.

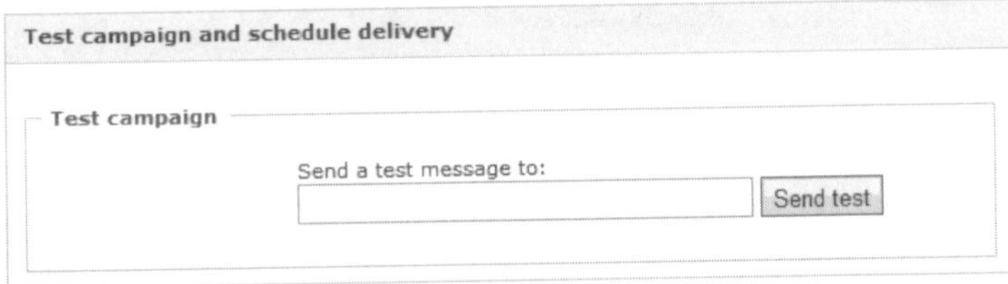

13. After you receive the test message and have approved the content and layout, you are ready to schedule the final distribution of the campaign. In the Schedule Delivery area (see Figure 9-13), choose whether you want to save the campaign for later, send it immediately, or schedule it for a specific date and time. Click the Calendar tool to choose the date for scheduling.
14. After you choose your delivery schedule, click OK to save your campaign.

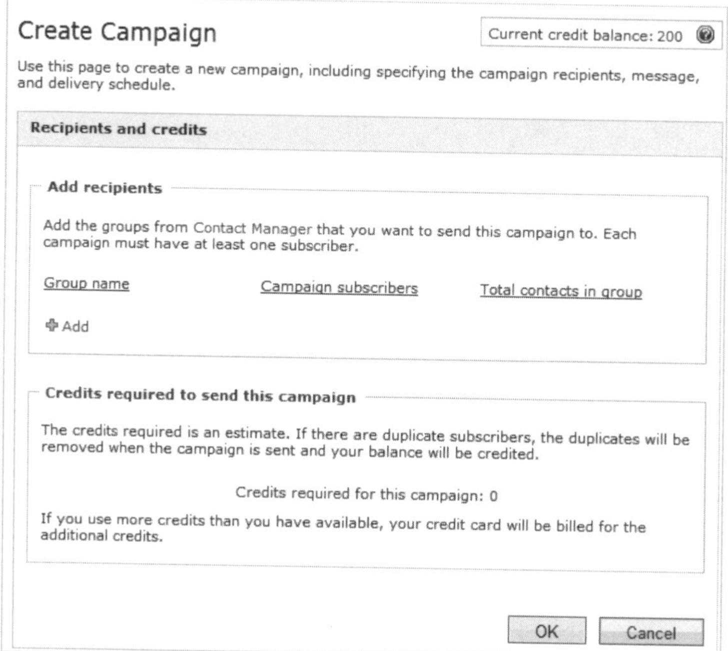

FIGURE 9-10 Use the Create Campaign page to choose recipients, select content, and set the delivery timeframe.

Add Subscribers by Group

Select the groups that you want to send this campaign to. If a subscriber is in multiple groups, the duplicate will be removed when the campaign is sent.

Group name	Campaign subscribers	Total contacts in group
☑ Customer	0	1
☐ Employee	0	0
☑ Lead or Prospect	0	1
☐ Newsletter Subscriber	0	0
☐ Vendor	0	0

Refresh OK Cancel

FIGURE 9-11 Select the groups you want to receive the e-mail marketing piece.

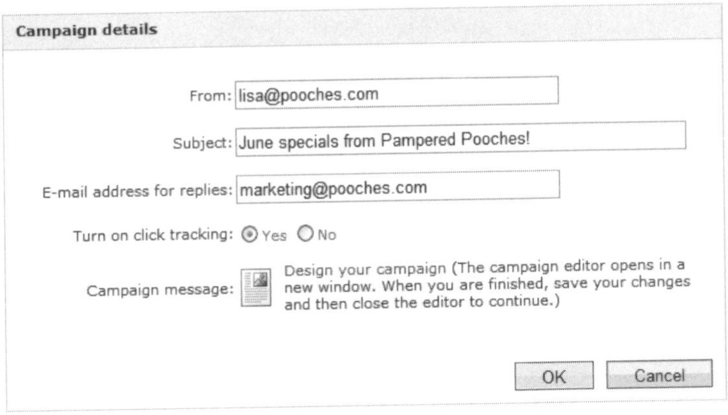

FIGURE 9-12 Add the From and Subject lines and choose whether you want the message clicks to be tracked.

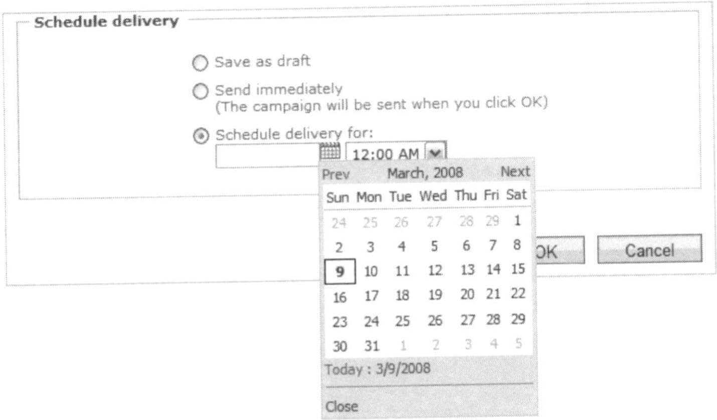

FIGURE 9-13 After you proof the campaign message, schedule the delivery.

The Campaign Details page appears, providing you with a quick overview of the choices you've made for the campaign. You'll see the Subject, the From e-mail address, the date and time the campaign is scheduled to be delivered, and the number of recipients who will receive the message. Click the Back To Your Campaigns button to return to a page listing the active campaigns in use with your site. This page displays all campaigns, the number of recipients receiving them, how many clicks have been generated, and whether any recipients have clicked the Unsubscribe link to remove themselves from your contacts list.

YOU KNOW YOU NEED TO ADVERTISE WHEN…

The choice about when to add advertising to your overall business strategy is sometimes a scary one for new business owners. Do you really need to advertise? Or should you just wait a little longer for your idea to catch on? What time is the right time—and how do you know?

Your decision may be influenced by a number of factors. Knowing things like what percentage of your sales come solely from your Web site is important. If you rely completely on your site for sales, you should be advertising from day one. If, on the other hand, you have a reliable stream of steady customers walking into your bakery every day and you simply want to augment that flow of traffic by making orders available online, you may not be in as much of a hurry to launch Web advertising and e-mail marketing strategies. In that case, adding the search ad and newsletter marketing features become important when you are ready to really grow your on-line presence and to expand and enhance your relationships with existing clients. They may not be as vitally important to keeping your business doors open.

Here are a few general guidelines for when you might seriously want to consider investing in the low-cost, low-risk promotion features offered in Office Live Small Business:

- **Word-of-mouth marketing doesn't seem to be working.** You've sent your business URL to all your friends and family, and asked the people close to you to chat up your new business and encourage people to come by for a look. But your Web stats are disappointing, and few people seem to be making the click to come to your site. Maybe it's time to go where the people are and to show them, through search ad results, that you have something that they're looking for.

- **Your main competitor is growing (and with an ugly Web site, too) and your own business isn't**. It's always a good idea to know who your competitors are and keep an eye on their progress online. If they seem to be enjoying an upswing in business while you hang on the low end of the curve, you may want to consider a few well-targeted keywords within a budget you can afford that put you on the page with the potential customers you're there to serve.
- **You have been relying heavily on print ads (expensive and time-consuming) and they aren't bringing good results.** Print ads are getting increasingly expensive and they can be hard to track. An e-mail marketing campaign is much easier, simple to modify, and low-cost. Plus, you can use the same campaign numerous times to different audiences, testing results from different customer groups, using slightly different messages.
- **You've reached a stage of readiness in your business where you're doing well with the customers you have and you're ready for more**. If you're just plain ready for more business and are happy with the growth you've had so far, why not create a budget you can afford and see what happens with search advertising and e-mail marketing? The costs—in time, money, and effort—are low, and you potentially can reap a big benefit: more customers, better relationships, and ongoing information that helps you continue to fine-tune, improve, and enhance the ads and marketing materials you produce.

What's Next

This chapter introduced you to two great (that is, low-risk and low-cost) promotion features in Office Live Small Business: adManager and E-Mail Marketing. The next chapter shows you how to get full benefit from the range of support Office Live Small Business offers you by exploring the Business Applications available as part of the core services.

Working with Business Applications

IN THIS CHAPTER, YOU WILL

- Get a quick look at business applications.
- Get started with Contact Manager.
- Work with Document Manager.
- Use the Team Workspace.
- Add other business applications.

YOU MAY be surprised to learn that once you get your business Web site up and running, open an e-commerce store, know how to work with e-mail and instant messaging, and learn how to market your business using adManager and E-Mail Marketing, you've only scratched the surface of the ways in which Microsoft Office Live Small Business can help you manage and promote your business. Sound impossible? This chapter focuses on the business applications that are available to you—free—as part of your Office Live Small Business core services.

A Quick Look at Business Applications

All businesses—like all business owners—are unique, so Office Live Small Business leaves it up to you to pick and choose from among the variety of applications you'd like to add to your account. You will find a few business applications set up for you by default, however. The business applications that are ready to use when you create an account in Office Live Small Business include these:

- Contact Manager, a customer-relationship management application that enables you to track all kinds of customer contacts, creating accounts, opportunities, products, and more

- Document Manager, a ready-made document library you can use to store, organize, and share files that are important for your business
- Team Workspace, a utility that enables your team to gather and share announcements, schedules, tasks, and links, whether you work across the office or around the globe

In addition to these three applications, you can tailor the services you need by adding any of the following business applications to your version of Office Live Small Business:

- Project Manager
- Time Manager
- Company Assets
- Competition Tracker
- Customer Support
- Employee Directory
- Estimates
- Expenses
- Jobs and Hiring
- Training
- Customer Workspace
- Basic Meeting Workspace
- Decision Meeting Workspace
- Social Meeting Workspace
- Wiki Workspace
- Blog

NOTE The blog feature in Office Live Small Business is not a public blog, like Windows Live Spaces, but rather an intranet/extranet blog you can use with password protection for your team workspace.

Because Contact Manager is such a far-reaching application, it has its own spot on the Office Live Small Business navigation bar. We'll start here. You'll find the other included programs by clicking Business Applications.

Getting Started with Contact Manager

Thriving businesses usually have something in common: They offer excellent customer service. If you want to make sure your customers know they are first in your book, treat them well by knowing who they are, following up on your promises, keeping track of their questions and purchases, and making online experiences on your site as easy for them as possible.

To take good care of your customers, you need to know who they are—and that's where Contact Manager really shines. Contact Manager in Office Live Small Business is a powerful (but free!) application that enables you to collect, organize, update, and follow up on the contacts that are the heart of your business.

With Contact Manager, you can organize and track information in a variety of ways, all designed to help you serve your customers better. This section introduces you to the features in Contact Manager you are likely to use most often. Click Contact Manager in the left navigation bar to get started.

Exploring the Contact Manager Window

The Contact Manager window (see Figure 10-1) provides all the tools you need to create, organize, and track contacts in Office Live Small Business. The navigation bar on the left gives you the tools for displaying different customer groups (after you create them, of course) and displaying information about personal contacts, companies, opportunities, and products.

The center column of the Contact Manager window displays a list of your current contacts. Below the Get Started With Contact Manager help box, you'll find the quick Add Contact box, which enables you to add basic customer information quickly. Finally, the column on the right side of the window shows you which team members are logged into the site and what items, if any, are shared with your Web site.

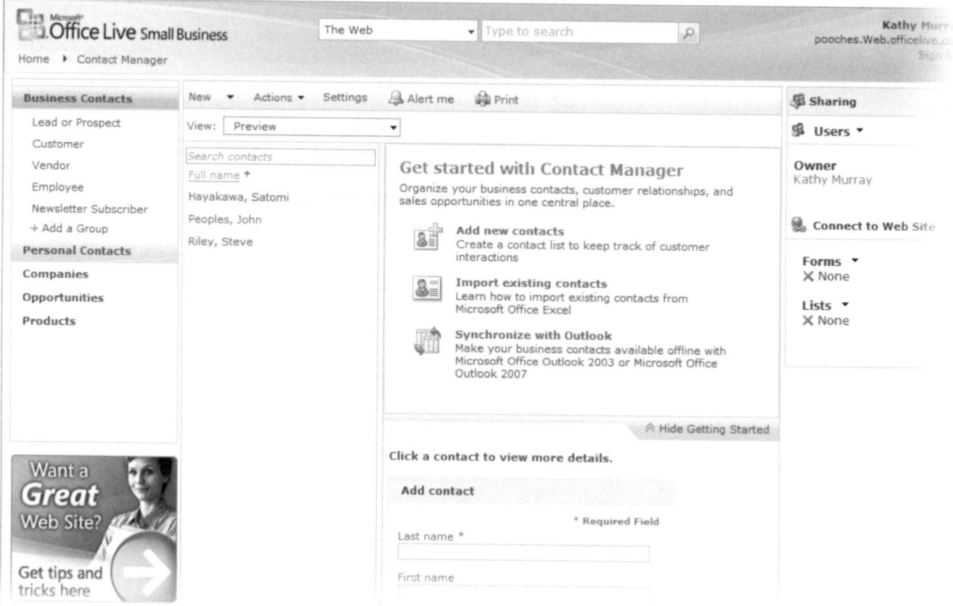

FIGURE 10-1 Contact Manager gives you a professional way to organize, track, and manage contact information for customers, vendors, and team members.

One of the first things you'll want to do in Contact Manager involves adding new contacts to your contacts list. Click the New arrow to display the options you need to create a new contact (see Figure 10-2).

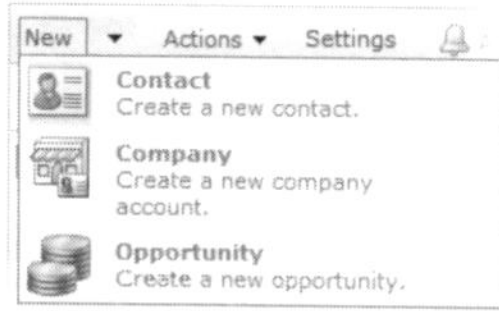

FIGURE 10-2 You can create a new contact, company, or opportunity in Contact Manager.

You can choose to add a contact, a company, or an opportunity. Here's what each of those items means in Contact Manager:

- A contact is an individual customer record that stores name, e-mail, address, and much more.
- A company account has vendor or client information and includes business contacts together in one company group.

- An opportunity enables you to create an item that tracks a bid, proposal, or sale that's in progress. You connect the opportunity to either a company account or an individual contact so that it gets tracked in Contact Manager.

Creating a New Contact

You'll create a new contact when you have information about a specific individual you want to add to your contact list. Suppose you just met someone at the coffee shop who might be interested in your product. You can create a new contact for him or her by using the information from a business card. Or perhaps someone new just ordered from your Web site. You can add that information directly into your Contact Manager so that you can follow up with future mailings and e-marketing pieces.

To add a contact in Contact Manager, follow these steps:

1. Click Contact Manager in the left navigation bar of the Office Live Small Business Home page.
2. Click the New arrow.
3. Click Contact. The New Contact window appears, as shown in Figure 10-3.

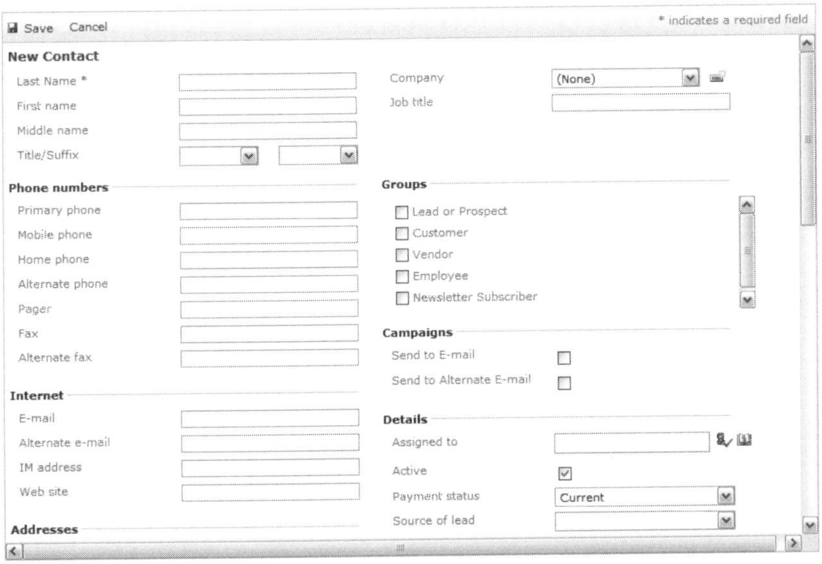

FIGURE 10-3 The New Contact window enables you to record all information you have about a new customer or vendor.

4. Click in the Last Name field and enter the contact's information. Press Tab to move through the boxes and fill in all the information you have available.
5. In the Groups area, click the check box of any group you want to add the contact to.
6. In the Campaigns area, click whether you want e-mail messages sent to the contact's primary or alternate e-mail address.

NOTE The e-mail and alternate e-mail addresses appear in the Internet area of the New Contact form.

7. Scroll down the page to display the Addresses, Personal, Activity, and Comments areas. Continue adding information as needed.
8. Click Save at the top of the form to save the new contact.

Creating a Company Account

The individual contact records are the building blocks that make up your contact management system, but creating company accounts enables you to group individual contacts and track your relationship with the entire company. Create a new company account by following these steps:

1. Click the New arrow and choose Company. The New Company window appears.
2. In the Company data fields, add all information that is relevant for your business.
3. In the Company Details area, you can assign a specific staff person to the new company account by clicking Check Names to the right of the Assigned To box; then choose the staff member from the list. Also in this area you can select whether the company is in good standing and indicate whether its accounts are current or overdue.
4. Scroll down to the Business Contacts area. In this section, you can add individual contacts into the company group by clicking Add New or Add Existing. Add New enables you to create a new contact entry for an individual and add it to the company group at the same time. Add Existing lets you add an existing contact to this company group. Click the check box of the contact you want to add and click OK.
5. Click Save to add the new company account.

Creating an Opportunity

All business owners love opportunities—they are those hopeful possibilities that can mean the next big client, an award-winning project, or professional acclaim for your business. Office Live Small Business enables you to keep track of your opportunities, which helps you think them through carefully and keep an eye on their progress. Here's how to create an opportunity:

1. Click the New arrow and choose Opportunity. The New Opportunity window appears, as shown in Figure 10-4.

2. Enter a title for the opportunity in the Opportunity Title box. For example, Pampered Pooches might use a title such as "Groomer training."

3. Click whether the opportunity relates to a company or a contact. After you make your selection, click the down arrow and choose the name of the company or contact from the list. This connects the opportunity to that company or contact's record.

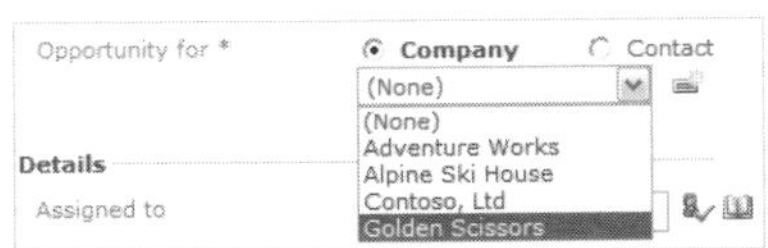

4. In the Status area, click the Sales Stage arrow and choose where you are in this opportunity process. You can choose from Prospecting, Qualification, Need Analysis, Proposal/Price Quote, Negotiation/Review, Closed Won, or Closed Lost.

Save Cancel
* indicates a re

New Opportunity
Opportunity title *
Opportunity for * Company Contact (None)

Status
Sales stage Prospecting
Probability 0.00 %
Close date 3/23/2008

Revenue
Total value 0.00
Total discount 0.00
Revenue forecast 0.00

Details
Assigned to
Payment terms None
Opportunity type Standard
Source
Competition
Delivery date
Expiration date

Products
+ Add new product + Add existing product
There are no items to show in this view of the "Opportunity Product" list.

FIGURE 10-4 Create an opportunity to track a proposal, bid, or project with a company or contact.

5. Add the Close Date if applicable, and fill in all other data as needed in the Revenue and Details areas.

6. In the Products area, you can add the specific products you are presenting to this client as part of the opportunity. You can add a new product by clicking Add New Product or select a product you've previously added by clicking Add Existing Product.

SEE ALSO The next section, "Adding a Product," shows you how to add a product to Contact Manager.

7. Click Save to save the opportunity and affiliate it with the company or contact you selected. This new opportunity will now appear in the Activity area of the company or contact.

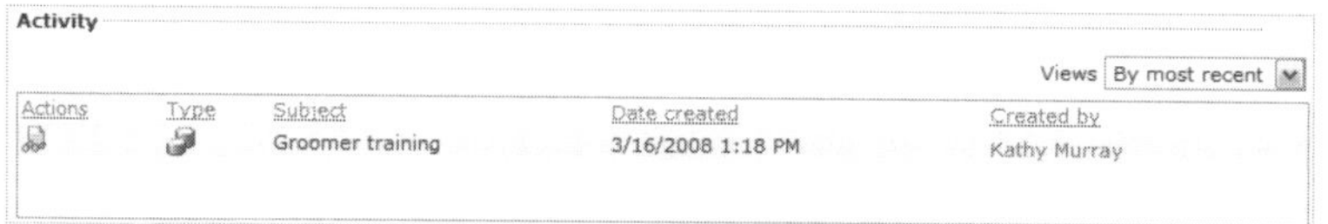

Adding a Product

Office Live Small Business also enables you to keep track of specific products in your product line. By creating product listings, you can stay on top of inventory, costs, discounts, and more. You can also import product listings from data sheets and spreadsheets and then export the information as needed—a great help for a small-business owner trying to single-handedly keep inventory and sales under control.

You can add a new product by clicking Add New Product in the Products area of the New Opportunity window or by clicking Products in the left navigation bar of the Contact Manager window, clicking the New arrow, and then choosing New Item.

In the New Product window (see Figure 10-5), enter the name of the product, a description, and the quantity you have on hand. In the Details area, enter the unit cost, unit price, and your discount percentage; and indicate whether the item is subject to a sales tax.

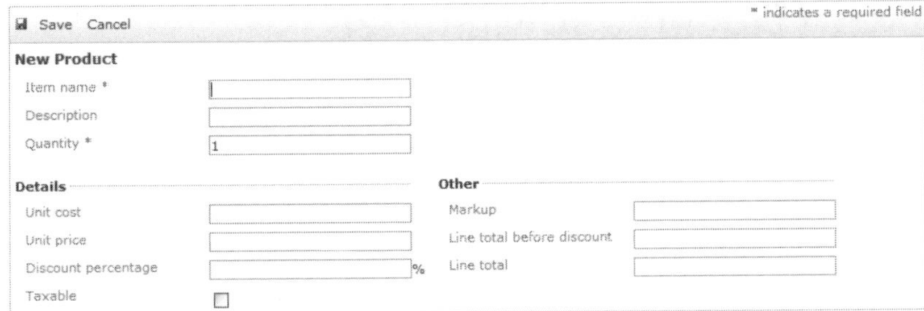

FIGURE 10-5 Enter your product in the New Product window to make it available when you add opportunities.

The Markup information items are calculated automatically for you to let you know how much you've invested in inventory for this item and how much you stand to gain at the point of sale.

Click Save to add the product to your available list. Now this product will be available when you click Add Existing Product in the Opportunities window.

A Quick Look at the Business Applications Window

As mentioned earlier in this chapter, you find all the other business applications by clicking Business Applications in the left navigation bar of the Office Live Small Business Home page.

The Business Applications page offers you a familiar layout. The Get Started area lists resources for the main tasks you're likely to try with the business applications. The Business Applications view in the lower portion of the window displays information from Document Manager by default. You can change what's shown here by clicking the links to the right of the Business Applications heading.

Working with Document Manager

Office Live Small Business makes it easy for you to work as a team—whether you are continually traveling from state to state and country to country or your staff is scattered around the world. If you have access to a Web browser, you can log in to your Office Live Small Business account and check your sales, send messages to customers, and work with your team.

One part of running a business remotely involves the ability to access, update, and share business-critical documents with others. You might be working on a draft of the business plan you need to share with your finance manager. Or perhaps you've just finished a new Microsoft Office PowerPoint presentation your field staff person has been waiting for. You can use Document Manager to upload, organize, and share the files your other team members need to help keep your business moving in a profitable direction.

Document Manager includes tools that enable you to do the following:

- Upload documents and pictures.
- Export documents and lists.
- Revise documents and pictures.
- Create customized libraries and folders for specialized documents.

Click Document Manager in the Business Applications window to display the program (see Figure 10-6). The documents are displayed in list form so that you can view and use them easily.

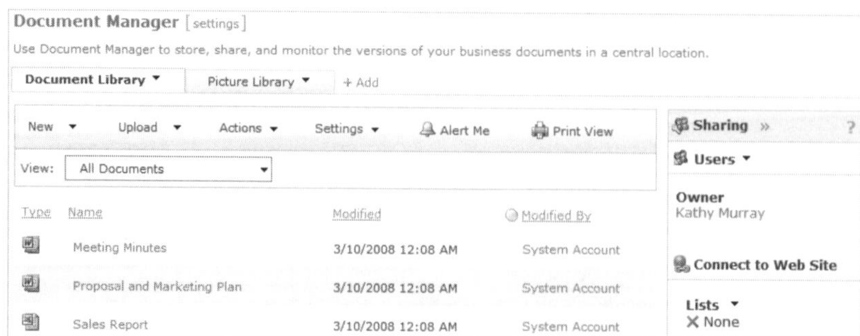

FIGURE 10-6 Document Manager enables you to create, store, organize, and work with files easily online.

CUSTOMIZING DOCUMENT MANAGER

You can tailor the look and feel of Document Manager to best suit the type of features you want to offer your own team. You can modify permissions and settings, change the items that are available on the menus, modify the appearance of the page, change what appears in the lists, and much more.

To customize Document Manager, follow these steps:

1. Click Document Manager in the left navigation bar of the Business Applications window.
2. Click [Settings] to the right of the Document Manager heading.
3. Scroll through the list of settings in the Document Manager Site Settings window and click the one you want to change.
4. Make any necessary changes.
5. Click Business Applications to return to the main Business Applications page.

Adding Documents

The first task you'll want to try with Document Manager most likely involves adding your own documents to the lists. The utility gives you the choice of adding documents one at a time or as a batch. Here's how to upload documents in Document Manager:

1. Click Business Applications in the Office Live Small Business Home page and click Document Manager.
2. Click the arrow to the right of Upload. A list of choices appears:

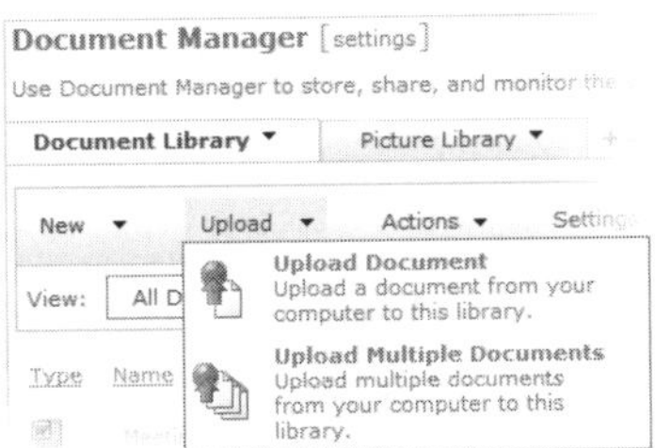

3. To upload a single document, click Upload Document. To upload a collection of documents, click Upload Multiple Documents. Each selection takes you to a different window:

   - If you choose to upload a single document, the Upload Document: Document Library window appears. Here you can click the Browse button and navigate to the file you want to upload.

   - If you choose to upload multiple files, a tree-like structure appears in the Upload Document: Document Library window so that you can choose the folder containing the files you want to upload and click the check boxes of all files you want to add.

4. Select the file(s) you want to upload and click OK. The new files are added to the Document Library and you can view, edit, or work with them as needed.

TIP

You can easily create new documents while you're working in Document Manager. Simply click the Document Library tab, click the New arrow, and choose New Document. The Microsoft Office Word window opens so that you can create, format, and save the new document. After you close the new file, it is added to the Document Library list.

Viewing Documents

The list view in Document Manager displays the files that are currently stored in your Document Library on Office Live Small Business. You can begin to view and work with those documents by following these steps:

1. Position the mouse pointer on a file you'd like to work with. The file becomes highlighted, and an arrow appears on the right side of the selection.

2. Click the arrow, and a menu appears (see Figure 10-7). One option, Send To, includes a second list of options you can use to send the file to another area.

3. Select the option that best fits the way you want to work with the document. Table 10-1 introduces the different choices in the list and explains what they do.

TABLE 10-1 Document Manager Choices

COMMAND	DESCRIPTION
View Properties	Shows you who created the file and when it was created and last modified
Edit Properties	Enables you to re-title and change the description of the document
Manage Permissions	Lets you assign permissions to allow (or restrict) access to the document
Edit In Word	Opens the document in Word
Delete	Removes the document from the Document Manager list
Send To	Enables you to send the file to another location
Check Out	Marks the document as checked out to you so that no one else can edit it simultaneously
Alert Me	Creates an alert so that you are notified if that document is accessed or modified

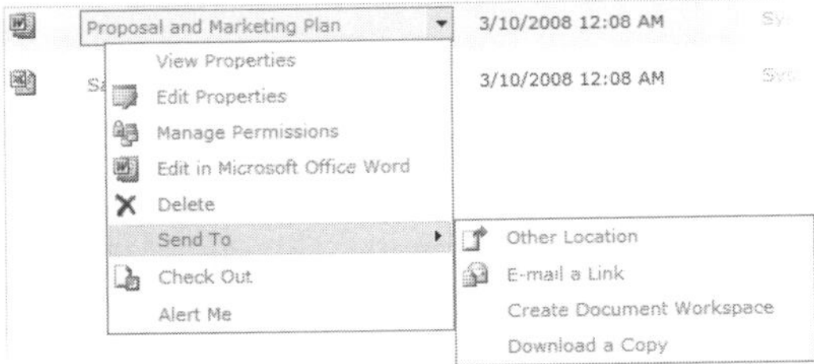

FIGURE 10-7 Click the arrow to the right of a document you want to work with and choose the option you want.

Managing Libraries

By default, Document Manager is set up to include two tabs: Document Library and Picture Library. To add your own library, click the Add link to the right of the Picture Library tab. A list of library choices appears so that you can click the one you want to add (see Figure 10-8).

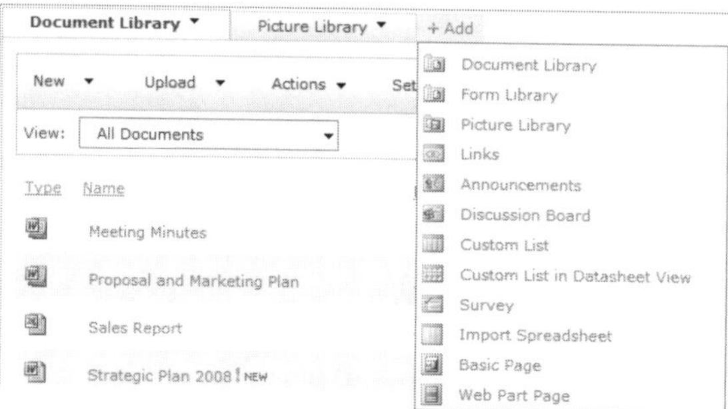

FIGURE 10-8 You can easily add a new tab to Document Manager by clicking the Add link and choosing the tab type you want to add.

You can change the names of tabs, hide tabs, or remove tabs completely by clicking the arrow to the left of the tab name and choosing the option you want from the list that appears.

Using the Team Workspace

A perfect companion to Document Manager, the Team Workspace gives you an easy way to keep your team in touch. By posting announcements for the group, assigning tasks, setting up meetings, and adding links and notes, you can make sure everyone in your group has access to the same information.

Click Business Applications in the left navigation bar and choose Team Workspace. The Team Workspace window appears, as shown in Figure 10-9. As you can see, the page offers a number of different information items. Here's a quick introduction to the tabs that appear by default:

- Dashboard displays the most current happenings from all tabs on the first page so you can see at a glance which items have most recently been added or updated.
- Announcements lists all the items team members have added, perhaps letting you know about an upcoming deadline, suggesting a marketing idea, asking for confirmation on a purchase, and so on.
- Calendar displays the monthly calendar for your business, complete with any scheduled events currently planned. (You can modify the calendar to show other views by default if you like.)

- Links lists all the Web links that have been collected by the team. Links might be to external or competitors' sites or to folders containing documents that team members want you to review.
- Shared Documents enables team members to share documents in a special library used for collaborative work.
- Tasks enables you to add, view, and update tasks that are assigned to specific members of your team.
- Team Discussion provides you with a space to have ongoing discussions about topics that are relevant to your business operations. For example, you might discuss a new marketing strategy, plan an upcoming meeting, or review a new product by creating a team discussion item.

To create a new item in the Team Workspace, simply click the Add link for the item you want to create. If you are working in one of the tabs mentioned previously, click New to open the New menu and then choose the item that reflects what you want to create.

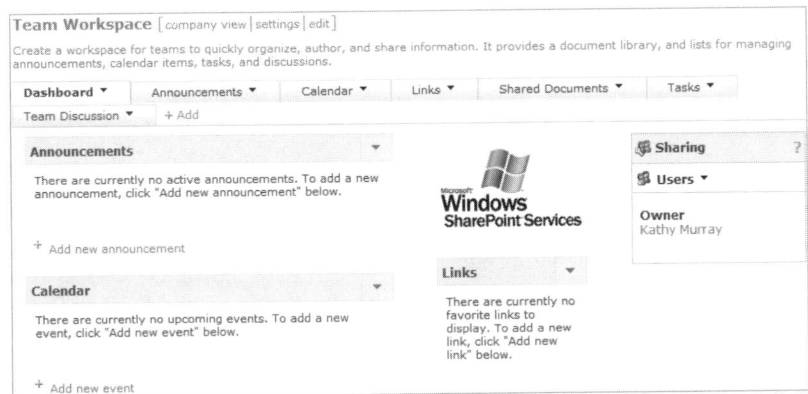

FIGURE 10-9 The Team Workspace helps you to keep your staff in sync and in touch.

> **NOTE** Much like you can in Document Manager, you can modify the default settings for the Team Workspace by clicking the [Settings] link to the right of the application name. Scroll to the item you want to change and click it; make your changes and then return to Business Applications.

THE TEAM WORKSPACE AND OFFICE LIVE WORKSPACE

When you are first getting familiar with the Team Workspace, you may wonder whether it is the same thing as Office Live Workspace. Although the two applications are both built on Windows SharePoint technology (which gives you the list-based approach to document and information management), they are meant to serve different purposes.

The Team Workspace is specifically designed for small businesses that need to provide a central hub of operations for team members who may be working at a distance from one another. For this reason, the options and features available in the Team Workspace are geared toward business applications and data management uses.

Office Live Workspace, on the other hand, is meant to be an online file storage, management, and sharing utility for people who use Microsoft Office 2007. Teachers, book study groups, students, soccer moms, and investment clubs are part of the audience for Office Live Workspace, as well as anyone else interested in organizing and storing documents for business or home use. You'll learn more about Office Live Workspace in Chapter 11, "Working with Microsoft Office Live Workspace." But when it comes to business applications for your company, the Team Workspace is the one to know.

Adding Business Applications

In addition to these three major business applications (Contact Manager, Document Manager, and the Team Workspace), Office Live Small Business includes more than a dozen additional applications you can add to tailor the services to your own business needs.

To add a business application to Office Live Small Business, follow these steps:

1. Click Business Applications in the Office Live Small Business Home page.
2. Click Add Application in the left navigation panel.
3. Choose one of the six application groups to see the applications that are available in that group. Table 10-2 introduces the groups and lists the applications available in each one.
4. Click the application you want to add (see Figure 10-10).
5. Click OK to add the application.

TABLE 10-2 Application Groups and Items

GROUP	INCLUDES
Collaborate With Co-workers And Clients	Project Manager, Customer Workspace, Team Workspace
Schedule Meetings And Events	Time Manager, Basic Meeting Workspace, Blank Meeting Workspace, Decision Meeting Workspace, Social Meeting Workspace
Manage And Share Documents	Document Manager, Wiki Workspace, Blog
Manage Your Business	Company Assets, Competition Tracker, Customer Support, Employee Directory, Estimates, Expenses, Jobs And Hiring, Training
Add Or Find Custom Applications	Upload A Custom Application, Find More Custom Applications, Upload Template
Your Custom Application	Blank Workspace

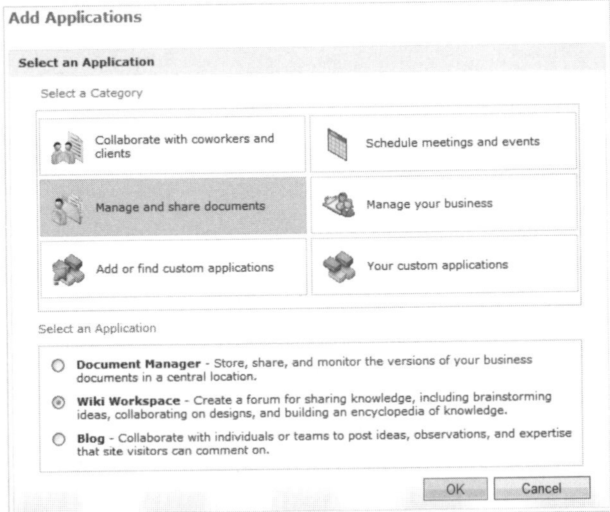

FIGURE 10-10 Click the category of the application you want to add, and then choose the application from the list.

Your new application is added to the list in the left navigation panel of the Business Applications page so that you can access it easily.

Deleting an Application

At some point you might realize that you have added a business application you don't really use. To clear up space on your navigation panel, you can delete unwanted applications. Here's how to do that:

1. Click Business Applications in the Office Live Small Business Home page.
2. In the left navigation panel, click the name of the application you want to remove.
3. Click [Settings] on the right of the application title in the window.
4. In the Site Settings page, scroll down to the Develop And Customize settings.
5. Click Delete This Application.
6. In the Site Manager list, find the application you want to remove (in this case, Wiki Workspace; see Figure 10-11), and click the Delete link in the right column.
7. Click OK when prompted to confirm that you want to delete the application.

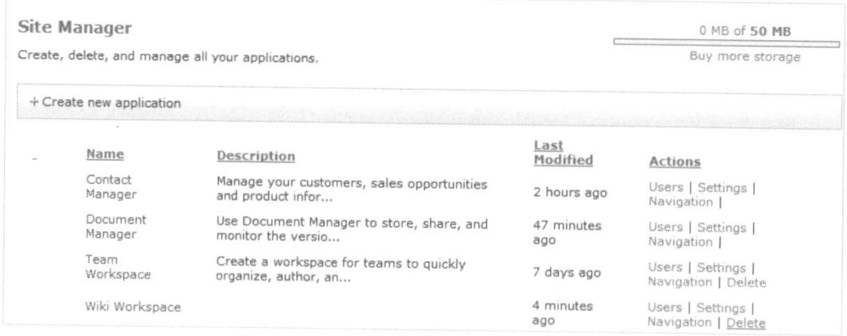

FIGURE 10-11 Click Delete in the right column of the Site Manager list to remove an application you no longer need.

There's no limit to the number of applications you can add to your Office Live Small Business account, and—best of all—the applications are free. In addition to all the utilities available in the program, you can create and add your own custom applications that help support the specific business tasks you need to accomplish.

KEEP AN EYE ON YOUR BUSINESS

For many of us, going into business for ourselves is the realization of a lifelong dream. You may have started out playing store as a child. Or perhaps you were the one in high school who was always looking for ways to get people to your events and parties. Whatever your focus, chances are that you've always been an idea person, a visionary with the desire to make things happen and a belief that one day things will really take off.

Once we begin taking steps to launch our businesses, we quickly learn that there's a lot more to business ownership than vision and passion. T's need to be crossed, and forms need to be filed. Data can't just run along on its own, unmanaged—we need to develop ways to track, record, and work with the information we amass. Otherwise, we may lose big opportunities—and potential (or repeat) customers.

Keeping an eye on business becomes not just a "want to" but also a "have to." In order to know how your business is doing—financially, practically, strategically—you need to be able to get an accurate picture of what's going on, today and every day.

The Office Live Small Business applications available to you offer a wide range of support services to help you get a clear sense of the big picture of your business. Take advantage of them—they're free! For little more than a few minutes of time invested, you can track the contacts you make with new customers, check inventory levels, propose a new service to a favorite client, add a comment to the marketing plan your team is working on, and set up a meeting with the bank to discuss funding for your next big thing.

Take a little time to investigate the different applications, and try them on for size. If you don't feel you'll keep up with them, delete them and use your old system; or if you think they fit nicely with the type of data you need to collect, assign someone to the task and make sure the data is tracked—religiously. The data you draw out of your business is only as good as the data you put in. So if you are inconsistent in tracking your phone calls, entering opportunities, scheduling meetings, and updating products, your data may be hit or miss, and it may come back to haunt you later. For example, when the bank is considering your application for funding, it will look much better if you have tracked all your data consistently over time rather than having to explain a two-month gap in your customer contacts.

After you settle on the applications that will help your business flourish, build them into your normal process. Make those applications a natural part of your business cycle. That way, as your business grows and you train new employees, capturing the important contact points and collecting the data you need becomes part of the fabric of your business. And that will leave you more time to realize your vision.

What's Next

This chapter introduced you to the business applications available for free within your Office Live Small Business account. The next chapter moves into the realm of the shared online world by giving you a tour of this service's close cousin: Office Live Workspace.

Working with Microsoft Office Live Workspace

IN THIS CHAPTER, YOU WILL

- Get to know Microsoft Office Live Workspace.
- Add documents to your workspace.
- Work with documents.
- Share your workspace.

IN THE previous chapter, you learned about the variety of business applications you can use with your Microsoft Office Live Small Business account to manage your customer contacts, files, opportunities, and more. Some of the business applications enable you to create online spaces that bring your team together to share events, tasks, announcements, and files. Other workspaces help you work collaboratively on documents, host meetings, and even plan a community event.

This chapter is about a different kind of online workspace: Office Live Workspace.

Office Live Workspace is an online space that enables you to seamlessly store, manage, and share files easily with others around the globe. Built to be a seamless online component for the applications in the 2007 Microsoft Office system, Office Live Workspace gives you a full range of features and supports designed to help you create, share, work with, and manage Microsoft Office Word, Microsoft Office Excel, and Microsoft Office PowerPoint files online. You can also easily create tasks, events, contacts, notes, and lists that help your group collaborate effectively.

The convenient and easy access from within Office Live Small Business means that you can access your files on Office Live Workspace from any computer with a Web browser. The security enhancements and permissions structure help ensure that the files are protected so that only those people with the necessary permissions can access them. Whether you're working on a new project, sharing a proposal, creating an event, or just helping the kids with their homework, Office Live Workspace gives you a private online area for the files you need to share with others who are helping you complete a project, organize an event, or reach a shared goal.

Introducing Office Live Workspace

If you have signed up for Office Live Workspace, you'll find Office Live Workspace at the bottom of the left navigation panel on the Office Live Small Business Home page (see Figure 11-1). If you haven't yet signed up for Office Live Workspace, you can go to *workspace.officelive.com/*to get started. (It's free and the sign-up takes only a minute.)

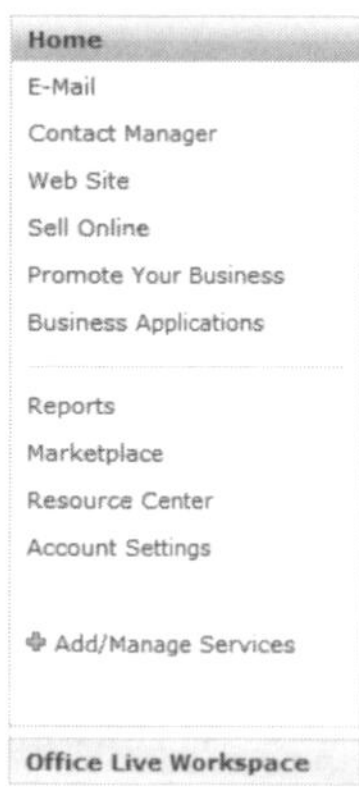

FIGURE 11-1 Access Office Live Workspace by clicking the button at the bottom of the left navigation panel.

Office Live Workspace gives you 500 MB of storage space, which could be up to as many as 1,000 files! You can upload almost any type of file—Word documents, Excel spreadsheets, PowerPoint presentations, and even PDFs. The service won't accept .exe files, however, which might contain elements that cause security problems. The size limit per document is 25 MB. Additionally, you can share the files you store in your workspace with as many as 100 people—giving you the ability to create collaboration among groups large and small, throughout an organization or around the globe.

NOTE Although Office Live Workspace does offer a password-protected environment for file sharing, exchange, and collaboration, you should check any document-storage policies your or other participants' organizations have in place before sharing your files. Be mindful of copyright and company security policies, whether you're collaborating for business or other causes.

SYSTEM REQUIREMENTS FOR OFFICE LIVE WORKSPACE

The requirements for Office Live Workspace are similar to those for Office Live Small Business:

- If you're using Internet Explorer, you need Internet Explorer 6, 7, or 8 on a Windows XP, Windows Server 2003, or Windows Vista system.
- If you're using Firefox 2.0 on a PC, make sure it's running Windows XP, Windows Server 2003, or Windows Vista.
- If you're using Firefox 2.0 on a Mac, you need Mac OS X 10.2.x.

Additionally, if you plan to use the multiple file upload tool, you'll need to use a browser that supports the installation of ActiveX controls.

Anatomy of an Office Live Workspace

When you click the Office Live Workspace button at the bottom of the left navigation panel, the Office Live Workspace window opens. The overall look and feel is identical to Office Live Small Business—so at first glance you might not notice you've changed programs! Figure 11-2 shows the first window you see after you click Office Live Workspace in the left navigation bar for the first time.

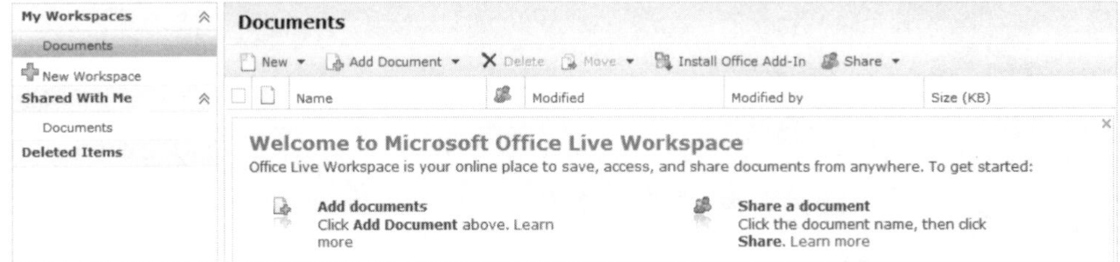

FIGURE 11-2 The Office Live Workspace window enables you to create workspaces and add and share documents with others.

Here are the key areas of the Office Live Workspace window:

- The left navigation panel in Office Live Workspace enables you to create and work with multiple workspaces and view and share documents in the workspaces you share.
- The toolbar across the top of the Office Live Workspace window includes the tools you'll use to create new documents in the workspace, add existing files, remove files you don't need, move files to other spaces, add Office Add-Ins, and share your files with others.
- The documents you add will appear just below the toolbar, in the document list (see Figure 11-3).

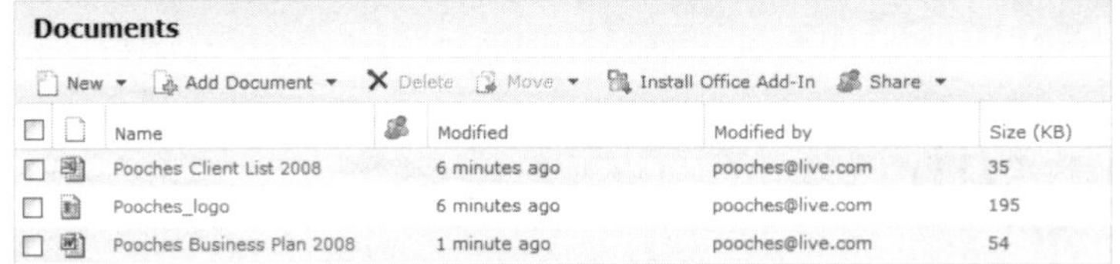

FIGURE 11-3 After you add files to the workspace, they appear in the document list.

With Office Live Workspace, you can organize your scout troop, gather documents for a spring event, work on a proposal for a new initiative, or give your students a way to turn in their book reports—all using this simple online Web space.

Adding Documents to a Workspace

Office Live Workspace enables you to add documents to the space two different ways. You can upload documents one at a time, or, if you're working with a collection of files, you can add them all at once.

If you decide to add multiple files, Office Live Workspace will download and install an ActiveX control so that you can choose the files you want and upload them at one time.

Uploading Individual Files

To add a single file to your Office Live Workspace, click Add Document and choose Single Document. In the Choose File dialog box, navigate to the folder containing the file you want to upload. Select it and click Open. The file is added to the documents list.

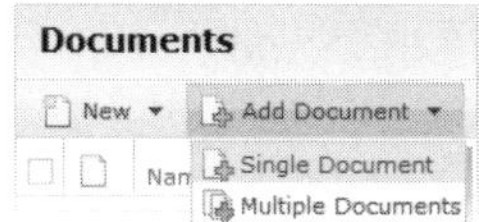

Notice that you can see all file types—not just documents—in the Choose File dialog box. This enables you to add spreadsheets, data lists, and any other file type you need to your documents.

The files you upload on Office Live Workspace are protected by Microsoft Forefront Security for SharePoint. Only people you grant permissions to can access the files, and they need to log in using a Windows Live ID and password. You make choices about the level of access and editing each person receives—you can determine whether people can view, modify, comment on, or remove files you place in the workspace.

Uploading Multiple Files

To upload a number of files at once, click Add Documents and choose Multiple Documents. You will be prompted to install the Multiple Document Upload Tool by clicking the yellow notification bar that appears at the top of your browser window and choosing Install ActiveX Control. The installation takes just a moment, and then you will be returned to the Office Live Workspace window.

Click Add Documents and choose Multiple Documents if necessary. (You might need to do this twice the first time you choose it; subsequently you'll be able to go right to the Multiple Document Upload Tool.) Click Install. The What Documents Do You Want To Add? box appears.

The What Documents Do You Want To Add? box enables you to upload documents two different ways:

- If you have folders open on your desktop, you can drag and drop files directly into the box and then click Upload.
- You can also click Browse For Documents to display the Select Documents To Upload dialog box. In this dialog box, you can choose multiple files (click the first file and press and hold Shift or Ctrl while clicking additional files); then click Open.

The files are added to the What Documents Do You Want To Add? box (see Figure 11-4), and you can browse for more documents in other folders or drag and drop additional files. When you're ready to upload the files to your Office Live Workspace, click Upload.

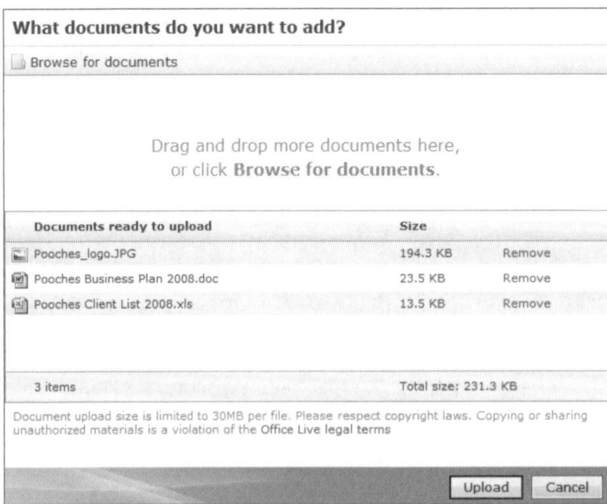

FIGURE 11-4 The files are added to the Multiple Document Upload tool.

Office Live Workspace displays the status of the uploading files; when the upload is complete, the files appear in your documents list.

Working with Documents

After you add documents to your workspace, you can easily view and even modify them online. This enables you to travel without carrying along a laptop full of files—you can simply log on wherever you have access, using your Windows Live ID and password—and work with the files stored in your Office Live Workspace.

To open a document in the workspace, click the file name in the documents list. The document opens in an area in the center of the window (see Figure 11-5).

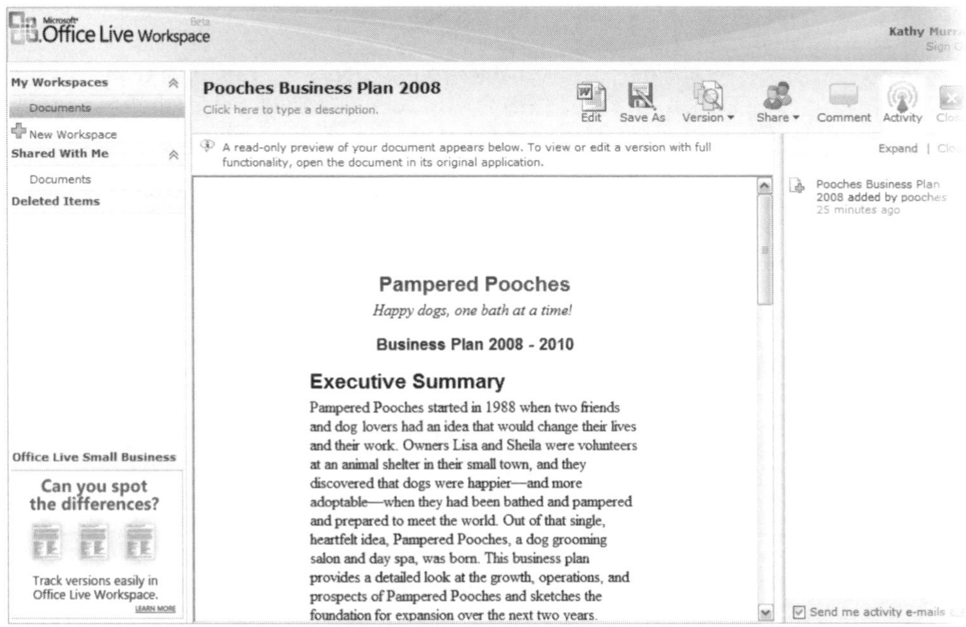

FIGURE 11-5 You can view a document in Office Live Workspace.

In the document window, the file itself appears in the center area of the window. It is displayed as read-only, meaning that you can simply view—but not edit—the content of the file. The Activity panel of the window lists the actions that have been taken for this particular file. Each time you view, edit, update, or move the file, another entry will be added to the actions column.

The tools in the top right side of the screen enable you to work with the file and share it with others. Table 11-1 gives you a quick description of each of the tools available to you.

TABLE 11-1 Document Tools in Office Live Workspace

TOOL	NAME	DESCRIPTION
Edit	Edit In Word	Opens Word so that you can edit the file in the original program. (Note: If you click an Excel spreadsheet in the document list, the icon here would show the Excel image, and the name of the tool would be Edit In Excel.)
Save As	Download To Desktop	Saves the selected file to your desktop (or any folder you select) so that you can edit it on your own system.
Version ▾	Versioning Option	Enables you to choose the version of the file you want to use, or upload and replace the existing version.
Share ▾	Share	Shares the current document or the current screen.
Comment	Comment	Displays the Comment panel so that you can add or review comments added to the current document.
Activity	Activity	Hides and displays the Activity panel along the right side of the work area.
Close	Close	Closes the current document and displays the document list.

Changing a Document

If you want to edit the document displayed in the Office Live Workspace area, you have two options:

- You can click Edit to open the document in Word (if it was originally created in Word; otherwise, choose the tool that reflects the created file type).
- You can click Save As and save the file to your desktop or another folder of your choosing.

INSTALLING THE OFFICE ADD-IN

You can download an Office Add-In to streamline the experience of using Word, Excel, and PowerPoint files with Office Live Workspace. The download is available in the Office Live Workspace tools at the top of the documents list.

Follow these steps to install and use the Office Add-In:

1. Click Install Office Add-In.
2. When the File Download dialog box appears, click Run. In the second box, click Run as well.
3. The Microsoft Office Add-In Setup Wizard launches. Click Next.
4. Accept the user agreement and click Next. Click Close to complete the wizard.

Editing a Document

When you click Edit, the document opens in the Office application in which it was created. You can edit the document as you normally would, and then press Ctrl+S to save the file. The document is saved to the Office Live Workspace site. Close the file to return to the document list in Office Live Workspace.

Saving, Modifying, and Uploading a Document

If you want to save a document to your computer in order to work on it, follow these steps:

1. Click the document name in the documents list.
2. Click Save As in the Office Live Workspace tools.
3. In the File Download box, click Save.
4. In the Save As dialog box, navigate to the folder where you want to store the file, and click Save.

Edit and save the file as you normally would. When you are ready to add it to your Office Live Workspace, follow these steps to update the file and replace the existing one:

1. Click the Version arrow.
2. Click Upload And Overwrite File (see Figure 11-6).
3. In the Choose File dialog box, navigate to the file you edited. Click it and click Open.

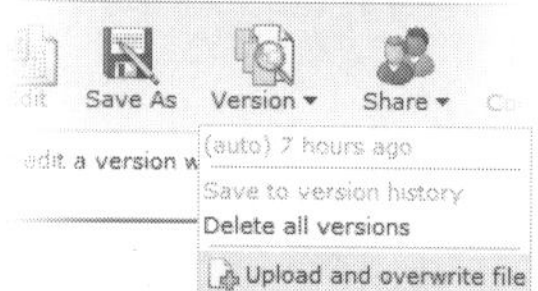

FIGURE 11-6 Replace the existing file with the changed one by using the Upload And Overwrite File option.

The file is added to the workspace, where it replaces the existing file with the same name. After the file is added, it appears in the workspace window.

Sharing Your Workspace

One of the best things about Office Live Workspace is the easy way in which you can share files with others. There are two different ways you can share items.

Start by clicking the Share arrow in the Office Live Workspace tools, and then do the following:

- Choose Share Document to share a document by sending others a link that enables them to log in to your space and view the shared file.
- Choose Share Screen to share your desktop or an application with others you invite.

NOTE To take advantage of the Shared Screen feature, you need to download and install Microsoft SharedView. Office Live Workspace prompts you to do this when you choose Share Screen.

Sharing a Document

To share a document in Office Live Workspace with another user, follow these steps:

1. Click the Share arrow.
2. Choose Share Document. Address lines appear at the top of the document window (see Figure 11-7).
3. Click in the Editors line and select or enter the e-mail addresses of those you want to assign editing permission (people who can view and modify the file).
4. Click in the Viewers line and select or enter the e-mail addresses of people you want to be able to view the file. These users cannot edit the file.
5. Click in the Message area and type text inviting the users to share the document.
6. Click Send.

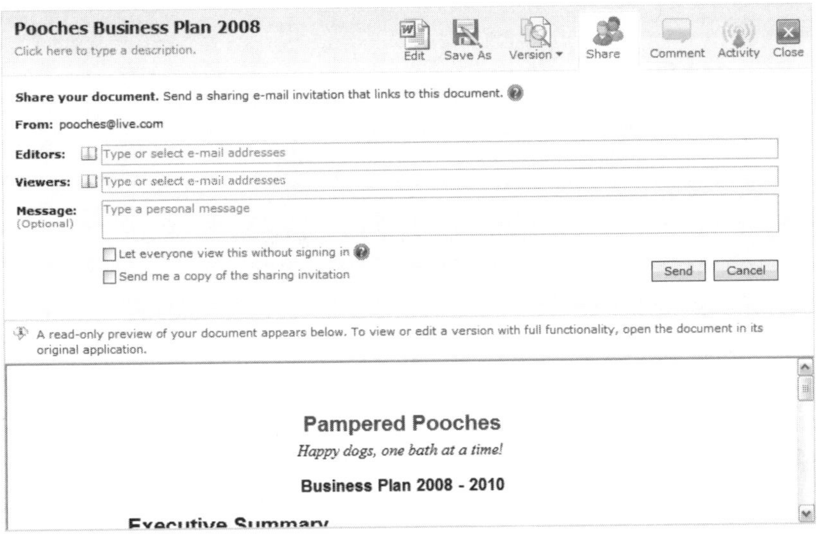

FIGURE 11-7 Send an invitation to others to enable them to share your document.

After the invitation is sent, a link appears at the top of the document window that enables you to review the sharing details for that particular file. Click View Sharing Details to see the list of users and the different permissions (Editors or Viewers) assigned (see Figure 11-8).

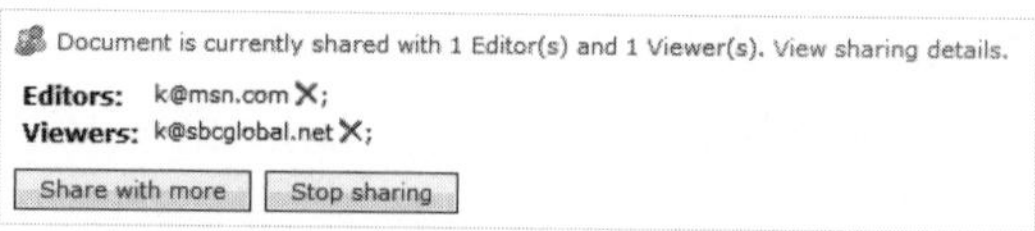

FIGURE 11-8 You can change sharing options by clicking View Sharing Details.

If you change your mind and want to rescind the invitation, you can click Stop Sharing to cancel the sharing permission. Additionally, if you want to stop sharing with a particular user, you can click the X at the end of the user's e-mail address to cancel sharing for that person.

The users you choose receive an invitation that looks like the one shown in Figure 11-9. To begin viewing the document, the user simply needs to click the Click Here To View It link.

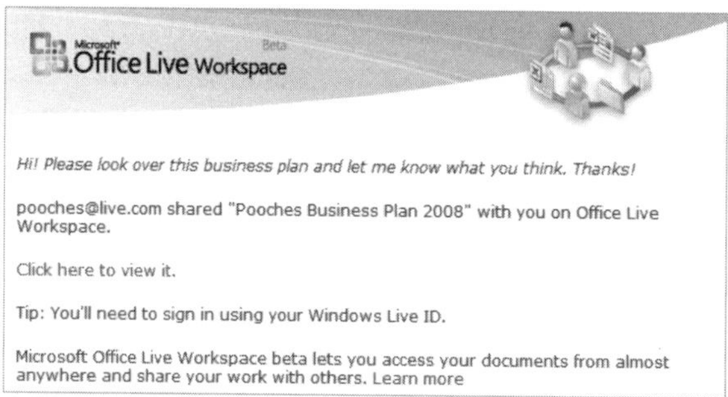

FIGURE 11-9 Users receive an invitation that provides access to the shared file.

Sharing a Screen

To use the screen-sharing feature in Office Live Workspace, you must download and install Microsoft SharedView. The prompt appears automatically when you click the Share arrow and then Share Screen in the Office Live Workspace tools.

When prompted to install Microsoft SharedView, click OK. You are then taken to the Microsoft Download Center. Click Download. Follow the prompts on the screen to run the installation utility. When prompted, review the user agreement and click to accept it. Click Install, and after a moment, the Microsoft SharedView Sign In dialog box appears (see Figure 11-10).

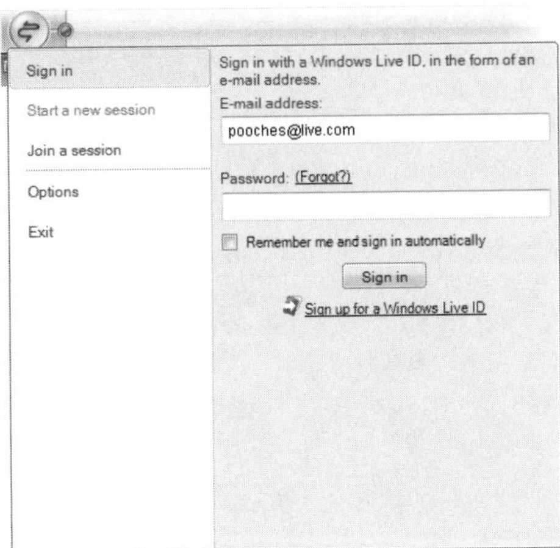

FIGURE 11-10 Before you can use Microsoft SharedView, you must provide your information in the Sign In box.

After you sign in, the Microsoft SharedView toolbar appears across the top of your Office Live Workspace window (see Figure 11-11). Here's what you use the tools in the toolbar to accomplish:

- Click Participants to add users to the shared session.
- Click Handouts to add handouts you've created to the session.
- Click Share to choose the applications you want to share.
- Click Stop Sharing to end the session.
- Click Preview to see how the session looks to others.
- Click Control to change the user who has control of the session.
- Click in the text box to enter a message other users can see.
- Click Send to send the text message.

FIGURE 11-11 The Microsoft SharedView toolbar appears along the top of the workspace window.

Click Stop Sharing to end the session. To close Microsoft SharedView, click the Microsoft SharedView button and click Exit.

FIVE TIPS FOR EFFECTIVE COLLABORATION

Whether you are using your Office Live Workspace to work collaboratively on a business plan, to set up an event for volunteers, to gather research for a new program, or simply to give your team an online space to store files and keep in touch, there are a few things you can do to help ensure that your collaboration goes as smoothly as possible.

1. **Have a plan**. Before you invite the first person to the shared space, know what your focus is, what you want to include on the space, and how you'll use it. Create a welcome document that explains the basic goals of the space and lets users know what to expect.
2. **Think through permissions**. Depending on the nature of your project or shared space, you may want everyone to have equal permissions—all editors or all viewers only. Or you may want to enable some people to do the reviews only, while others make edits, create spreadsheets, and pull together presentations. Plan out the permissions before you invite users so that you don't have to take away permissions—and need to explain yourself—later.
3. **Keep your versions straight**. If you are working on a large document that includes the collaboration of a number of people, it's important to make sure you are working with the latest versions of your files. For example, perhaps your gardening group is working on a grant proposal that involves half a dozen editors and reviewers. Take extra care to ensure that the draft of the proposal includes all collaborators' comments, that the financial statements are as complete as possible, and that users are working with one file that is continually updated with the most current information. This ensures that no one's contribution gets left out of the mix as you finalize the proposal.

4. **Communicate clearly**. If you have questions about tasks, versions, or process, be sure to communicate clearly with the rest of your collaborators. You can use your planning document to anticipate and answer questions up front (sort of like a FAQ), but invariably questions will arise, mistakes will happen, and courses need to be corrected while you're working on your project. Use Office Live Small Business to e-mail or instant-message teammates; offer to host sharing sessions using Microsoft SharedView to show collaborators just what you want them to do. When in doubt, ask your questions and communicate as completely and clearly as possible. When everybody knows what to expect, collaboration goes more smoothly.
5. **Check in daily**. Even though collaboration takes time and effort, it's a good idea to check in daily to stay on top of changes in the space. By default, Office Live Workspace sends you activity e-mails that let you know when documents are changed in the workspace. But in addition to the e-mail notifications, you can make it part of your routine to visit the site regularly and see how things are progressing in the workspace.

What's Next

This chapter focused on Office Live Workspace, a complementary cousin to Office Live Small Business. As an add-on to the wide range of features you've already added to your site, Office Live Workspace enables you to integrate Microsoft Office applications seamlessly into your online business support services. The next chapter rounds out the book by introducing you to the range of options at your disposal for learning more about running a small business, getting your questions answered, and participating in a community.

Using the Resource Center

IN THIS CHAPTER, YOU WILL

- Learn about phone and e-mail support.
- Explore the Resource Center.
- Find how-to articles and resources.
- Take an online seminar.
- Participate in the Microsoft Office Live Small Business community.
- Read and subscribe to blogs.
- Learn about additional small business resources.

BY NOW you are most likely well on your way to using Microsoft Office Live Small Business features to get your business online; promote your business; and manage people, projects, sales, and more—all from a single simple Web interface. How's it going so far?

The developers of Office Live Small Business recognize that starting and running a small business is more than a doing-it-once kind of activity. A business needs constant attention and care. You are always tracking your data, correcting course, and trying new things. You are managing people, adding features, and expanding your data lists.

A thriving business gives you a lot to manage—and that's a good problem to have! Luckily, Office Live Small Business includes a comprehensive Resource Center that provides you not only with software support but also with practical suggestions for business setup, management, and promotion. This chapter rounds out the book by introducing you to the Office Live Small Business Resource Center.

Getting Free, Fast Phone and E-Mail Support

You're probably used to getting phone support for major purchases such as new computer systems, digital devices, and more. But how often do you get phone support for software or Web services—free? Even more, where will you find free phone support for a free Web service? You've got to admit, that's unusual.

Office Live Small Business knows that you have a lot on your plate as the owner of a small business. The last thing you need to do is lose time while you struggle with setup or Web design. For that reason, Office Live Small Business offers free phone support for 30 days after sign-up. After that, you receive toll-free, ongoing phone support if you purchase one of the add-on services: adManager, E-Mail Marketing, or premium e-mail. In the United States, call (866) 591-LIVE (5483) toll free to take advantage of the phone support.

Another source of support for you as a small business owner and Office Live Small Business subscriber is available via e-mail. The Office Live Small Business team has set a standard of responding to all customer e-mail within 48 hours. If you can't find answers to your questions online in the Help system, the Community forum, or the Office Live Small Business blog, you can click the Contact Us link at the bottom of the Resource Center page and submit your question or issue on the online form.

Exploring the Resource Center

You'll find the Office Live Small Business Resource Center by clicking the Resource Center option in the left navigation panel on the Home page. As you see in Figure 12-1, the Small Business Resource Center page lists all the different resources available and provides quick links to the key help areas:

- Customer Stories takes you to a page with customer video clips and stories about how Office Live Small Business is used by other small businesses like yours.
- Sign Up For The Newsletter enables you to add your name to a subscriber list so you receive tips, ideas, and project suggestions in the Office Live Small Business newsletter.
- Seminars displays a page listing a number of small business resource seminars in a variety of topic areas.
- Get Help From Your Peers takes you to the community forums where you can post a question, respond to others' posts, and review recently added items.

- Resources For Women takes you to a page with resources compiled especially for women entrepreneurs.
- FAQs displays the Office Live Small Business frequently asked questions in all areas of Office Live Small Business.

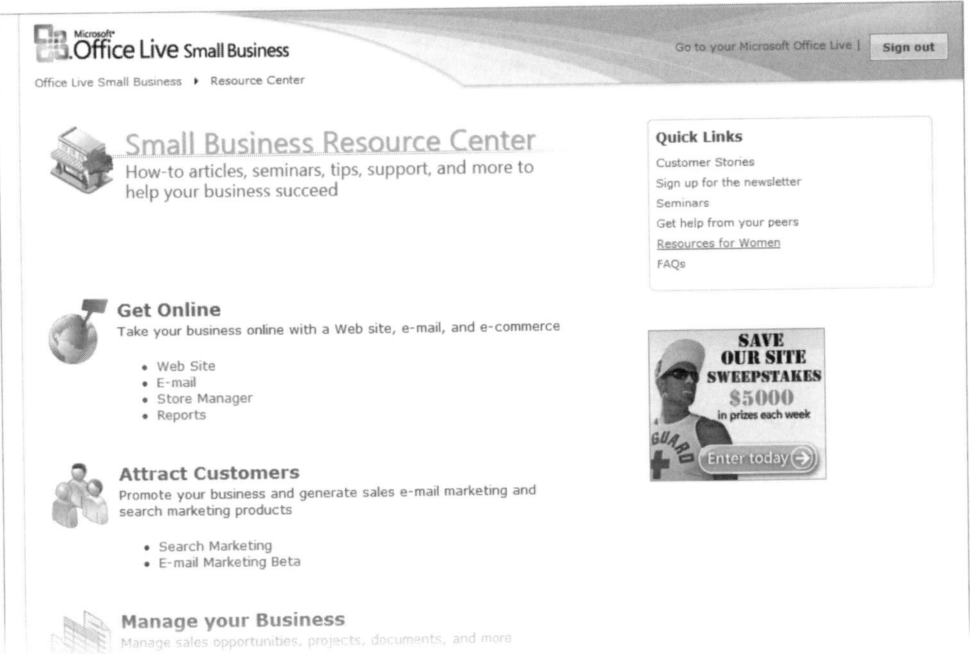

FIGURE 12-1 The Resource Center provides suggestions, training, and more for the different tasks you accomplish with Office Live Small Business.

Displaying How-To Articles

Office Live Small Business includes a comprehensive set of how-to articles that provide the specifics of tasks that help you set up your account; get your Web site online; promote your business; and manage people, projects, and more. Simply scroll through the list of topics and click the link you want. A subpage offers additional links to specific articles, as Figure 12-2 shows.

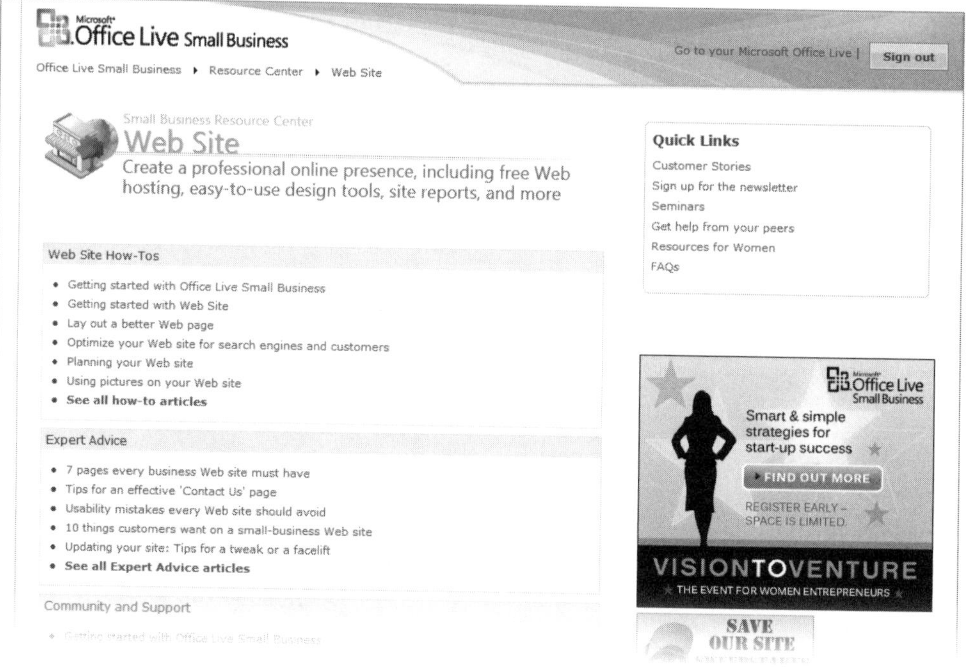

FIGURE 12-2 Each category lists a variety of resources to help you find what you need in specific topic areas.

> **NOTE** The Resource Center offers a number of on-demand seminars you can download and watch at any time on the Office Live Small Business site. The seminars are designed with busy business owners in mind and focus on a variety of specific business topic areas, such as online marketing, tax tips, and ideas for women entrepreneurs. Click Seminars in the Quick Links area and navigate to the seminar you'd like to see. Click View Online, Download Video WMV, or Download Audio MP3 to watch the seminar online or save it in video or audio format.

Getting Help from Your Peers

It's a great feeling of support to know that you're not the only small business owner who has ever dealt with startup worries, staffing troubles, financing challenges, and Web struggles. The Office Live Small Business community brings together business owners like you in all stages of business operation—from novices to experienced business owners.

You can use the Community Forums to find answers to your questions about the way the software works, to connect with other users, and to share what you've learned about running and growing a business online.

Getting Familiar with the Forums

The great thing about discussion forums is that it's easy to ask and answer questions that other Office Live Small Business users may also be wondering about. You can find ideas, new techniques, tips, and solutions by reading what others have posted; and you can learn a lot about what other users use to enhance and promote their sites.

The Discussions area of Office Live Small Business includes the following categories:

- Get Online (see Figure 12-3) includes threads about the basics of setting up and designing your site and managing contacts.
- Attract Customers covers information about marketing and promoting your business.
- Manage Your Business Online contains conversations about working with the business applications in Office Live Small Business.
- Special-Interest Group Conversations includes a group specifically for women entrepreneurs.
- Others provides a category for questions and ideas that don't fall within any of the other subject areas. If you have an idea about how to improve Office Live Small Business, you can post it in this discussion area.
- About This Community Site offers discussions where you can provide feedback about the site, add your own comments, or read about people who have become "masters" of Office Live Small Business.
- Articles includes hundreds of articles that provide practical ideas for creating, managing, improving, and promoting your site.

The last two categories, Who's Online? and Forum Statistics, give you a sense of the community itself, showing you who is currently online with you and how community members are using the discussion forums.

Discussions

Get Online

Forums	Last Post	Threads	Posts
Create a Great Site Exchange questions and ideas with your peers on the design and creation of sites.	Re: Content question by royster Saturday 10:35AM	130	576
Show and Tell at the Customer Gallery Show your work, ask for advice or check out what others have done, and ask them how they did it.	Re: Would appreciate any feedback by jann1033 Saturday 9:42AM	58	366
Sell Products and Services Online Customers are here, how do you sell to them? Exchange best practices with your peers.	Re: admanager by Mike Monarch (MSFT) Saturday 10:21AM	27	173
Use Email Mail is an important business tool; share (or ask) to other customers how to use it in the most efficient and advantageous way!	Re: email not working! by DEA Friday 1:49PM	42	148
Beginners Forum	Re: What is the cost of using Office Live Small Business? by shedivy Saturday 9:19AM	85	364

FIGURE 12-3 The Discussions forum includes categories with ongoing conversations in each of the major areas of Office Live Small Business.

Reading a Forum Post

You can easily scan the posts in a particular discussion thread and reply to one that interests you, or you can start a new thread with a new question or tip.

To view all posts in a thread, click the name of the thread you want to view in the Forums column. For example, clicking Sell Products And Services Online displays the screen shown in Figure 12-4.

Office Live Small Business Community Forums

Microsoft Office Live Small Business » Microsoft Office Live Small Business Community » Get Online » Sell Products and Services Online

Sell Products and Services Online

Write a New Post

Page 1 of 2 (27 items) 1 2 Next >

Topics

Thread	Replies
admanager Last post by Mike Monarch (MSFT) on Mar 15, 2008 10:21 AM	1
Online presence Last post by Filiberto-MSFT on Mar 15, 2008 2:04 AM	1

FIGURE 12-4 You can review the posts in a discussion thread.

To view a specific post, click the title. The post opens in the Office Live Small Business window and you can read through it, click Reply to display a message window to add to the thread, or click Contact to compose a private message to the person who posted the item.

Adding a Forum Post

To add a new post to the discussion, click the Write A New Post button at the top of the message list. The Write A New Post window appears (see Figure 12-5).

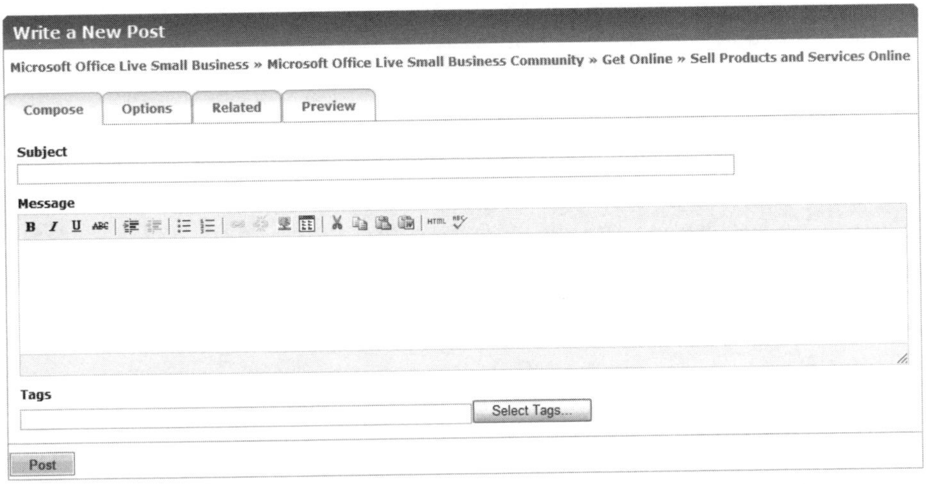

FIGURE 12-5 Type a subject line for your post and enter your question or comment in the Message area.

Add your post by following these steps:

1. Click in the Subject line and type a title for the post.
2. In the Message area, add the comment, tip, or question you want to add. You can use the formatting tools to change the look and format of the text if you'd like.
3. Click in the Tags line and type any tags that apply to your post. For example, if you are asking a question about templates, you could type **templates** in the Tags line.

TIP If you'd rather select tags from a list already included in Office Live Small Business, click the Select Tags button. In the Select Tags dialog box, click the check boxes of the tags you'd like to include; then click OK. The tags are added to the Tags line on your post. Tagging a post in this way enables other users to find your post when they search for items that include the tags you specified.

4. Click the Preview tab to see how your post will look when you post it.
5. Click Post to add your item to the discussion thread.

NOTE By default, Office Live Small Business Discussions enables other users to reply to your posts and e-mail you directly via the Contact button. If you want to change these settings, click the Options tab and click Do Not Allow Replies to disable the Reply button and click the Email Me Replies To This Post check box to disable the Contact button on your post.

Viewing Blogs

You'll also find blogs in the Office Live Small Business Resource Center, as part of the Get Help From Your Peers page. Click Get Help From Your Peers in the Quick Links box and scroll down to the bottom of the page to find the latest blog posts. Blog posts are written by members of the product group, usually in answer to questions they see popping up regularly on the discussion forums.

The most recent posts appear in the Latest Blog Posts box. To see all blog posts related to Office Live Small Business, click More Blog Posts. A listing of blog posts appears on the screen. When you click the title of the one you want to read, it opens in the Office Live Small Business window (see Figure 12-6).

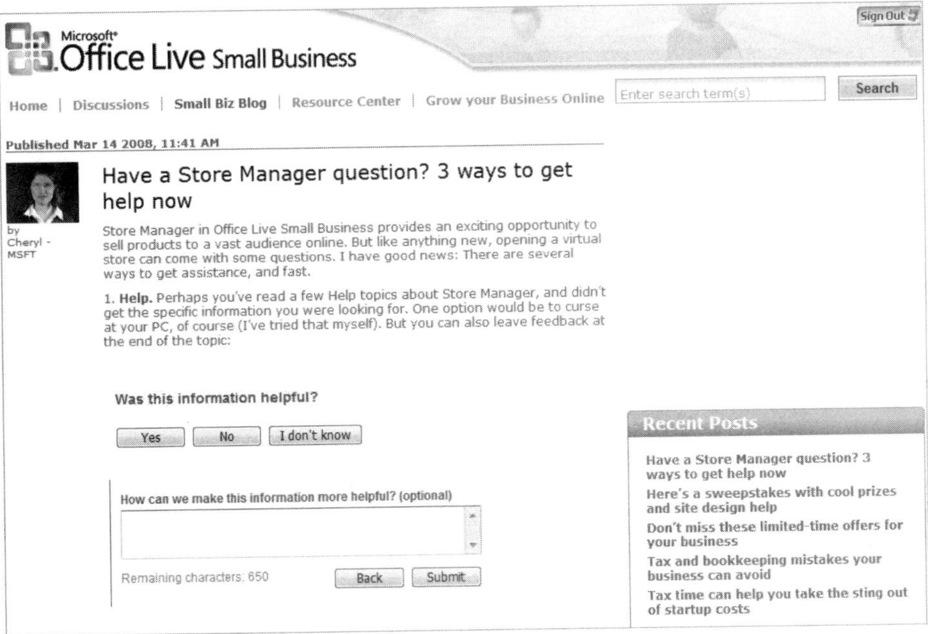

FIGURE 12-6 Blog posts give you additional ideas on using Office Live Small Business features.

TIP Be sure to take a few seconds and respond to the feedback at the end of the blog post so that the team gets good feedback about the information posted on the blogs. If you are looking for a topic that you can't find the answer to, tell the team about it by adding a comment in the text box and clicking Submit.

SIGNING UP FOR BLOG RSS FEEDS

If you want to receive blog posts automatically whenever they are added to the site, you can sign up for Really Simple Syndication (RSS) feeds. You'll know an RSS feed is available for a particular blog whenever you see the small RSS icon:

In Internet Explorer 7 or 8, you can click the Subscribe To This Feed link to add the RSS subscription to your Favorites Center. Click Subscribe in the Internet Explorer box to add the feed to your Feeds folder.

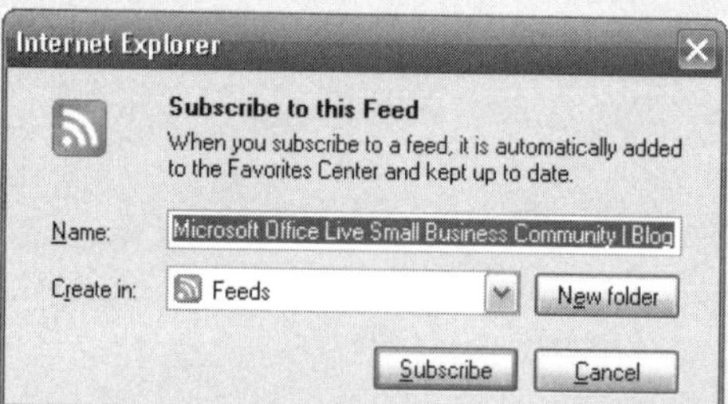

When new content is posted, the information is pushed to your Feeds folder automatically. You can read the content by clicking Favorites Center in your browser and clicking the Feeds button at the top of the Favorites Center.

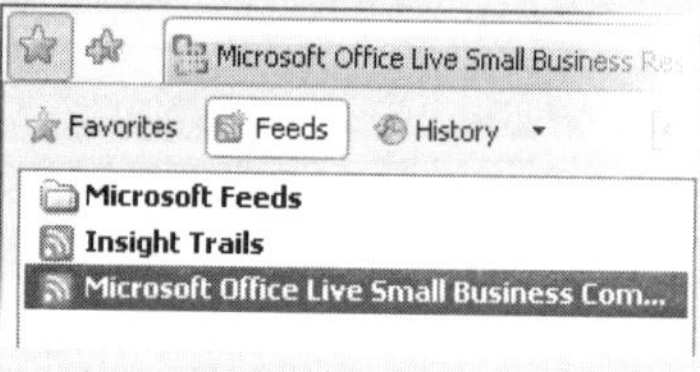

ADDITIONAL RESOURCES FOR SMALL BUSINESSES

With just a few searches, you will no doubt find an almost inexhaustible list of sites that offer a wide range of help resources for small businesses. This list offers just a few of the sites I visit that have provided reliable information. I can't vouch for all the content they post today or will post in the future, but you may want to visit them to see whether they have anything helpful for you:

- **Startup Nation** (*www.startupnation.com*). Startup Nation is a community "for entrepreneurs, by entrepreneurs" that partners with Office Live Small Business to provide a thriving set of forums, online articles, and more for business owners. There's a huge amount of information here, as well as a real sense of community with other small business owners.
- **Inc Magazine** (*www.inc.com*). The popular business publication *Inc Magazine* has a comprehensive Web site that includes how-to articles, in-depth analysis, a resource center, blogs, and more.
- **Small Business Administration** (*www.sbaonline.sba.gov*). This is one you'll want in your Favorites folder. The SBA offers a huge amount of information (all free) that ranges from business news to legal information, as well as important information about various loan programs.
- **Microsoft Startup Center** (*www.microsoft.com/smallbusiness*). This site is designed specifically for startup businesses and offers a startup checklist, business financing ideas, business plan basics, tips on building your brand, and much more.
- **Business Week Small Business** (*www.businessweek.com/smallbiz*). The popular business magazine *Business Week* offers a section focused on small business that provides the latest news, features, and resources.
- **Wall Street Journal Small Business** (*www.online.wsj.com*). The Small Business page of the *Wall Street Journal* provides features focused on small business as well as market analysis tools, links, and more.

Now It's Your Turn

Throughout this book, you've learned about the various features of Office Live Small Business designed to support you as you get your business online, attract customers, and manage your business. Now that you know the program, it's up to you to make it work!

Remember that with Office Live Small Business, you have numerous resources to turn to as well as program and real-people support for stepping into the unknown as you grow your business. Take the risk, invest yourself, and be sure to drop us a note in the Community forums and let us know how you're doing.

Good luck! (And don't forget to have some fun along the way.)

Index

J

K

L

M

N

O

P

T

U

V

W

Y

Z

About the Author

Katherine Murray is the author of more than 50 books on a variety of topics related to digital lifestyle, Web technologies, and Microsoft Office products. An avid writer, blogger, and editor, Katherine loves software that enables users to be more creative and productive. In addition to writing books, Katherine owns and operates reVisions Plus, Inc. (*www.revisionsplus.com*), a small business providing publishing services to companies throughout the United States. The mother of three and grandmother of one, Katherine lives and works in Indiana where she writes surrounded by her four-footed friends: two dogs, three cats, and a turtle.